Analyze a Survey with Microsoft™ Excel™

Jeff Walden

PLEASE NOTE: TO BUILD THE DATA DASHBOARD MODEL AS SHOWN IN THIS BOOK, **YOU MUST USE EXCEL 2010 OR LATER.**

Version 2010 of Excel introduced the *AGGREGATE* function, which the model uses extensively for **query-sensive calculations** such as standard deviation and mean.

There may be alternative ways to calculate standard deviation and mean (or other statistics) that are sensitive to whether the model is showing or hiding a specific group of records, but this book does not cover those methods. The techniques shown here may not work in versions of Excel earlier than 2010.

CONTENTS

Chapter 1

We Need a Survey...

You don't have to be a big company to do a meaningful survey, and you don't need a PhD in statistics to convert your raw data into information that you can use to better understand your customers, to develop your market, or to drive sales. **This book will show you ways to look at your survey data in Microsoft Excel and derive useful information from that data.**

We include some sophisticated formulas for your use in Excel spreadsheets, as well as some tips and tricks about how to arrange your data on a spreadsheet. We found these tips and tricks while researching this book. But... a word of caution: this book is not a general Excel tutorial. There are many — and we mean *a lot of* — great Excel tutorials available in print and on line that help you learn Excel basics up to, through, and beyond advanced statistics.

This book is about looking at *surveys*.

Maybe your organization has just finished a survey, and you're sitting at a desk right now looking bleakly at 872 responses and wondering how to make sense of them. **This is the book that will show you where to start.**

That said, this book is about squeezing useful information from *relatively simple surveys* — surveys that you or your company might do.

What do we mean by a "simple survey"? It is a survey where all the respondents answer the same set of questions. Programmers call this type of data file "flat." You may have seen complex

> ### What? You *already* have data from a survey?
>
> If you already have data from your survey, **and** it's in the form of a CSV (comma-separated values), tab-delimited, or Excel file, why wait?
>
> Jump to "Importing Your Own Survey Data from a CSV File" on page 110, import that data into Excel, and get cracking!

surveys — surveys where some respondents follow one path through the survey and others follow a different path based on how they answer certain questions. Those surveys require a *relational database manager* (perhaps the Microsoft Access program) and some higher-end statistical analysis.

But, if you want to get a handle on what your customers think and aggregate their answers in ways that you can present and that your organization can understand and act on, **you've come to the right place.**

Note: **This book requires Excel 2010 or later and recommends Excel 365.** It assumes that you *generally* know how to use Microsoft Excel — how to enter and edit formulas and make references between cells, how to *replicate* (copy) formulas along rows and columns, how to format cells as percentages, and control the number of decimal places. It expects that you know the difference between absolute cell references (references using $ such as $M$23 that always point to one cell) and relative references (those than increment when you copy, paste, and fill, such as plain old M23). Some specific instructions are covered in the Appendices. **You do not need to be an expert spreadsheet jockey,** although you may feel a bit like one when we're done.

Surveys begin with knowing how big a sample you need for the accuracy you want to achieve. We show you how to calculate that. If you have already completed your survey, you can estimate the accuracy that your survey achieved.

Surveys require some skill at crafting questions. We provide survey writing guidelines, example questions, and a sample Widget survey that works with the Data Dashboard example worksheet.

We show you how to build, modify, and use the Data Dashboard survey analysis model. At some level, every part of a survey is connected to every other part. People do not answer questions in a vacuum. For our own work, we needed an easy-to-modify tool that could isolate the responses for any answer or group of answers and show how the remainder of answers depended on them.

We built the Data Dashboard to help us analyze that kind of question dependency. You can't get that information from gazing at big columns of numbers. You need a tool that's *lively* and *responsive* and that can tell you how statistics change. See "What Do We Mean When We Say "The Statistics Change"?" on page 7 for a sample.

Once we saw how data changed in response to other data, we could move on to developing more complex, calculated tables of data, graphing the data, exploring Excel's wealth of built-in statistics, and applying those techniques to the survey material.

WHAT'S IN THIS BOOK?

- **Chapter 1: "We Need a Survey..."** is an overall introduction to the concept of the Data Dashboard and what it shows you.

- **Chapter 2: "Let's Do a Survey"** What can you learn from a simple survey? What about anonymity? How many responses do you need for accuracy?

- **Chapter 3: "Question Time"** How many questions should you put in a survey? Figuring out your "audience." What *kinds* of questions should you include? How can you gather and use data that isn't precisely a question? We build a demo survey.

- **Chapter 4: "Create the Data Dashboard"** Step-by-step, with formulas and explanations.

- **Chapter 5: "Running Advanced Filter Queries"** Looking at your data through the Data Dashboard. What queries can tell you. Other analyses you can do with the Data Dashboard.

- **Chapter 6: "Handling Text Fields in Surveys"** Open-ended text fields are tricky and time-consuming for the analyst, but they can divulge great information if you handle them correctly.

- **Appendix A: "How-To: Various Tasks"** Use our example data. Bring data into Excel from a CSV file. Add ID numbers. Add your own data to an existing Data Dashboard.

- **Appendix B: "Become a Query Ninja"** Eight different ways (at least) to execute Advanced Filter queries.

- **Appendix C: "Explaining the Data Dashboard's Most Important Formula"** Does just that and in detail.

A WORD ABOUT STEP-BY-STEP INSTRUCTIONS.

The author has documented software for many years. It's one thing to introduce all the functions of a new program to the world step-by-step when all users are equally unfamiliar with the software. But it's a *real* challenge to illustrate a specific task — such as analyzing a survey — using a well-known program like Microsoft Excel that has been available and has had every single function thoroughly documented *for decades*.

Because of its task-orientation, readers of *Analyze a Survey* may be of any experience level with Excel — people who want to pick up interesting ideas on how to think about and interpret their recent survey data... and others who need every step laid out for them because they find themselves in new and unfamiliar territory.

We've tried to strike a balance by getting out of the way (as much as possible) of those folks who just want the concepts and formulas and who don't always need to be reminded to "insert column here," and those folks who may "know" Excel, but who may need a little extra coaching.

To that end, we've moved some of the longer and necessarily more detailed how-to sections — such as how to import CSV data, alternative ways to create Advanced Filter queries, and an in-depth explanation of a very important but non-intuitive formula — to a series of appendices. Other step-by-steps we've left in place for everybody to follow — or just to skim. We hope we've made the right decision in each case.

Feel free to jump over all those details you already know to find those details you may not.

A QUICK TOUR OF THE DATA DASHBOARD

The Data Dashboard helps you put your finger on all the Basic Statistics about your data — counts, percentages of response for each answer to questions, averages, and means. In addition, it shows the interrelation of your data and how statistics change when you select subsets of your survey data in *ad-hoc* queries. Do respondents from higher-revenue organizations answer differently than do respondents from lower-revenue organizations? *Let's have a look.*

Figure 1.1 on page 5 shows an overview of the Data Dashboard worksheet we'll be developing. You can customize your version of the Data Dashboard using the formulas we supply (or any other formulas you want to create), and we'll suggest ways you can do that. The Data Dashboard lets you filter your data using queries to ask questions like:

- How did CEOs (or VPs, or HR, or the people in London) answer your survey questions (and what are the important statistics derived from those answers)?

- What are the sizes of responding organizations in the New York market?

- Which location's customers tell you they have the best customer support experiences? Which say they've had the worst? How did the answers to other question vary with those customer support scores?

Let's look at the different parts of the Data Dashboard (follow along on Figure 1.1):

1. **Queries.** The Data Dashboard uses Excel's Advanced Filter queries to examine your survey data, and these queries go here at the top of the model. We'll cover how to create these queries — and note a couple of confusing items to watch out for. If you find that you use specific queries over and over, we'll show you how to prepare them ahead of time for a quick copy-and-paste. If you really want to hone your query skills,

Appendix B can turn you into a "Query Ninja."

2. **The Survey Data.** In the example, we use data from only 20 responses, each answering 15 questions. We confess that this is so that the Data Dashboard can fit in one image (and so you can type this example data into Excel if you want to). Our specific numbers are not critical — you can make up your own. However, in the real world, *everything* derives from your data. The example data contains a *screening question*, *context questions*, *four survey body questions* (in two groups representing grouped topics), and *four demographic questions*. We explain this information in the next few chapters. We expect that your own surveys will have much more data and — of course — will include real questions that are meaningful to you.

Note: Want to use our data while building this model? Easy. You can find that data in a simple table in "Want to Use Our Data? Here it is…" on page 109.

---

3. **Basic Statistics (aka "Full Counts").** These values include a count for each column (to show you if you have any inadvertent blanks), a total (useful for bar charts), Median (middle) values — but only for columns where they matter — Means (averages, where they matter), and standard deviation (where that information matters). You can, of course, include any additional statistics you want. *Basic Statistics always show the counts and statistics for all data in the model as a reference.* Thus, you can see how only the people in Oshkosh answered the survey versus the survey population as a whole.

Figure 1.1: The Data Dashboard overview — you will build this worksheet, *but no one expects you to read this image*

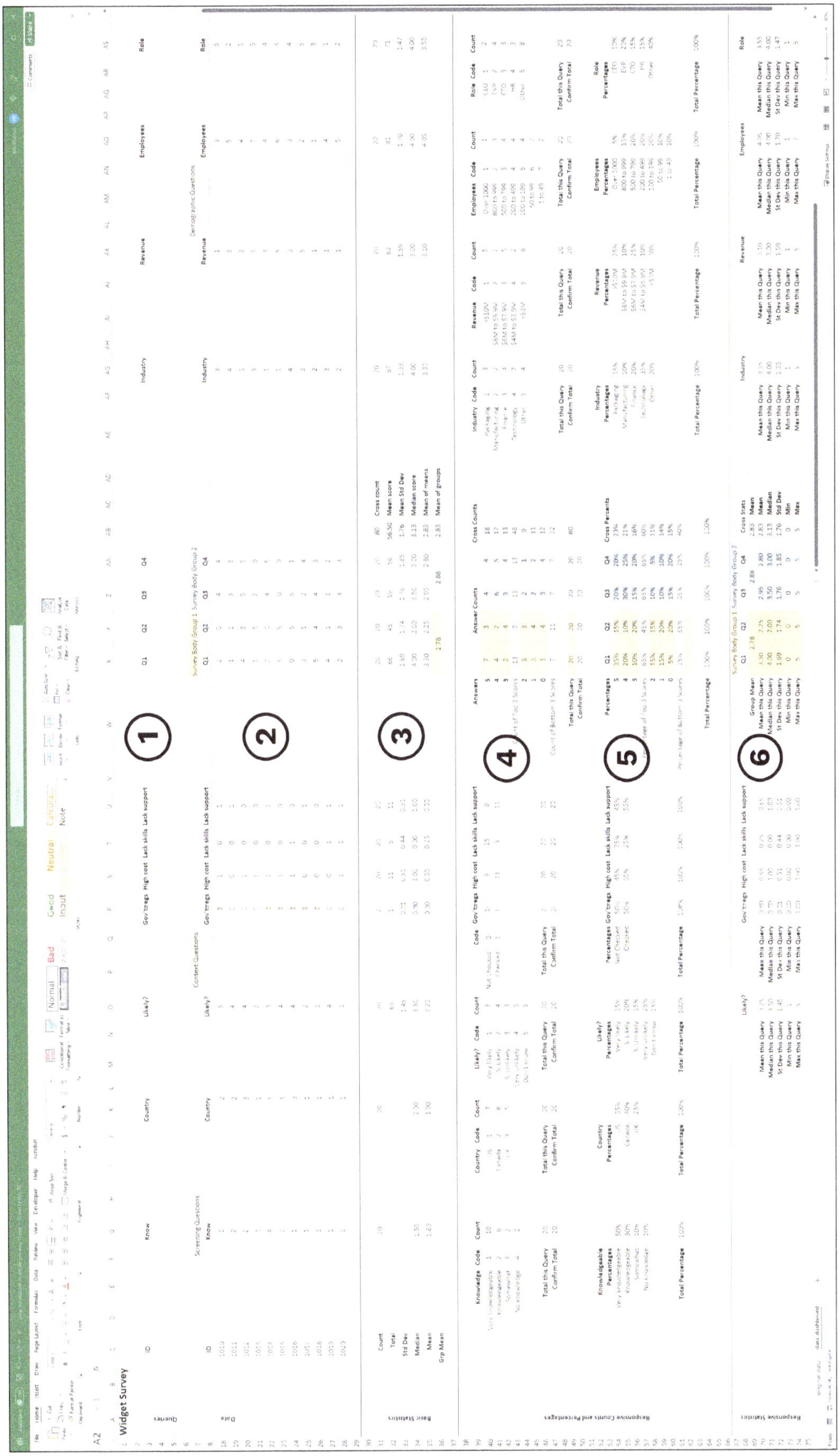

1. Queries. Controls what information is calculated below.

2. Data. The Data Dashboard example uses only 20 records.

3. Basic Statistics. Counts, Media, Mean, and similar statistics for the whole of the data.

4. Responsive Counts. When queries hide and show data, these fields reflect the changes.

5. Responsive Percentages. How the data changes in response to queries.

6. Responsive Statistics derived from the changes in data caused by queries.

4. **Responsive Counts** and...

5. **...Responsive Percentages** both change when you filter your data in ways that hide some of the data rows and show others. The example model uses data from only 20 simple responses; but when your query filters the data (to show only US data, for instance), the Data Dashboard responds by showing **a subset of rows**. The Responsive Counts automatically recalculate when you query the data and change that subset, and the Responsive Percentages change according to those counts.

6. **Responsive Statistics** also change when you query your data.

Some survey questions don't require all these statistics. It makes little sense, for example, to produce a numerical average of the values representing the three locations (1, 2, and 3). Calculations are easy to add if you find that you need them.

WHAT DO WE MEAN WHEN WE SAY "THE STATISTICS CHANGE"?

In our sample survey data for the Data Dashboard, three countries are represented: the US, Canada, and the UK. These might be five cities or ten store locations you're using in your survey. There are only 20 returned surveys in our small database. Figure 1.2 shows the demographic information for all responses. (The data are off-screen in this image for simplicity.) Compare this information to Figure 1.3 on page 8.

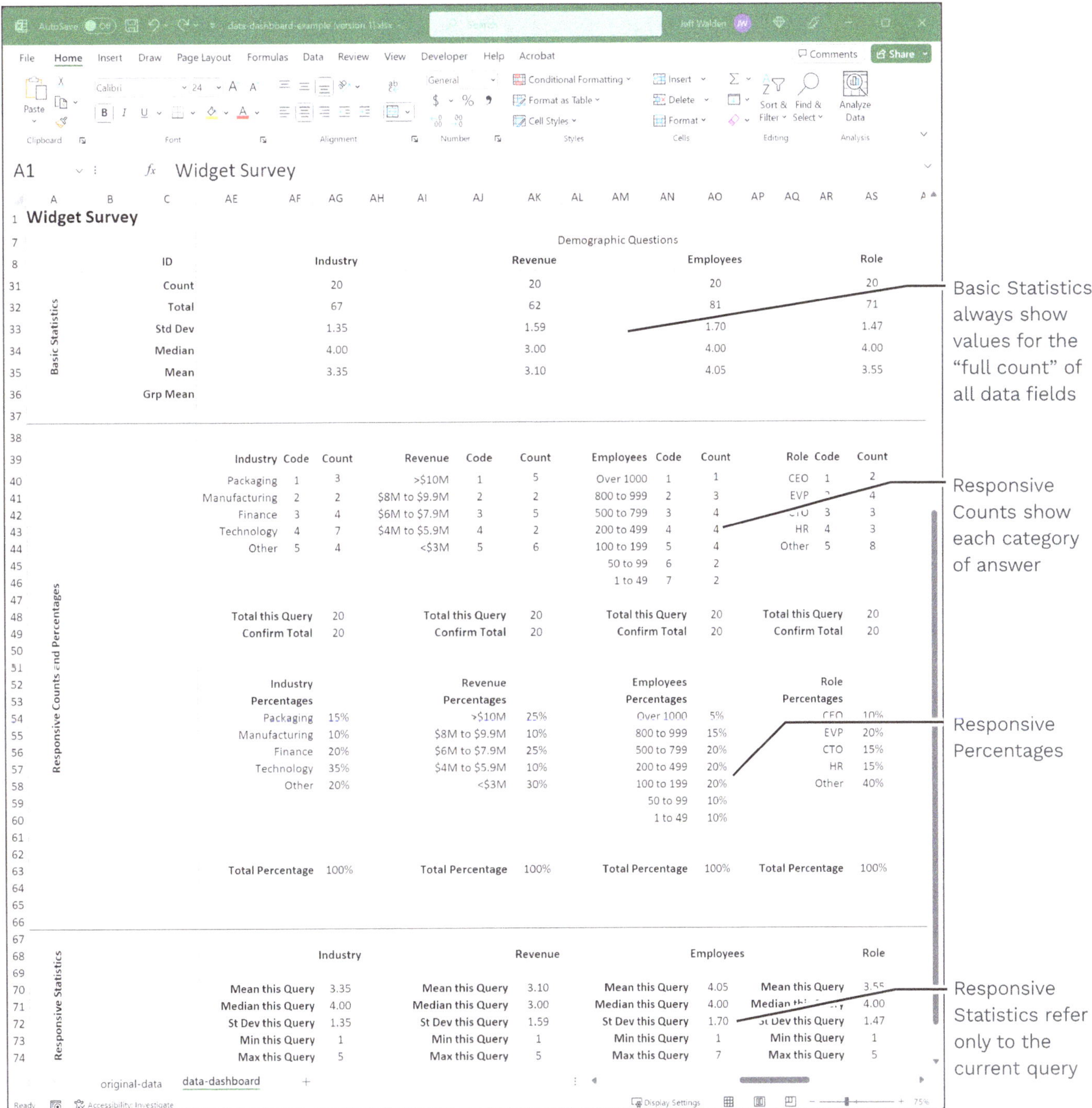

Widget Survey

Basic Statistics

	Industry	Revenue	Employees	Role
Count	20	20	20	20
Total	67	62	81	71
Std Dev	1.35	1.59	1.70	1.47
Median	4.00	3.00	4.00	4.00
Mean	3.35	3.10	4.05	3.55
Grp Mean				

Responsive Counts and Percentages

Industry	Code	Count	Revenue	Code	Count	Employees	Code	Count	Role	Code	Count
Packaging	1	3	>$10M	1	5	Over 1000	1	1	CEO	1	2
Manufacturing	2	2	$8M to $9.9M	2	2	800 to 999	2	3	EVP	2	4
Finance	3	4	$6M to $7.9M	3	5	500 to 799	3	4	CTO	3	3
Technology	4	7	$4M to $5.9M	4	2	200 to 499	4	4	HR	4	3
Other	5	4	<$3M	5	6	100 to 199	5	4	Other	5	8
						50 to 99	6	2			
						1 to 49	7	2			
Total this Query		20	Total this Query		20	Total this Query		20	Total this Query		20
Confirm Total		20	Confirm Total		20	Confirm Total		20	Confirm Total		20

Industry Percentages		Revenue Percentages		Employees Percentages		Role Percentages	
Packaging	15%	>$10M	25%	Over 1000	5%	CEO	10%
Manufacturing	10%	$8M to $9.9M	10%	800 to 999	15%	EVP	20%
Finance	20%	$6M to $7.9M	25%	500 to 799	20%	CTO	15%
Technology	35%	$4M to $5.9M	10%	200 to 499	20%	HR	15%
Other	20%	<$3M	30%	100 to 199	20%	Other	40%
				50 to 99	10%		
				1 to 49	10%		
Total Percentage	100%	Total Percentage	100%	Total Percentage	100%	Total Percentage	100%

Responsive Statistics

Industry		Revenue		Employees		Role	
Mean this Query	3.35	Mean this Query	3.10	Mean this Query	4.05	Mean this Query	3.55
Median this Query	4.00	Median this Query	3.00	Median this Query	4.00	Median this Query	4.00
St Dev this Query	1.35	St Dev this Query	1.59	St Dev this Query	1.70	St Dev this Query	1.47
Min this Query	1	Min this Query	1	Min this Query	1	Min this Query	1
Max this Query	5	Max this Query	5	Max this Query	7	Max this Query	5

original-data | data-dashboard | +

Figure 1.2: **BEFORE** All demographic information for the (very small) Data Dashboard example. Note that values for Basic Statistics are the same as those for Responsive Statistics. The counts and percentages show the general distribution of respondents' data.

Figure 1.3 shows the Data Dashboard information *after* we've executed an Advanced Filter query to show only UK (Country 3) data. The Basic Statistics remain the same, but counts and percentages now show only information for the UK responses, and Responsive Statistics show values solely for the UK.

When you do a query, the information on the Data Dashboard spreadsheet changes to show counts and statistics just for the subset of data you have chosen.

You can expand your version of the Data Dashboard worksheet to any practical number of fields and survey questions. This book shows you how.

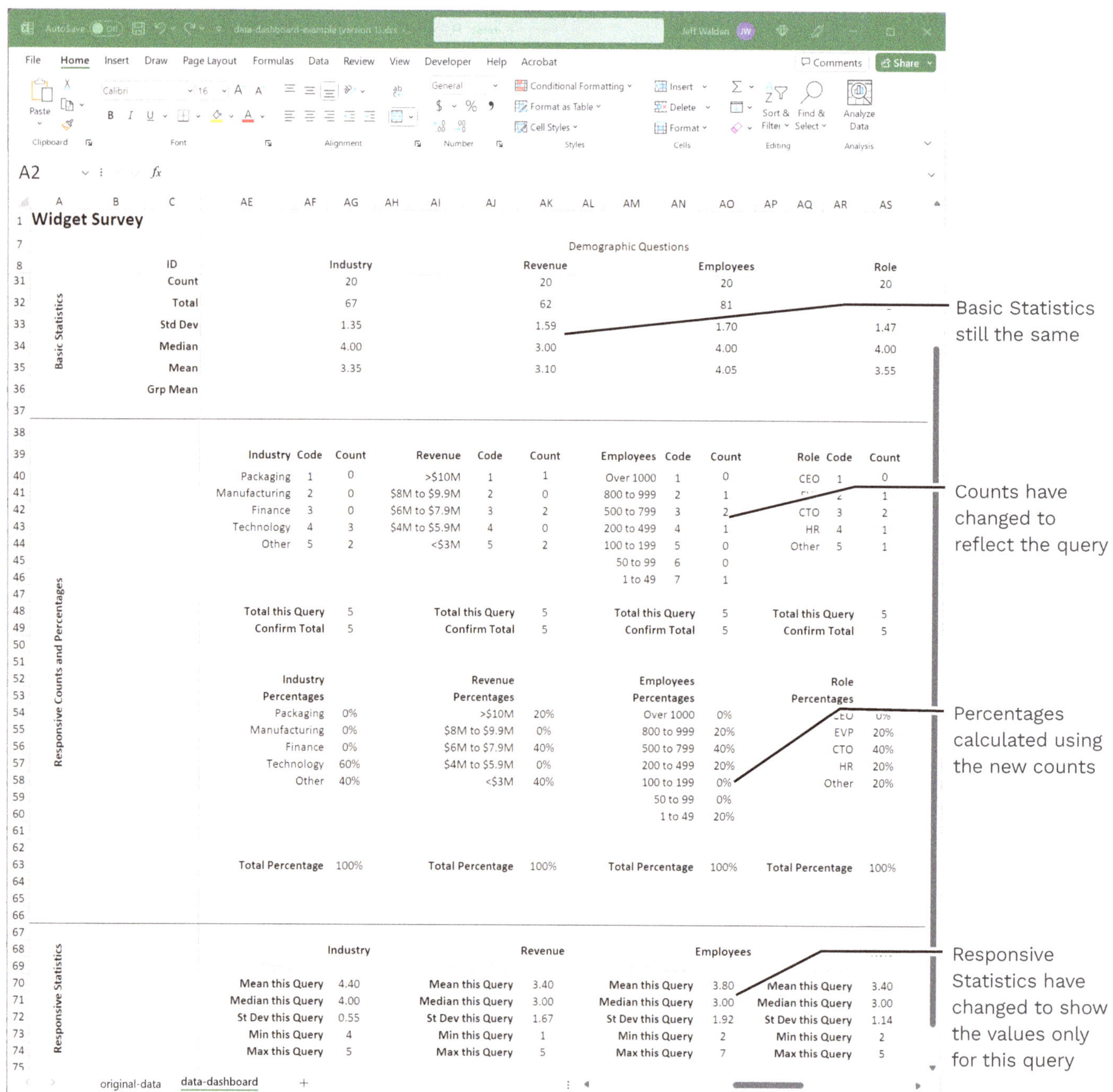

Figure 1.3:   AFTER Now the Data Dashboard shows only Country 3 (UK) data, the counts, percentages, and statistics have all changed to reflect the selection of records made by the query

Chapter 2

Let's Do a Survey

Here are some of the items you can learn or infer from even a simple survey:

- **Concentrations of customers, clients, or users — or concentrations of potential customers.** Learn where sources of new clients can be found by looking at where you have successfully found existing customers. This can open up new markets for you.

- **Find out how customers like or use various products, services, or features.** Feedback is always useful.[1]

- **How your clients do what they do.** Learning more about what your clients do and how they currently do it can give you insight into new products or services that you can create to serve them better.

- **Who your customers are.** How large is your typical (business) customer in terms of revenue or number of employees or some other measurement that is meaningful to your business? (How many brooms do your customers buy annually?) What are the industries in which your clients function? Your business may deal with a single industry (bicycle manufacturing) or may work across many different kinds of industry (HR departments).

- **Whom you reach and who responds.** You have control over the person to whom you send your survey — but who responds? For example, is the typical respondent to your survey the president of the organization, a senior or department manager... or someone from the mail room? To whom (or at least to what role) does your respondent report?

- **How knowledgeable are your clients** about their own business or about yours? Where do they get their information? Knowing this can help you advertise and communicate better.

A few minutes writing down these kinds of ideas and discussing them with your associates will begin to clarify for you the types of information you might like to find out from a survey.

You can't find out *everything*. No one will tell you *everything* and you will have to keep your survey short enough for people to be willing to complete it and respond. But you will find that many people are surprisingly open about sharing their information with you.

---

1   Be careful with soliciting or acting on outside suggestions. Existing company projects have been "contaminated" for organizations that have read outside suggestions or received ideas that were essentially similar to products already under development. It can be difficult to prove later where the original idea came from and who really owns it. You don't want someone to claim you stole their idea. If your organization wants to solicit external product ideas, consider having a third party vet them for you first.

SHHH! ANONYMITY

There are two kinds of anonymity: *Yours* and *Theirs*. Table 2.1 discusses the advantages (and disadvantages) of each combination.

Table 2.1: Who's Anonymous?

YOU	THEM	COMMENT
Anonymous	Anonymous	This is the best way to assure the highest returns and most honest responses. If you're surveying an industry (local or national) or a similar business function across several industries (companies that have an HR department, for example), this is your best bet.
		Assuring your own anonymity can take some doing, however. Obviously, you can't send the survey on corporate stationery and still remain anonymous, but you also can't send an email from a corporate IP address or put the survey on a known corporate website and still maintain anonymity. There are third-party companies that will do blind mailings, emailings, or provide links to an anonymous survey website for you and who will anonymize the results. This puts you at one remove from the responses and assures both your and their anonymity.
Anonymous	Not Anonymous	Respondents — generally — want to remain anonymous. Wouldn't you? This approach is *least likely* to elicit responses in the quantity you may want. Respondents will be unwilling to declare their identity while responding to an anonymous party, no matter how wide the welcoming smile.
Not Anonymous	Anonymous	If you're surveying groups such as a trade association, a dealer network, a real estate community, or clubs where your organization is already well known, easy to guess, or even expected to do periodic surveys, you may benefit from revealing your identity while assuring all respondents of their own anonymity. Do not ask for any identifying information. A third party may help here to with respondent anonymity.
Not Anonymous	Not Anonymous	A known organization surveying its own identifiable customers (say, because of a recent service appointment) is a good example of a mutually non-anonymous survey — both organization and customer know who the other is. If you want to ask a specific individual or organization (or a set of them) to comment on your business or project, ask directly. That's a kind of survey, too. Neither organization is anonymous. You can still obtain, organize, and analyze good responses if there are enough of them.

As your returns come in, apply a sequential number to each so that later you can find and re-confirm (if necessary) the responses that each return contains.

Such numbers do not identify the respondent. They allow you to audit the accuracy of the response if you need to. You will not know whose response it is — only that you can confirm that response #748 contains the answers that your records show it did.

HOW MANY RESPONSES DO YOU NEED?

The Rule of Thumb. Statisticians say that you'll need somewhere between 10% (of a population) up to (about) 1,000 valid responses, but generally not fewer than 100. This is called a *sample size*. Such rules of thumb must always be imprecise.[2]

The sample size is based on the size of the entire population you're surveying (if known), the margin of error you are willing to tolerate, and how confident you want to be in the results.

Sample size can vary, dipping as low as (say) 50 responses or rising to (say) 1100. There is more to this simple-seeming question than a rule of thumb, however, and we'll grind those numbers in the next few pages so that you can feel more confident.

Sample size is like the resolution of a computer monitor.

Think of sample size in terms of the resolution of a computer monitor. Computer monitors (and newspaper photos) display their images as dots, with the number of dots expressed as dots-per-inch (dpi). For your survey, you need to figure out what resolution — how many dpi — is detailed enough to produce the picture you want to see, yet is grainy enough not to cause excessive expense or processing effort. Mailings or survey websites of any type cost money; processing of any type requires resources such as personnel time, which in turn costs money. We want this book to make the processing task much, much easier, more cost-effective, and much more understandable.

Here are some facts of life to consider about your required sample size:

- **What is the population of the group you want to survey?** For example, there are about 6300 gas stations in the State of Alabama (according to Google). In Alaska, there are fewer than 400. This may be achingly obvious, but there is a larger total population of gas stations you can survey in Alabama than there is in Alaska.

You may or may not know the size of the population — and that will affect your ultimate sample size.

- **Not everybody you invite is going to respond to your survey.** Even if you're surveying a troop of Boy Scouts who promise to do their duty and obey the Scout Law, not all of them will answer your survey. It's just human nature. You have to factor into your calculations what percentage of recipients of your survey invitation you think **will not respond** — and that percentage may be *big*. If your organization has done similar surveys in the past, those surveys can guide your expectations. *You want a safety margin.*

- **Not everybody who responds is going to respond with honest answers.** Sorry. Some people will simply check off the first or last item in every list or mark all answers the same. Some will not finish the survey, but will send it back anyway. Some may try to be outlandish with any comments you allow (one reason we don't like free-form answers). You'll have to ignore suspicious responses (but may wish to retain them for any audit). *Suspicious responses can invalidate that respondent's whole survey;* you can't use just one part of someone's survey. You'll have to factor into your calculations what percentage of people may respond in a non-useful or non-usable way. *Safety margin, again.*

- ***At most*, you want responses from 10% of the survey-able population, or 1000 responses, whichever is *smaller*.** This may be counter-intuitive. For those 6300 gas stations in Alabama, that would be a useful maximum of 630 responses. In Alaska, you might just want to survey all 400 gas stations and see how many responses you get, because 10% is only 40

---

2   https://survicate.com/blog/survey-sample-size/

stations (not the ideal 100 rule-of-thumb lower limit) and it will be impossible to get 1,000 valid responses because the entire population of gas stations does not number 1,000.

On the other hand, there are over 72,000 commercial bank branches in the US. (Google again.) Ten percent of that number is 7,200 — so you may not need to invite all 7,200 to reach the 1,000-response goal. Of course, you might get *neither* 10% nor 1,000 responses from the banks. *Have we mentioned a safety margin?*

- **What response rate do you *think* you'll get?** It's difficult to know in advance — especially if you've never surveyed this group previously. In direct-mail advertising, a 3% response rate is considered good, but with advertising, you're selling something that (presumably) somebody else wants to buy. That's direct-mail motivation.

In surveys — especially where your name is known or you're dealing with a trade association or a large club that is interested in responding and finding out the result — you might get a response rate *much greater* than 3%. And then... we recently worked on a lengthy survey that emailed an invitation to over 22,000 people who performed the same business function but across several different industries. About 3.5% of them responded

with valid surveys. That was a usable number — around 750, with about a 3.5% margin of error at 95% confidence. But it took 22,000 invitations to get those 750 usable surveys. *Safety margin.*

- **Minimum responses give you rough estimates.** If you think that most people you're surveying will respond the same way (little variation between responses), then a minimum response may be "good enough." Or perhaps the answers you want are not vitally important to your business. You can save some money.

- **Maximum responses give you high-resolution, high-accuracy results.** Maybe you think that the people you survey will give very different answers with high variability. *AND*, you're doing the survey because the answers are keenly important to the future of your organization. *AND*, you have the time and resources to invest in those important answers.

- **All bets are off when you can't guess the population size.** Sample sizes get much larger when you don't have an idea of the size of the population you're surveying. As you'll see from our sample size calculation, the sample size needed from an unknown population can be **several times** the size of that required from a known population. *And you still need that safety margin.*

Time-Value for Responses

There is a time-value for the responses you get back in a survey. Ideally, all your responses will come back in a single group at more-or-less the same time. But what if they don't?

Let's say that on October 1 you send out a survey to 2,000 bicycle shops (there are 7,000 in the US — Google) but only get 100 responses back within the next two weeks. Another week goes by, and nothing more comes in. You can see from Table 2.2 that this gives you a margin of error a little better than ±10%. Is that "resolution" good enough? Do you need more responses to achieve higher resolution? If so, you'd better send out those invitations right away.

The risk you run is that the conditions under which people answer the survey may change during the time interval, and you'll get a different *kind* of answer from the later group than you did from the earlier group.

Interest rates go up and down. Markets change. Supply chains dry up or over-produce. Pandemics happen. Products go in-and-out of fashion. Model years change. News stories appear that affect opinions.

How much of a difference does that make to your survey? We can't answer that for you, but the two sets of responses you get can rapidly become two very different sets of answers because of that variable, time.

OH, NO! *MATH*!

Yes... but this is some math that is going to help you, and you won't need to do the figuring because Excel will calculate everything for you. Promise.

HOW BIG A SAMPLE DO YOU NEED?

Remember that rule of thumb: 10% or 1,000, whichever is smaller, but "no fewer than" 100 responses.

Table 2.2 shows sample sizes for different populations at different margins of error (and all at a 95% confidence level). A **population** is the entire group. A **sample** is the subset of the population that represents it, and sample size is what

Table 2.2: Sample size required for various populations at 95% confidence level

MARGIN OF ERROR	POPULATION SIZE					
	>5000	5000	1000	500	200	100
±10%	95	94	88	81	65	49
±5%	361	357	278	217	132	79
±3%	906	879	516	340	168	91

you need to have in-hand when all the validity dust has settled and you have discarded those responses that you can't use.

The samples with margins of error ±10% are all under 100, but in this table all sample sizes also are under 1,000.

Don't take our word for these numbers. Figure 2.3 on page 15 shows you how to calculate a custom sample size estimate for your own needs using Excel.

NEW TERMS FOR THE RECORD

- **Population:** The total number of people, organizations, Alabama gas stations, or other survey-able items.

- **Sample size:** The number of *valid* and usable responses you need to have

returned to achieve the margin of error you want at the confidence level you require.

- **Margin of error:** Expressed as a percentage plus-or-minus, margin of error is an indication of accuracy — the lower the margin of error, the more accurate your survey will be. You will only reach 0 if you survey everyone in a population *and* if everyone responds truthfully and accurately. *<sigh>* In other words, **you can never reach a margin of error of 0.**

- **Confidence level:** How confident you are (or would like to be) about your data. Confidence level is expressed as a percent; 95% is common. A related statistical concept called *confidence interval* reflects the uncertainty that results because you are not surveying an entire population. Confidence level and confidence interval are corresponding values, although they are not the same thing.

BRACE YOURSELF: HERE COME THE CALCULATIONS

This is not a book about statistics. Really. It's not.

There are plenty of great books available and many excellent websites you can resort to if the science of statistics is what you want to learn. Community colleges offer (relatively) inexpensive courses.

We want to be as *simple* and as *practical* and as *prescriptive* as possible... but sometimes even we can't escape the math. Our aim is to obtain a **ballpark estimate** of how many valid responses we need to receive for a given population.

There are two generic formulas that don't involve calculus (statistics textbooks can get very finicky when they address this topic). Figure 2.1 shows the formula for determining sample size where you have **a known population** — that is, if you can obtain a reasonable estimate of the number of gas stations in Alabama or bank branches in New Jersey.

Figure 2.2 shows an equivalent formula where you have **an unknown population** — the number of stage magicians in Canada (some professional, some amateur, some learning, just to imagine an unknown and possibly unknowable population).

We pick both these formulas apart in Figure 2.3 on page 15, and show you how to calculate them using Excel.

$$sample\ size = \frac{\dfrac{z^2 \times P(1-P)}{e^2}}{1 + \left(\dfrac{z^2 \times P(1-P)}{e^2 N}\right)}$$

Figure 2.1: The calculation for determining sample size when you have a "known" population. Note that there is a "top part" (numerator) and a "bottom part" (denominator) that look very similar. **Source:** https://blog.remesh.ai/how-to-calculate-sample-size

$$sample\ size = \frac{z^2 \times P(1-P)}{e^2}$$

Figure 2.2: The calculation for determining sample size when you have an "unknown" population — it looks simpler, but requires a *much bigger* sample. **Source:** https://blog.remesh.ai/how-to-calculate-sample-size

Here is what the terms in the formula mean:

- **sample size** is the number of *valid* responses you need.

- **z** is the z-score. Z-scores are standard deviations in a normal (bell-shaped curve) distribution, and they're related to confidence levels. Because you have not yet done your survey, you don't know the standard deviation for your sample. To overcome this, we use a z-score table. See Figure 2.3 on page 15, which shows the higher part of a z-score table. Much as with margin of error, you cannot reach 100% confidence.

- **P** is the standard deviation for your population at large. Standard deviation shows how widely the response data diverges from the mean (average) — some people answer 12 and others answer 47 (big divergence); or maybe some people answer 12 and others answer 13 (small divergence)... you don't know, yet. You probably *can't* know the standard deviation for an entire population in a business survey. The more surveys you do on that same population, the closer to knowing that standard deviation you will get. We'll be starting with a standard deviation of 0.5. You can adjust that standard deviation to suit. Smaller is tighter; larger is looser.

- **e** is margin of error, expressed as a percentage. Your responses should be in a range of plus-or-minus the margin of error. If a group's responses average 80 on a scale of 1–100 and your margin of error is ±3%, the number in the "real world" for that answer is going to fall somewhere between 77 and 83. You cannot reach a margin of error of 0.

- **N** is population size. For example, the 6300 gas stations in Alabama or the 72,000 branch banks in the US or the 200 member organizations of your trade association. In some cases, you may have to provide an educated guess.

SAMPLE SIZE CALCULATION

Figure 2.3 shows you how to set up the sample size calculation from Figure 2.1 and Figure 2.2 on page 14.

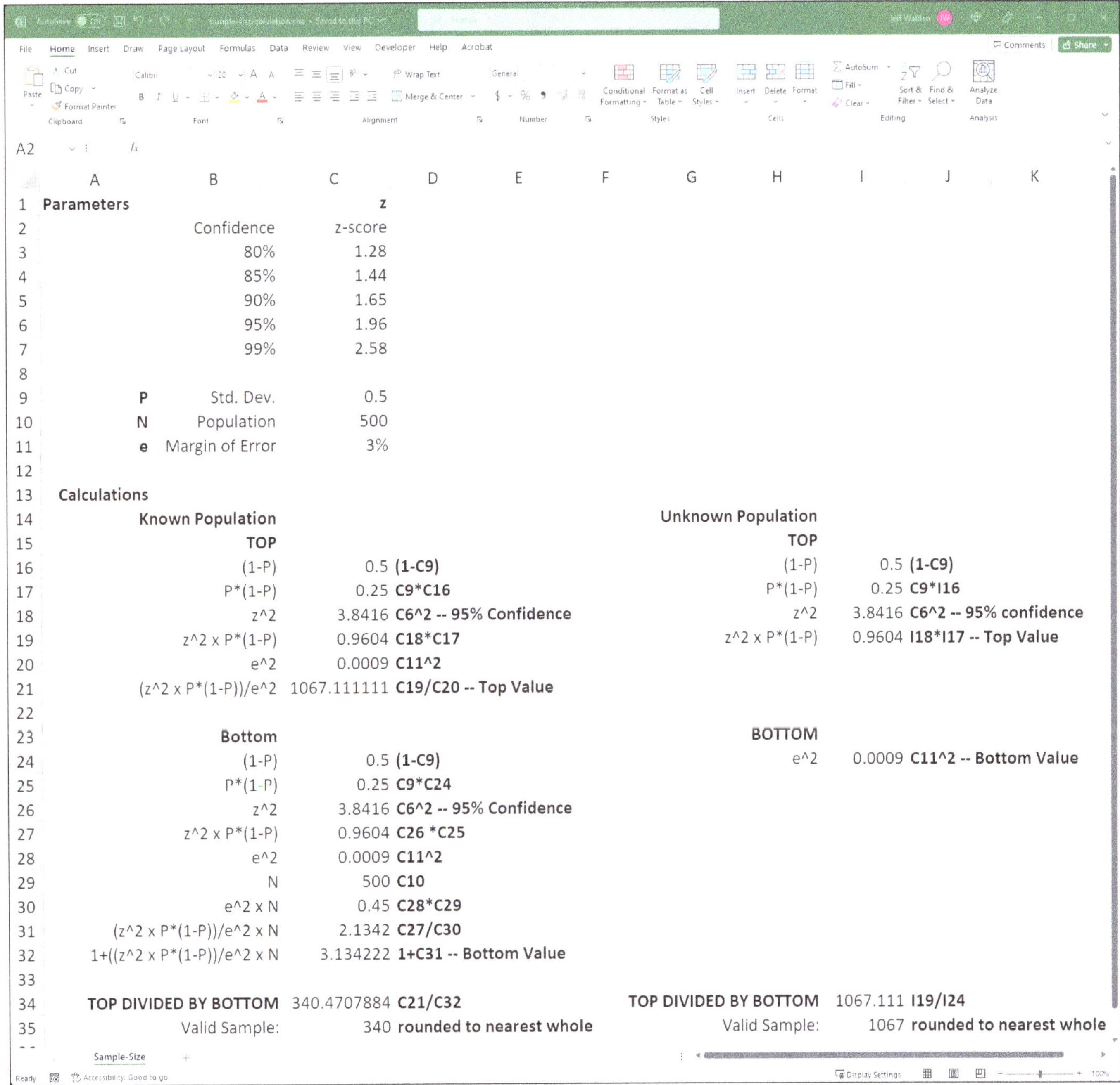

The spreadsheet in the figure contains the following (column labels A–K shown across the top; row numbers 1–35 down the left side):

Row	A	B	C
1	**Parameters**		**z**
2		Confidence	z-score
3		80%	1.28
4		85%	1.44
5		90%	1.65
6		95%	1.96
7		99%	2.58
9	**P**	Std. Dev.	0.5
10	**N**	Population	500
11	**e**	Margin of Error	3%
13	**Calculations**		

Known Population (columns A–D):

Row	A	C	D
14	**Known Population**		
15	**TOP**		
16	(1-P)	0.5	**(1-C9)**
17	P*(1-P)	0.25	**C9*C16**
18	z^2	3.8416	**C6^2 -- 95% Confidence**
19	z^2 x P*(1-P)	0.9604	**C18*C17**
20	e^2	0.0009	**C11^2**
21	(z^2 x P*(1-P))/e^2	1067.111111	**C19/C20 -- Top Value**
23	**Bottom**		
24	(1-P)	0.5	**(1-C9)**
25	P*(1-P)	0.25	**C9*C24**
26	z^2	3.8416	**C6^2 -- 95% Confidence**
27	z^2 x P*(1-P)	0.9604	**C26 *C25**
28	e^2	0.0009	**C11^2**
29	N	500	**C10**
30	e^2 x N	0.45	**C28*C29**
31	(z^2 x P*(1-P))/e^2 x N	2.1342	**C27/C30**
32	1+((z^2 x P*(1-P))/e^2 x N	3.134222	**1+C31 -- Bottom Value**
34	**TOP DIVIDED BY BOTTOM**	340.4707884	**C21/C32**
35	Valid Sample:	340	**rounded to nearest whole**

Unknown Population (columns G–J):

Row	G	I	J
14	Unknown Population		
15	**TOP**		
16	(1-P)	0.5	**(1-C9)**
17	P*(1-P)	0.25	**C9*I16**
18	z^2	3.8416	**C6^2 -- 95% confidence**
19	z^2 x P*(1-P)	0.9604	**I18*I17 -- Top Value**
23	**BOTTOM**		
24	e^2	0.0009	**C11^2 -- Bottom Value**
34	**TOP DIVIDED BY BOTTOM**	1067.111	**I19/I24**
35	Valid Sample:	1067	**rounded to nearest whole**

Figure 2.3: How to set up Excel calculations for sample size when you have populations of "known" and "unknown" sizes — note that the calculation for an unknown population makes no use of the value for N (population) in the parameters list. Remember that Excel formulas begin with the equal sign (=).

In Figure 2.3 on page 15, how can a valid sample size (for an unknown population) *possibly* be twice the size of the *entire population size* for a known population? Because by definition *the population size of an unknown population is unknown.*

With a known population size (N = 500), we can choose the confidence level, set the standard deviation and margin of error, and end up with a usable subset of the overall population. But the unknown population calculation does not require a value for N. It *must calculate without it.* That level of uncertainty, even with the same confidence level, standard deviation, and margin of error — mandates a valid sample size larger than we believe the population might actually be (as used in the known population calculation).

If 1067 is too large a number of valid responses for your unknown-population survey, you can pick a different confidence level, and set standard deviation and margin of error in such a way that you end up with a number for valid samples that pleases you... and that fits your budget. But that number likely will be of a lower confidence level and greater margin of error, and possibly a greater standard deviation.

Remember the statistician's rule of thumb: About 10% of a population or 1000 valid responses. Even the known population calculation requires a sample size of 68% for the level of confidence and margin of error we want. Want a smaller sample? Juggle the numbers. This is why we created the sample-size calculation to begin with, to make these numbers easier to juggle.

We'll run into this uncertainty effect again on the Data Dashboard — using functions that thankfully are built into Excel — with standard deviation for a sample (STDEV.S) versus standard deviation for an entire population (STDEV.P).

In Figure 2.3 on page 15, the calculation for a population of unknown size (just how many gas stations *are* there in Alabama, anyway?) must allow for the uncertainty that we may not be obtaining a sufficient sample.

It's a good idea to have at least some idea of the population size you'll be sampling. A best guess will help.

A lot.

HOW DOES THE SAMPLE SIZE CALCULATION WORK?

Recall the formulas in Figure 2.1 and Figure 2.2 on page 14. First, the Excel spreadsheet calculations shown in Figure 2.3 on page 15 separate out any fixed values (**z**, **P**, **N**, and **e**) so that we can **(a)** adjust them — all except for z, which we can only pick — and **(b)** easily refer to them in the calculation. The calculations then use your choice of those parameters to calculate the top part (numerator) and bottom part (denominator) step-by-step so that you can more easily see and verify what these models are doing.

Finally, both models divide the top part by the bottom part — and there's the answer to how large a sample you need.

The formulas for each step appear in bold to the right of the values. Don't forget to begin Excel formulas with a = sign.

You *select* the z-score corresponding to the confidence level you want for your survey. In Figure 2.3, that's the value located at cell C6, which corresponds to 95% confidence. **The z-scores are specific numbers; you can select from among them, but cannot change the z-scores themselves.** Deriving z-scores is beyond the scope of this book. You can find tables of z-scores for additional confidence levels as well as how to derive them in textbooks and on the Internet.

The standard deviation is a measure of how widely the data diverges from the Mean (average). Standard deviation (for a normal distribution "bell curve") is between 0 and 1. Smaller is narrower; greater is wider. We picked a standard deviation in the middle — 0.5. You can alter this value to suit your own model and see how it changes your sample size.

Population is your best guess at the number of total people or organizations that make up the group you are surveying — for example, those 6300 gas stations. You can alter your assumed population to suit your model — but the farther your population size value strays from reality, the less accurate your sample size number will be. Finding a population number may take some research.

Margin of error is the level of accuracy you're willing to accept. The less critical your survey is to vital decision-making, the higher the margin of error you may be willing to tolerate and the "grainier" the image you see (in our analogy of the computer monitor). Similarly, if you believe strongly that most of your population will answer the same way ("Everyone drinks water, don't they? Who would say no?") you can accept a greater margin of error and require fewer valid responses. This will save you money. You can alter the margin of error to suit your model and needs.

On execution, the formula may end up displaying a number that includes a decimal component — 340.4707884 in the actual case of Figure 2.3 as presented. We rounded the decimal component until we had a whole number. You can't have 0.47 of a response. You can increase or decrease the number by one or leave it to Excel. Your call.

Note: Remember, this is all a big approximation for figuring out the number of valid returns you need for the level of accuracy you want to achieve — and are willing to pay for.

Once you have Figure 2.3 implemented in Excel, you can fiddle with the input numbers. Alter the confidence level (select a different z-score), set a slightly higher or lower margin of error. Change the population to conform to your best information about the size of that population. You can follow as the calculations ripple down through the formula and all the way to the *Top Divided by Bottom* — which is the number of *valid* responses you need to receive based on the parameters you have set.

Oh — and this is about as difficult as the real math will get.

SUMMARY

- A simple survey can help you learn more about your customers, clients, and suppliers, and help you work better with all of them.

- It's best if you and your survey recipients remain anonymous. Failing that, you can be public, but your recipients still may want to be anonymous.

- The rule of thumb is that you need valid responses from 10% of the population or 1,000, whichever is less, and that you should gather at least 100 valid responses. You can use Figure 2.3 on page 15 to more accurately calculate the number of valid responses you need.

  - Remember that not everyone will respond and that some responses will not be valid (or usable).

Chapter 3

Question Time

How many questions should you include in your survey? This might appear to be another "ballpark item" with an easy-to-use rule of thumb, but this time the thumbs seem to be missing. Question count depends on several judgment calls.

- What is it you want to find out, and who is best suited to answer?

- How many questions will it take to ferret out what you need to know?

- What is the tolerance of your recipients in terms of number and complexity of questions and giving you their time?

- How important learning the results of your survey may be to the *recipient* (not to you).

Figure 3.1:   Like much else in life, you have to balance how many questions you can ask against the time your recipient may be willing to spend — for free, remember — to answer your survey

No survey will work if the recipients of your survey won't take the time to complete it. You must make it as easy as possible for them... and still find out what you need to find out.

Note: If you're known to your survey population, if you're surveying a trade association or a club (and not trying to assemble proprietary marketing information), perhaps you can offer the eventual survey report — or at least part of it — to respondents. If respondents must be anonymous, you can offer a downloadable report from your website. The idea is that invitees will want to participate in the survey so that they can see the aggregated results later.

Real World: A survey that required the knowledge of multiple people

We recently analyzed a survey that contained over 70 questions of different types. There were eight main groups of questions, plus demographic, context, and screening questions. The survey was sent to a large number of recipients in over a dozen industries.

The results of the survey were of great interest to the participants — and they had to be.

Although there was one official respondent per survey, the questions were of such complexity that subject-matter experts were required from around the recipient organizations. It was unlikely that any one person could answer everything. The survey respondent had to gather and collate answers before the survey could be filled in on the survey web site. Responses took a couple of weeks to assemble.

If the aggregate answers had not been so overwhelmingly important to the participants, such a major survey might have faced difficulties.

Before preparing your survey, consider the traditional journalistic questions of *Who, What, When, Where, Why,* and *How:*

- **Who is the "audience" of your survey?** What is the composition of the recipient population? Are they senior management personnel in large corporations, small business owners, government functionaries, club members, enthusiasts, or factory hands? This is the same kind of question you'd ask yourself before preparing a brochure or an advertisement.

- **Who is the "audience" for the *results* of your survey?** Who gets to see the information when you're done, and how do you intend to present it? Will you be publishing the results as a booklet or PDF (Portable Document Format) report, or doing an internal presentation or white paper? Who are the stakeholders of the results? Do you need to deliver actionable information to another department, such as marketing or sales? What information do *they* need? Have you consulted them?

- **What is the survey topic?** What is it that you want to discover or learn? Can you state it in a single sentence? The answer to this will drive the composition of the survey questions. The overall topic should be concise and defined. *What challenges do corporate HR departments face? How well-run are the bicycle dealers of the Four Corners region?*

- **What is your process for developing the survey questions?** Is it a group effort? Will one person draft the questions and others critique? Who has final say over the question set and how they're asked?

- **Why is it important** for your organization to know this information (or to publish this information)? What are the *stakes*? Will the business fold without knowing this information, is it "nice to know," or somewhere in between? How much of a difference will the survey make in how you run the business (or club or trade group)? We've already related the importance of the information to the margin or error and level of confidence that you can accept (or afford) when obtaining the data. Is a ±10% margin of error and a 90% confidence level good enough? *Your call.*

- **When will you execute the survey?** No survey lives in a vacuum. It swims through a sea of other activities that claim recipients' time and attention. How long are you going to allow the survey to remain live or "open" (how long will you continue to accept responses)? A quick scan of the Internet finds *opinion* that late morning (local time) on a Monday or Tuesday during the last week of the month is the best time to initiate a survey in terms of response rate. Fair enough. You'll still need to temper this with your own knowledge of seasonal activities, major holidays, business events, conventions, or industry trade shows — and when your target recipients may return from them or can otherwise give you their attention. People often return to full inboxes (even on Mondays); but a trade show itself may be a good place to conduct some surveys.

- **Where — to what locations — will you send your invitations?** How widespread do you want your invitees? Is your survey local, national, or international in scope? Does location even matter to your survey? That is, are responses from New York going to be lumped in with responses from Vancouver (because location has no real bearing), or is the difference between New York (US) and Vancouver (Canada) a key to what you're trying to find out? Does time zone matter? What about observing local holidays?

- **How are you going to execute the survey?** By phone, on paper, or electronically via email and website? This book is about *analyzing results*, but execution to obtain those results must be part of your planning.

Note: Time-test your survey on your own people.

PARTS OF A SURVEY

There are at least four parts to the "simple survey" we're imagining:

- **Screening questions.** Exclude potentially inappropriate respondents and gives you a sense of the range of respondents.

- **Context questions.** Gauge where the respondent fits into the survey's concerns.

- **Survey body questions.** The main survey questions.

- **Demographic questions.** A snapshot of the respondent.

Sometimes a question can fit into more than one part of a survey. How you view such questions is up to you; these four parts can be fluid.

SCREENING QUESTIONS

It's difficult enough for an honest surveyor that not all invitees will respond and that some who do respond will provide thoughtless, incomplete, or useless responses. On top of all that, you may have honest, well-meaning people, flattered that they have been mistakenly invited, offering you sincere but unusable data because they are outside your survey population. You don't need such responses, but you *do* want such respondents to identify themselves — somehow — if possible.

Be bold. Be direct. Be ruthless. **Ask screening questions.** For example:

- **How knowledgeable are you about the care and maintenance of mountain bikes? (Please choose only one.)**

    - A master of anything with wheels
    - Very knowledgeable
    - Somewhat knowledgeable
    - No knowledge

You've seen these types of questions before. They ask about the business function you perform, what you buy or recommend, and from what information sources (magazines, social media, blogs) you get your information about the survey topic. Only you can decide at what level you want to cut off respondents to your survey.

If you lack an abundance of responses ("We don't have enough mountain bike masters!") you can decide to include the next level, those who are merely "Very knowledgeable" and still exclude the *somewhats* and the *nots*.

If you do that, you must include all valid responses marked *very knowledgeable* or a random subset of them if there are too many. You can't cherry-pick. The aim is to reach or better your target sample size (or accept a greater margin of error or a lower confidence level, or both).

Of course, you also can use such a question just to *monitor* the knowledge level of your respondents and not specifically to exclude otherwise valid responses.

The Data Dashboard model that we'll build allows you to see each set of answers separately or in combination.

Here are a few more sample screening questions for your consideration:

- **Which entry most closely describes your function in the organization? (Please choose only one.)**

Let's say that the topic is managing Human Resources and that your purpose is to find out the key difficulties that HR experiences across a variety of businesses.

The choices for "function" might be Chief HR Officer, Senior HR Manager, Divisional HR Manager,

---

An Upside-Down Screening Question?

Screening questions are put into surveys to *exclude respondents* — but remember the first bullet at the beginning of this chapter: "What is it you want to find out, and who is best suited to answer?"

What if you want to know the opinions of people who *know nothing* about mountain bikes? The same screening question then works the other way, and you would seek out those respondents who have the least knowledge... The "Master of Anything with Wheels" finds himself ignored.

Screening questions. They're for screening.

Assistant HR Manager... down to HR Staffer, and None of the Above.

If the answer is *None of the Above*, you may want to exclude that survey response — that person is not involved in HR at any level. Perhaps they received the invitation in error. However, **only you can decide at what level** your respondents stop being *knowledgeable enough* to answer your questions acceptably.

Another way to ask that same kind of question, but focused on a particular business function, is:

- **In what way are you involved in Widget engineering for your organization? (Choose one)**

... followed by a set of responses such as: Leads Widget Engineering, Manages Widget Engineering for several divisions, Widget Engineer, Widget Engineering Advisor, Widget Engineering Consultant, Other.

- **Where do you turn for information about trends in modern waste and recycling management? (Check all that apply.)**

There follows a list of magazines, newspapers, newsletters, websites, social media, blogs, streaming media — whatever you think is appropriate (you know your own industry, region, or club best). Because this list is all factual, the list can be relatively long (max 15 to 20). If nothing else, the information will be useful for your marketing department. At the far end is our friend *None of the Above*. You can also allow the respondent to enter the name of a news source not listed. Who knows? You might find a new advertising venue.[1]

You can slip into the list a couple of dummy "information sources" that do not actually exist. This way, you can catch some folks who are just checking names off at random that "sound good."

And exclude those respondents if you wish.

- **Do you buy or do you recommend commercial hair preparations? (Yes/No)**

By now you are probably getting the picture about the use of screening questions. The opinions of someone who is knowledgeable, a senior manager, and who reads the correct blogs can still be less useful to you if they do not "buy or recommend."

You can separate the two so that the respondent can differentiate between *buy* and *recommend* or choose both or neither.

You can really put someone on the spot:

- **What dollar value of widget manufacturing equipment does your office approve annually?**

...after which you provide, say, half a dozen purchase ranges for the respondent to select (with items *Above X* and *Below X*). Or... *How many Widget units do you purchase* [or produce] *per quarter?* Provide a set of answers. Later, you can correlate purchases with revenue or the number of employees or some other measure relevant to your business that can show you how best to target your sales efforts (or recruitment).

All this inclusion and exclusion activity is your call, of course. A club or trade association may be inclusive by its very nature and need little or no screening, but the information can still be valuable to contextualize the respondents and their responses.

CONTEXT QUESTIONS

Context questions allow surveyors to gauge what the surveyed organization is doing or where it fits into the survey's major concerns. Context questions can make up most of — or all of — the survey and can be extremely important to the surveyor.

Context questions often are single-issue questions, rather than a set of questions focusing on a topic (see "Survey Body Questions" on page 24).

---

1   Allowing open text entry into your survey questions can complicate matters for your analysis. For one thing, you must review each entry. Text cannot be aggregated because each such entry is unique by definition. There are ways to classify open text entries so they can be handled numerically, but — for the simplest surveys — we advise against using text fields *casually*. See "Here's a Real (but Short) Survey" on page 26, and also Chapter 6, "Handling Text Fields in Surveys" on page 97.

Context questions can include:

- **Over the next 12 months, how likely are you to...**

To answer such a question, you can provide a limited set of responses (*Very Likely, Somewhat Likely, Somewhat Unlikely, Very Unlikely, Don't Know*) or a scale (scales of 1–5 or 1–10 are popular).

You can ask a set of such questions — new equipment purchases, or management practices in different departments, for example. However, a linked set of such topic-based questions may be more appropriately put into the Survey Body. As we say, Context questions and Survey Body questions are fluid.

- **How confident are you that...**

- **How easy is it for you to...**

- **How hard would it be for you to...**

What's the Difference Between a Screening Question and a Context Question?

Purpose is the difference. For example, if you're using Revenue to include or exclude a specific size organization (too big; too small), it's a Screening question.

If you're using Revenue to classify the various sizes of organization that have responded to your survey, it's Demographic.

Similarly, if you ask *What's Your Industry?* with the intent of making sure you do not include organizations selling bicycles, it's a Screening question. If you want to know which types of organizations have responded to your survey, it's Demographic.

Questions such as *How likely are you to...* or *How difficult is it for you to...* or *Which of the following reasons...* are usually Context questions because they throw light on the current practices of the respondents. Unless, of course, you're using them to exclude a set of respondents.

So, *purpose* determines the "classification" of the question.

Oh... and all that including and excluding can also be done after-the-fact when you're analyzing your data.

Again, these are scalar questions (1–5 or 1–10) reflecting some aspect of the survey respondent or the respondent's business, understanding, or practices.

One interesting technique is to ask a question (*How likely are you to...*) and then provide a series of check-all-that-apply statements that relate back to it.

For example:

- **How likely is your dealership to switch completely to electric vehicles in the next five years?**

You can include a range of checkable questions that relate to the original question:

- **Check all reasons for your answer that apply:**

  - Electric vehicles have no place in the dealership network.
  - Customers are interested but MSRP is still too high.
  - Electric vehicles are the future.
  - We have no facilities to diagnose and work on electric vehicles.
  - The investment in electric vehicle repair is too great.
  - We get great support from our manufacturer.
  - All dealerships must switch to electric vehicles.
  - Production is still too limited.

Such a question set can provide insight into the rationale for the respondent's original answer.

In your analysis report, you can make such statements as, "The X percentage of respondents who said they would switch to electric vehicles within five years gave these reasons," and, "The Y percentage of respondents who said they would not switch to electric vehicles within five years gave these reasons." And you can provide percentages for both sides and each reason. Thus, you can derive a great deal of detailed information about your survey population from a relatively small set of questions. See "Respondents Who Said This, Also Said That..." on page 94 for an example of how you can tabularize this kind of information from the Data Dashboard.

SURVEY BODY QUESTIONS

Context questions flow easily into Survey Body questions. There is little difference in the questions themselves. Usually, Survey Body questions consist of several similar questions grouped by topic. For example, you can ask:

- **Number these five product features in order of importance to you from 1 to 5 with 1 being most important.**

Or...

- **Rate how frequently you use each of these five software features in your daily work on a scale from 1–5, with 5 being most frequent.**

...and then follow that question with more detailed questions organized around each of the features.

Or you could divide the Survey Body questions into several categories — supply chain, manufacturing, distribution, sales — and ask questions about the respondent's business that focus on each of those categories.

How complex you want to get depends on what you want to find out and how tolerant your recipient is about answering your questions. Some surveys can get very complex. See "Real World: A survey that required the knowledge of multiple people" on page 19.

Why bother to organize Survey Body questions by topic or category? Organizing by category focuses the attention of the respondent on a particular area or set of information. A respondent can think about supply chain issues or their most recent service call, — or in the case of a more complex survey, the respondent can submit that subset of questions to the supply chain expert and not bother that expert with extraneous issues.

Later, when analyzing responses, the surveyor can produce an overall or *Mean* (average) value for the category as a whole. The Mean value becomes a stand-in value for questions about the entire category, useful for cross-tab tables and simplified graphs. Of course, the values for each question remain available for analysis, too. It depends on the level of detail that you want to examine.

Do I have to group questions like this? Of course not. This is why we say that Context questions — which are mostly stand-alone or that deal with a single issue — can flow into the more topic-oriented Survey Body questions. Your surveys will always be different from the simplified and generalized model we present here.

DEMOGRAPHIC QUESTIONS

Your survey invitees will include a range of persons or organizations that you believe best reflect the survey population and from whom you want to gather your data. No doubt you have engineered an excellent mix and balance of recipient *invitees*. However, you ask demographic questions to understand the mix and balance of those who have, in fact, *responded*. Not everyone you invite will respond, and you can't control whose responses you will receive (or who ultimately did the responding).

> *You ask demographic questions to understand the mix and balance of those who have responded.*

Demographic questions help determine the respondents' position in the survey.

In your later analysis, you can see the percentage of one group relative to another, and how answers of one demographic group differ from — or are similar to and reinforce — the answers of a different demographic group.

Demographic questions can include anything that's meaningful to know about your survey population... as long as your respondents are willing to answer those questions. Not all of these example questions may be pertinent to every survey.

- **Revenue (or income) range.** Provide a set of ranges suitable for your survey — don't expect respondents to write-in a value.

- **Age of respondent.** This may not be pertinent in every (or even in most) surveys, but it might be pertinent to *yours* — for example, if you're surveying rock concert ticket buying patterns or skateboard users, or if your answers must come from someone who is a legal adult.

Again, provide reasonable ranges; don't expect a write-in.

- **Number of employees.** Provide a set of ranges suitable for your survey population.

- **Industry classification.** In the US, there are two main industrial classification systems: SIC and NAICS, each of which includes over a thousand industry and business types at a dizzying level of detail. You probably won't need more than a dozen classes for even the biggest of simple surveys, and your invitees may not even know their own classification (and *almost certainly will not know it* offhand, by number, or at the level of detail offered by these high-power classification systems). Provide a selection of the business types that are meaningful to you as *names* (not as numerical codes), plus Other. You can convert them to a code later for your analysis, if you even need it.

- **Years the organization has been in business/Time it has been doing this particular function/Year founded/Year function was started.** We've found it interesting to consider Years versus Revenue or Number of Employees as an indicator of "business acceleration" — how fast an organization is moving and growing. A growing high-tech company easily can add 1,000 employees in a year; an ice cream factory, not as many. If an organization reaches a level of effectiveness and maturity in its industry after 3 years that other organizations require 15 years to reach, this provides important insight into the organization and its industrial sector.

- **Number of locations/offices/branches/factories/clubs within a geographical area.** You need to define what an *area* means. It might be a county, a state, a province, a country, or a region such as "west of the Mississippi."

- **Your role in the organization.** Who is responding? Provide a meaningful set, along with Other: CEO, President, Manager,

---

Real World: Survey Time-to-Completion

This is a survey item that is not a question but which you may wish to consider as an option for electronic data collection (via website/URL).

With a website survey, a respondent often clicks a button such as "Begin Survey" to start, and then "Complete Survey" to end. This gives you the ability to calculate the time it takes the respondent to complete the survey. You can't do this with a paper survey and it may be meaningless even with an electronic survey that many people must work on.

Some surveys allow a respondent to stop and save the survey and come back to it later. A timer can be part of such an arrangement, too.

Is this information meaningful? *It can be*, even if the survey is not a timed test of any kind.

We worked on a survey where the scalar scores given by the respondents slowly decreased so that they were lower in the latter part of the survey when compared to the beginning of the survey. Were these scores lower because the topics towards the end of the survey were more difficult to assess or were the respondents just getting tired at that point?

Interesting question, and no good way to tell. One reason for this is because the survey recorded no start-stop time tick. If we had had a start-stop time tick, we might have calculated an average time-to-completion and then measured the scores against that average. Did people who took longer to complete the survey provide lower scores? Higher? Was there no correlation?

Possibly, people might work more slowly as they fatigued. *Possibly*, the answers they provided might go down as they fatigued. *Maybe. Possibly.* Ultimately, we just don't know. We *do* for next time…

At the very least we might have seen where the break-point was in terms of number of questions before fatigue set in and could use that info in planning future surveys.

Club President, Branch Manager, etc. This can act as a check against the screening question, *What is your function in the organization?*

- **Who respondent reports to.** This question can provide insight into the structure of the organization being surveyed, and can also serve as a check against both the *Your Role* and *What Function* questions.

SURVEY DATA ITEMS THAT ARE NOT QUESTIONS

Make room in your data collection process for non-question items that may help you later during your analysis. These items may not actually appear on the survey or be answered by a respondent; your data entry process itself can capture them.

- **Code number/ID number.** Add a unique sequential code number to each anonymous survey response. You can do this as the responses come in or after you have arrived at your set of valid responses. You'll be better able to audit your results later if you need to do so. **A code number DOES NOT identify the respondent** — only the response. The operation of the Data Dashboard routinely hides and shows different sets of responses. The code number can verify that response #2311 was indeed from a CEO and was not incorrectly transcribed or otherwise corrupted. How else could you know if you can't identify

and check against the original information? We recommend this as a must-have.

- **Survey date/Return date.** Perhaps your survey is time-sensitive; a late return date might be a reason to reject it. Attaching a date to the responses as they come in also can aid archiving.

- **Location.** Location can be part of the survey questions (Choose the closest large city to you from this list...), or you can set up two or more as-needed survey websites and provide separate URLs to invitees in different locations, thus obtaining the location that way. Location is valuable if you're doing **THE EXACT SAME SURVEY AT THE EXACT SAME TIME** in multiple locations. Only if all questions are the same at the same time can you validly compare locations.

HERE'S A REAL (BUT SHORT) SURVEY

As we were writing this book, we received a real survey — a short one — from a real company seeking to find out how their technician performed on a recent service call. (The technician did very well and we said so.)

We've concealed the company name and the identity of the technician.

Note that:

- The organization knows who we are and we know who the organization is. (Neither of us is anonymous to the other. That's Okay for this purpose.)

- The organization has access to area demographics — income distributions, real estate valuations, etc. — from other

sources. They don't need to ask qualifying questions. They know whom they visited.

- The organization knows the product they serviced and its pricing, which they can map against demographics.

- The organization knows the identity of their technician and responses about that technician from other customers.

Note: We gave the technician top grades (truly, the tech was good). We suspect that if we had given lesser grades, we would have been asked to describe in a text field what had gone wrong or what could have gone better — but that's not a survey path we explored. A second technician did arrive, but whether this was the "company specialist technician" as described in the survey or just a helper we don't know.

Here are the questions:

- How satisfied are you with [technician's] ability to assist you with your service request?
  1 - Very DISSATISFIED
  2 - Dissatisfied
  3 - Neutral
  4 - Satisfied
  5 - Very SATISFIED

- How satisfied are you with [technician's] knowledge and expertise?
  1 - Very DISSATISFIED
  2 - Dissatisfied
  3 - Neutral
  4 - Satisfied
  5 - Very SATISFIED

- Was [technician] able to fully resolve your request?
  1 - Yes
  2 - No

- Thinking about your most recent Technician visit, please indicate how likely you are to recommend [company] to friends and family. Please respond with a number from 1 to 5.
  1 - Definitely would NOT RECOMMEND [company]
  5 - Definitely WOULD RECOMMEND [company]

- On your recent service request, did you have a [company specialist technician] in addition to your [company technician] helping you, and if so would you be willing to answer two additional questions?
  1 - Yes
  2 - No
  3 - No [company specialist technician]

- How satisfied are you with the service that the [company specialist technician] provided you? Please reply with an answer from 1 to 5.
  1 - Very DISSATISFIED
  5 - Very SATISFIED

- Can you briefly describe what you felt was the most beneficial aspect of what the [company specialist technician] provided to you?
  [text entry follows]

As we have said, we're not fond of text entries in surveys because each entry is unique and each one must be assessed separately — which means "more processing" for the survey and more expense for the surveying organization. In this case, the organization is judging the work quality of their own service technician. They need the input. If customers have something to say, they should have a way to say it.

GUIDELINES FOR QUESTION WRITING

If you're reading a book called *Analyze a Survey with Microsoft Excel* (and we believe that you are), it's unlikely you're in the business of doing surveys professionally. You're just trying to get a job done.

People who *are* in the business of doing surveys professionally often run surveys just to determine how best to ask questions when they run a real survey for a client. They run surveys to determine what set of answers to provide for a given question and how best to phrase them. They massage their questions to eliminate any phrasing that might bias the answers. *They test continually.*

It's unlikely that you will go to such extremes, but you can still write a decent survey. The following items are not rules, just advisories.

It's very, very much easier on you if everything reduces to a number. You're about to do an analysis of your data in Excel, a spreadsheet that's superb at handling numbers, but it is not a word processor. Having free-form text answers of various lengths in your data certainly is doable as part of this analysis, but it's going to complicate matters for you. Therefore, it is best if all the answers to your survey questions can reduce to a number.

For example, a *Yes/No* question becomes 1/0.

A *How Likely* question (*Very Likely, Somewhat Likely, Somewhat Unlikely, Very Unlikely, Don't Know*) reduces to 1–5 (or even to 4–0 if you want Don't Know to be a 0). The sequential direction of numbers is not critical.

Note: The Data Dashboard as presented presumes that all your questions will result in number values, although you can import (almost) any text attached to a record as a cell in Microsoft Excel. See Chapter 6, "Handling Text Fields in Surveys" on page 97.

Ask the most important questions first. Pollsters say that questions of lesser importance when asked early may accidentally bias answers to the more important questions if you ask those important questions later in the survey. So **ask the important questions up front** for the freshest, least-biased answers. We suggest you put such questions in the Context questions section.

Ask one question at a time. For example, **do not ask**, *What do you think of XYZ's steel tube and their carbon fiber bicycle frames?* Opinion about the steel tube frames may differ from opinion about the carbon fiber frames, making this double-barreled question difficult to answer with a single response. If you need both answers, ask both questions.

Keep response choices to a small number. Five choices is a good goal. You can provide a larger number of choices when the answers are matters of fact rather than opinion. The question *What is your role in the organization?* easily can have a dozen responses because the respondent falls into one category or another — and which category is not open to very much debate. Opinion questions need to stick as closely as possible to that goal of "around five" choices.

Simplicity and neutrality. Use neutral wording. Do not try to lead the respondent. You should be doing a survey because you want to find something out, not force confirmation of a pre-existing opinion. **Do not start a question with**, "Wouldn't you agree that..." or "Most people think..." Do not use casual idioms (*fishing expedition, bang for the buck*), sports analogies (*drop the ball, skin in the game, half-time talk*), or undefined acronyms (*SPF, MSDN*). Your survey may be completed by someone who is not a native English speaker, by someone who does not follow sports (or not *your* sports), or by someone who is unaware of your acronyms. Finally, avoid biased or "loaded" words. Do we really need to hammer on those?

Yes/No questions apparently bias people towards Yes. People seem to want to please surveyors and will say Yes even if that answer is not *exactly* true. Save your *Yes/No* questions for matters of fact (Was the technician able to resolve your problem? Does your organization include an on-site HR department?) rather than opinion.

Offer respondents a choice rather than ask agree/disagree. Much as with *Yes/No* questions, people like to be agreeable and this can provide incorrect data. Rather than ask a debating-club question, such as: "All organizations need an on-site HR department (Agree/Disagree)," instead, ask something like:

- **Does your organization include an HR department?"**
  - We have an on-site HR department.
  - We have an off-site HR department.
  - We have no HR department.
  - What is an HR department?

OUR WIDGET INDUSTRY SURVEY QUESTIONS

Bearing in mind all the foregoing collection of DOs and DON'Ts and with our apologies in advance for such a small collection of survey data (this just keeps it easy for you to enter it yourself if you wish), here are the questions that correspond to the simple survey we'll later work with in the Data Dashboard. We've labeled the parts of the survey where the questions appear for your information — not something that you'd do on an actual survey.

Because all these questions reduce to numbers, we've also shown you the number that corresponds to each response. Adding number values to the responses is likewise something that you *ordinarily* would not do on an actual survey unless you're asking for a specific numeric score such as 0-5.

SCREENING QUESTIONS

This question establishes whether the respondent can answer with an adequate level of knowledge, at least for our purposes.

- **How knowledgeable are you about overall widget operations at your organization?**

  - Very knowledgeable (1)
  - Knowledgeable (2)
  - Somewhat knowledgeable (3)
  - No knowledge (4)

Our survey and analysis is set up for this question with a 1-2-3-4-style correspondence between response and number. However, you may want the correspondence to work the other way, so that *No knowledge* is equivalent to a 0 (maybe that's more meaningful to you). It's your call. The direction of the numbering doesn't matter as long as you keep track of it and don't always assume that 1 is "best" in your analysis. "Best" number and direction may have a bearing when you're comparing Means and Medians between questions. For example, can a Mean (average) value of 3.5 in question A and a Mean value of 2.5 in question B actually be equivalent? Sure, if question A is valued from 5–1 and question B is valued from 1–5. Direction doesn't matter until you start comparing the directional apples to the directional oranges.

CONTEXT QUESTIONS

Context questions establish the location of the business and "ask the important questions" of the survey. If you're sending your invitations to the gas stations of Alabama, the members of the Chamber of Commerce in Reno, NV, or the banks of Union County, NJ, you already know the location of the respondents.

Because we set up only one website page for our fictional widgeteers to complete our widget survey, it's necessary for respondents to tell us their location. If we had set up different websites — one for invitees from the US, one for Canada, and one for the UK — or if we filtered connections to our single website by the email link that the respondent clicked, we would not need to ask this question explicitly. There are several such ways to attach this information to the response, but here we ask it outright:

- **In what country are you located?**

  - US (1)
  - Canada (2)
  - UK (3)

We could also ask this question in terms of what large city is nearest to you (especially for respondents in a single country) or your time zone. Be aware that someone in the middle of Pennsylvania may not know whether Pittsburgh or Philadelphia is the nearest city to their location.

The "Important" Question

The following pair of questions asks about the organization's attitude towards a new practice in the widget industry. As mentioned earlier about this type of approach ("How likely is your dealership to switch completely to electric vehicles in the next five years?" on page 23), the first question asks for a direct answer and the second question (actually a set of check-all that apply selections) provides insight into the main question.

- **How likely are you to institute the new practice of electronic widget management within the next 12 months?**

  - Very Likely (1)
  - Somewhat Likely (2)
  - Somewhat Unlikely (3)
  - Very Unlikely (4)
  - Don't know (5)

- **Which of the following reasons apply to your organization's approach to electronic widget management? (Select all that apply.)**

  - Government regulation has mandated a conversion to electronic widget management in our region.
  - We are concerned about the high cost of conventional widget management, and want to reduce costs by going electronic.
  - We lack appropriate skills to convert to full electronic widget management at this time.
  - We lack management support for electronic conversion.

If one of these statements is selected, it signifies 1. If a statement is not selected, it signifies 0. The statements are not mutually exclusive. A respondent could check all, none, or any. For example, it might be true that government regulation mandates electronic widget management **AND** that the organization lacks appropriate skills to convert.

Because the potential reasons are matters of fact (not opinion), you can provide more than the few statements shown here, so that you can cover the set of potential reasons that may concern businesses and organizations, and get a better sense of the pulse of the industry.

Nor does this preceding pair of questions constitute the only way to ask the survey's "important" questions.

Depending on what you're trying to find out — level of management support or organizational intention to implement — you might otherwise have asked, "How active is senior management in making the decision whether to convert to electronic widget management?" (0–5) Or, "How supportive is senior management in making the

decision…" Or, "On a scale from 1 to 5, with 1 being very easy and 5 being very difficult, how difficult [or how easy — ask only one way] is it for your organization to convert to electronic widget management?"

If electronic widget management is important to the industry, you might ask more than one of these questions.

Or, there might be two important questions or three. *This is your survey*; all that we're doing here is concocting imaginary questions about an imaginary industry to make the data sample feel more realistic — and provide additional examples on how to write survey questions.

SURVEY BODY QUESTIONS

As we've pointed out, Context questions can flow into Survey Body questions and they can appear minimally different. Context questions tend to revolve around single issues and Survey Body questions tend to form groups around topics. What we've done with our survey is create two *groups of Survey Body questions* (sorry, only two questions each; this is just a tiny demo) — one set built around widget *production* activities and one set built around widget *distribution* activities.

Grouping focuses the respondent's attention on specific aspects of a topic or category.

For the body of the survey, we want to focus the respondent's attention on specific aspects of a topic or category. We can use this grouping idea later on when analyzing the data. For example, in a category with five or even ten questions, we can create statistics for the group as a whole, as well as for individual questions. This provides summary information for the question group that makes it easier to tabularize and graph.

You'll see how this summary process works as we build the Data Dashboard, beginning with "Create the Data Dashboard" on page 33.

In our case, each of the Group One and Group Two questions is *scalar*, using a scale from 0–5. These scales can signify anything you want, as shown in Table 3.1 on page 31. **You must define the meanings of each gradient for your respondents.** Don't leave it to the respondent to imagine a gradient. Be specific.

Note: When using scalar questions, it's important to identify the specific scale you're using — and the meaning you've attached to each gradient — so that your respondent can refer back to this information as they complete the survey.

Table 3.1: Possible meanings for a 0–5 scale

SCORE	DOES YOUR COMPANY…	HOW LIKELY…	ARE YOU…
5	Significant, Focused Activity	Yes, Definitely	Continuously Involved
4	High Activity	Likely	Involved Often
3	Average Activity	Neutral	Involved Sometimes
2	Low Activity	Unlikely	Involved Rarely
1	Minimal Activity	No, Definitely	Minimally Involved
0	No Activity	Don't Know	Not Involved

Note that in Table 3.1 our "top score" is the highest number. Thus, a "bigger number" means "better" in this case during later analysis.

You can offer scalar responses in a variety of ways: as Yes/No (1–0, 1–2), as High-Low (1–2 or 2–1 or 1–0), as 1–3, 0–5, 1–5, 1–10, 1–100, or even — *shudder* — 1–1000… That said, on that 1–1000 scale, do you really care about an opinion response difference of 856 versus 857? Do you think that your respondents can differentiate precisely enough between the two scores (or that individual respondents will respond consistently enough) to make it meaningful? They will probably end up mentally processing their scores as 1–5. We like 0–5 because it allows for an obvious "no" or "zero" response when that is appropriate (the 0) and still allows for 1–5 gradations, or 20% per score value. People who've grown up with the decimal system generally find that easy to manage.

Note: According to Wikipedia[2] some regions of Asia and Africa use duodecimal (base 12) counting. We couldn't resist checking.

2   https://en.wikipedia.org/wiki/Duodecimal

Question Group One (Widget Production)

Answer on a scale from 0–5, where 0 indicates no activity and 5 indicates significant activity, as in Table 3.1.

- **We use best-practice electronic widget management during production.**

- **We consider lubrication for the widget during stamping to be a critical factor in production quality assurance.**

Both questions bear on important aspects of widget production and best manufacturing practices for widgets. Thus, these questions are grouped together.

Question Group Two (Widget Distribution)

Answer on a scale from 0–5, where 0 indicates no activity and 5 indicates significant activity, as in Table 3.1.

- **Our contracts help assure the financial stability of our authorized widget suppliers.**

- **We always use refrigeration for shipping widgets, even though some models may not strictly require it.**

Group Two questions are concerned with widget supply and distribution best practices and use the same 0–5 scale.

Not Limited to 0–5

We hope it's obvious that Survey Body questions are not limited to 0–5 scalar answers. We chose 0–5 because that scaling makes it easy to show how questions can be grouped and aggregated during analysis.

You can use Yes/No, Agree-Disagree, 1–10, or any other form of answer that's meaningful for your questions. We've already discussed various options for structuring questions.

As a best practice — and to make it easier on your analysis later — asking questions whose answers reduce to a number is an excellent approach.

We discuss how to deal with open-end text responses in Chapter 6, "Handling Text Fields in Surveys" on page 97. It is *not* as easy as dealing exclusively with numbers.

DEMOGRAPHIC QUESTIONS

The Demographic questions of the widget survey provide a snapshot of the respondents' organizations. They are generally straightforward and not opinion-based. Therefore, such fact-based questions can have more than the "ideal" five answers. For example — and if you think you need it — you might have a dozen or 16 responses to Primary Industry to get the granularity you want.

- **Which of these answers best describes your organization's primary industry classification? (Select one)**

  - Packaging (1)
  - Manufacturing (2)
  - Finance (3)
  - Technology (4)
  - Other (5)

- **What best defines the revenue of your organization? (Select one)**

  - More than $10M (1)
  - $8M – $9.9M (2)
  - $6M – $7.9M (3)
  - $4M – $5.9M (4)
  - Less than $3.9M (5)

- **How many employees are in your overall organization? (Select one)**

  - Over 1,000 (1)
  - 800 – 999 (2)
  - 500 – 799 (3)
  - 200 – 499 (4)
  - 100 – 199 (5)
  - 50 – 99 (6)
  - 1 – 49 (7)

- **What best describes your role in the organization?**

  - CEO (1)
  - EVP (2)
  - CTO (3)
  - HR (4)
  - Other (5)

SUMMARY

Number of questions. The number of questions you put into your survey depends on what you need to find out, how important it is to you that you find it out, and how many questions your respondents will tolerate. It's a judgment call.

Before you begin. Be guided in your planning by the journalistic questions of Who, What, When, Where, Why, and How.

Surveys generally have four parts. *Screening questions* to exclude unneeded or unwanted respondents, *Context questions* to ask the "important" questions of the survey, *Survey Body questions*, and *Demographic questions* to obtain a snapshot of respondents.

Survey data that may not be questions. These can include a code or ID number for each returned response, survey date or time, and location (if meaningful to your survey).

Guidelines. It is easier to manage the survey if everything reduces to a number. Ask the important stuff first. Keep the questions and responses neutral and simple, and keep response choices ~5 for opinions. Yes/No and Agree/Disagree are Okay... but have been found to bias opinion responses.

Chapter 4

Create the Data Dashboard

You have completed writing your survey, you have executed it, and have received an adequate number of valid responses to satisfy your requirements for margin of error and confidence level (see "How Many Responses Do You Need?" on page 11). You have ruled out the obviously incomplete surveys and the surveys filled with junk data and those that otherwise don't meet your requirements. You have made an executive decision about whether to accept surveys where all (or almost all) the answers are the same — for example, all responses are number 1, or all 5, or all in the middle. These may be legitimate but it's hard to know — which is why it's an executive decision. As a practical matter, it might all boil down to how many valid responses you have *with and without* the questionable responses. Only you can decide. But here we are! It is time to create the Data Dashboard.

WHERE'S THAT DATA?

Depending on how the data was created — accumulated from phone calls, on paper forms, drawn from a web site, or produced via the services of an e-mailing or survey company — your data may already have been delivered to you as an Excel spreadsheet. If so, great. More frequently, the data were sent to you as a comma-separated-value (CSV) or tab-delimited text file.

Or, your junior assistant (um... or *you*) may have spent a few late nights entering the values into Excel from paper.

Note: Want to use our data — just to play with? There's not much of it (it's just a small sample), and you can quickly enter it into a blank Excel worksheet. See "Want to Use Our Data? Here it is..." on page 109. Otherwise, feel free to use your own data. Of course, you will need to modify your Data Dashboard accordingly — field names and length of data columns in particular.

IMPORT YOUR DATA INTO EXCEL

If your data is already in a CSV file or an Excel worksheet, save that file as **Original-Data** (or some similar name) to your computer. We will copy from it or import from it, and we may need to return to that original copy later. **Don't touch it or modify it otherwise** (until it's successfully in Excel).

Other than copying and saving, we won't alter the original. Put it into the cloud or save it to disk or a thumb drive, and place that thumb drive on a purple velvet cushion in the office safe. Original data is precious. Don't lose it.

Now, **let's work with the copy of that original data** that you have put on your computer. Even then, it's wise to leave the original data on its own worksheet tab... and then copy that data to a "working-data" tab. **Can you tell that we like redundancy and save frequently?**

Instructions for importing a CSV file. We've documented the multi-step process of importing and *un-formatting* the data from a CSV file in the section "Importing Your Own Survey Data from a CSV File" on page 110.

Why do we say "unformatting"? Excel automatically anticipates your needs and formats imported CSV data for you in a particular way as a *table*, but Excel's way of formatting the data is not needed by the Data Dashboard, and so we remove the formatting that Excel adds during the import process.

A short refresher on importing an Excel file. Find it here: "Importing Your Data from an Excel File" on page 113

THE STARTING POINT: YOUR DATA IS IN EXCEL

Our sample data is meager. We have only 20 rows. Your data — for almost any reasonable survey — will be much more extensive. You may have *several hundred* rows of data and one column for every question's answer. Figure 4.1 shows our sample data imported into Excel.

Each row is called a *record*. Each row holds all the answers from a single respondent.

Each column is called a *field*. There are several fields in each record.

The intersection of row and column (a cell) holds a single response for a single question from its individual record. Each intersection corresponds to an answer given to a question in the survey.

We'll be using the terms *record* and *field* frequently from now on.

Note: It is important that all data rows and columns contain data. **Why?** This confirms that there are no incomplete records. Incomplete records already should have been set aside as invalid. The Data Dashboard worksheet includes a column count and a percent value to re-confirm this as you work with the data.

	A	B	C	D	E	F	G	H	I	J	K	L	M	N	O	P
1	ID	Know	Country	Likely	Reason1	Reason2	Reason3	Reason4	Q1	Q2	Q3	Q4	Industry	Revenue	Employees	Role
2	1001	1	2	3	0	0	1	1	4	0	0	4	5	2	3	5
3	1002	1	2	2	1	0	0	1	5	2	5	4	4	4	4	3
4	1003	5	3	2	1	1	0	1	4	2	4	3	4	5	3	3
5	1004	2	3	5	1	1	0	0	5	3	4	0	4	1	2	2
6	1005	4	2	5	0	1	0	1	1	2	5	0	4	3	5	4
7	1006	2	2	5	0	1	0	0	5	0	0	5	5	5	2	5
8	1007	2	2	3	0	0	0	0	5	3	3	1	4	5	5	2
9	1008	3	3	1	0	0	0	0	3	4	1	5	5	5	7	3
10	1009	1	2	5	1	0	1	1	5	1	3	3	1	2	6	1
11	1010	1	2	5	1	1	0	1	2	0	4	4	3	1	3	5
12	1011	2	2	4	0	0	0	1	1	1	3	3	4	3	5	2
13	1012	2	3	4	0	1	0	0	4	3	5	5	5	3	4	5
14	1013	1	1	2	0	1	0	0	1	5	2	0	3	3	7	5
15	1014	4	1	3	1	1	0	1	2	0	4	5	1	4	4	4
16	1015	2	1	4	1	1	0	0	5	5	0	0	1	5	6	5
17	1016	1	3	4	1	1	1	0	0	5	5	1	4	3	3	6
18	1017	1	1	2	1	0	0	1	3	1	2	4	3	5	2	5
19	1018	1	1	1	1	0	0	0	5	4	4	3	2	1	1	5
20	1019	1	1	4	0	0	1	1	4	1	1	2	3	1	4	6
21	1020	1	1	1	0	1	1	1	2	3	4	4	2	1	5	2

Figure 4.1: Survey data in Excel after it was imported from a CSV file and un-formatted

Note: Our data imported with an existing sequential ID number for each record. To find out how to create your own ID numbers, see "Add Your Own ID Numbers" on page 114. The sequential ID allows you to refer to a specific (but otherwise anonymous) record.

If you want to rename your columns, now is a good time. We added a question mark after *Likely?* to remind us that these (and the four following) answers correspond to the question *How likely are you to institute the new practice of electronic widget management within the next 12 months?* We changed the names of the *Reason1* through *Reason4* fields to *Gov't regs*, *High cost*, *Lack skills*, and *Lack support* to remind us of the four reasons provided in the survey that people might select (or not select). The fields *Q1* through *Q4* remain the same; these are Survey Body questions — you might have 4, 25, or 50 of these — it's your survey.

LET THE DATA BREATHE

A quick look at Figure 4.1 on page 34 and at the finished Data Dashboard in Figure 4.2 on page 36 shows a big part of how we'll create the Data Dashboard — adding extra columns and rows to allow room for the addition of informative labels and concise calculations on the data. The data is a lot easier to look at, work with, and comprehend when it has "room to breathe" and has been "prettified."

Note: Again — it's *your* data. We prefer a "pretty" version of the Data Dashboard worksheet for presentations and reports (and general ease of use). If you find all that annoying... be our guest. We take our cue from professional programmers who "pretty-print" and thoroughly comment their code.

To start, we added 3 or 4 columns between most fields to make room for the labeling on the bottom part of the Dashboard. How many columns you add is not critical (and you can add or subtract columns and adjust the width of individual columns as we build the Data Dashboard so that the layout looks good to you). The number of spacing columns is up to you — and if your data uses short field names and brief responses, your own Data Dashboard can be much "tighter" than the example shown here.

An organized Data Dashboard makes it easier to spot changes and makes a better "presentation" to management.

A Word About Named Ranges

You may already know that Microsoft Excel includes a feature called Named Ranges, with which you can — for example — name a data range (such as Revenue) and then use that name in calculations rather than laboriously specifying the beginning and ending cell locations of the range in every formula that uses it.

The Data Dashboard worksheet as shown in this book does not use Named Ranges because they can make initial development more difficult and confusing for someone with less familiarity with Excel.

Named Ranges can help when adding updated data to the Data Dashboard. When you name a range in this way, you only need to make more row-room for any additional data you get and then need to redefine the named range in only one place — the Name Manager.

Calculations that use the Named Range automatically understand that the data range has been changed. This makes the Data Dashboard more flexible for surveys that frequently change their size of data set (survey results are bigger or smaller, but have the same fields), *but Named Ranges are not more flexible when surveys change the number and kinds of their fields.*

If you're very familiar with Named Ranges, feel free to use them. However, during the creation of the Data Dashboard worksheet, you'll be copying and replicating formulas. Named Ranges can complicate that because they are fixed and absolute. If you plan on modifying the Data Dashboard worksheet for a variety of surveys, Named Ranges can make those changes more difficult.

We suggest that if you want to use the Named Ranges feature, that you develop and perfect the Data Dashboard as you want it, first, and only after you are confident you have finished apply Named Ranges to the data and to your calculations.

ADDING ROOM FOR QUERIES AND BASIC STATISTICS

We're about to examine each section of the Data Dashboard in close-up detail. Before we do, take a look at the *overall* arrangement of the data and its calculations. **It is too small to read** in Figure 4.2 — we know this. This is an overview so that you can see general organization — how the columns line up, for instance. We'll use close-ups so that you can read the text.

Screening questions and Context questions appear on the left; Demographic questions appear on the right. In the middle we've grouped the Survey Body questions, coded by yellow and blue to signify the two topic groups.

This organization may or may not reflect the order in which your survey asked its questions.

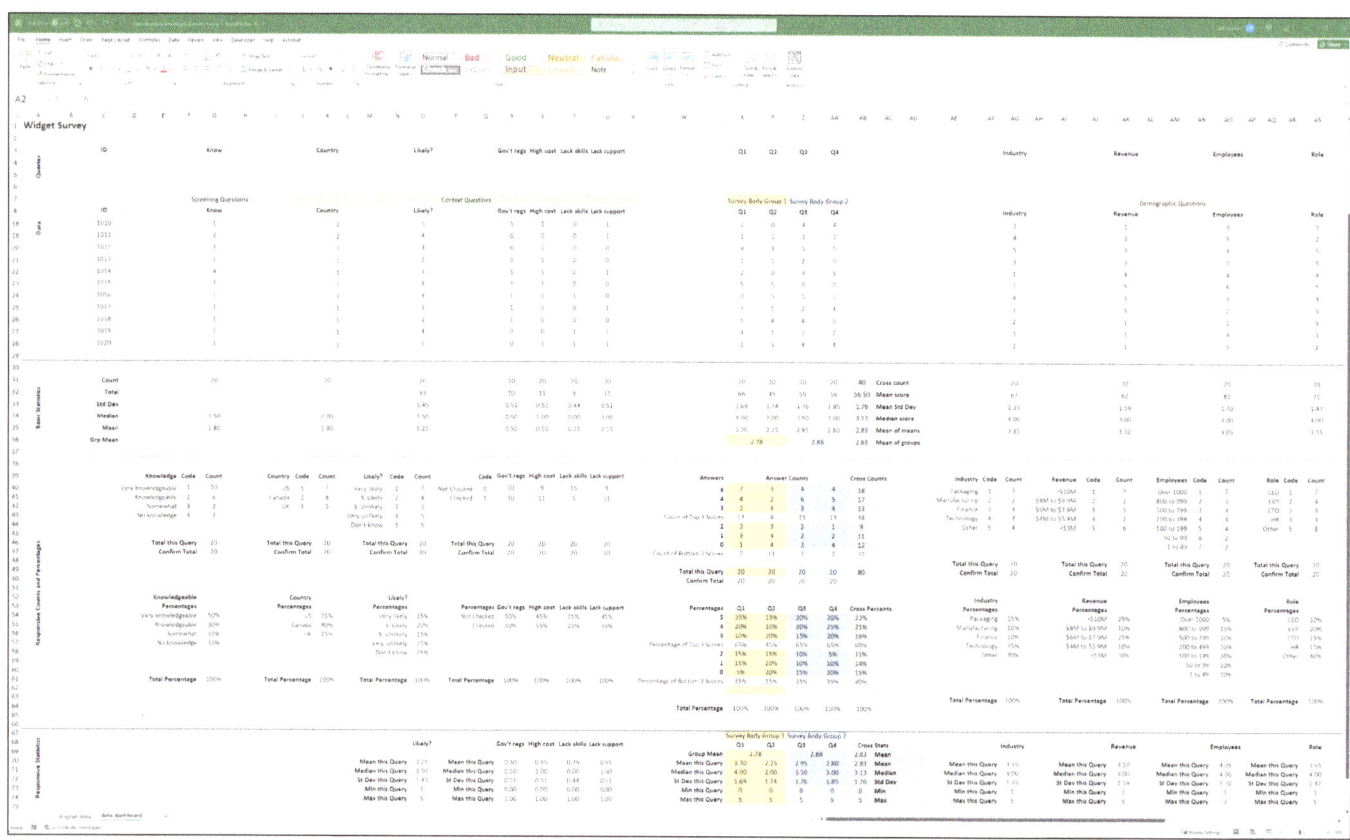

Figure 4.2:   The completed Data Dashboard, columns expanded and arranged to look "pretty"

ADD ROWS FOR QUERIES UP TOP

The Data Dashboard worksheet uses Microsoft Excel Advanced Filter queries to hide and show data according to the criteria you provide (show Canada-only responses, for instance). We leave room for them at the top of the model, as shown in Figure 4.3 on page 37.

Note: The top of the Data Dashboard is a good place for queries, but you *can* put the query area elsewhere. See "Running Advanced Filter Queries" on page 67 and Appendix B, "Become a Query Ninja" on page 119 for that. For now, we strongly suggest *up top*.

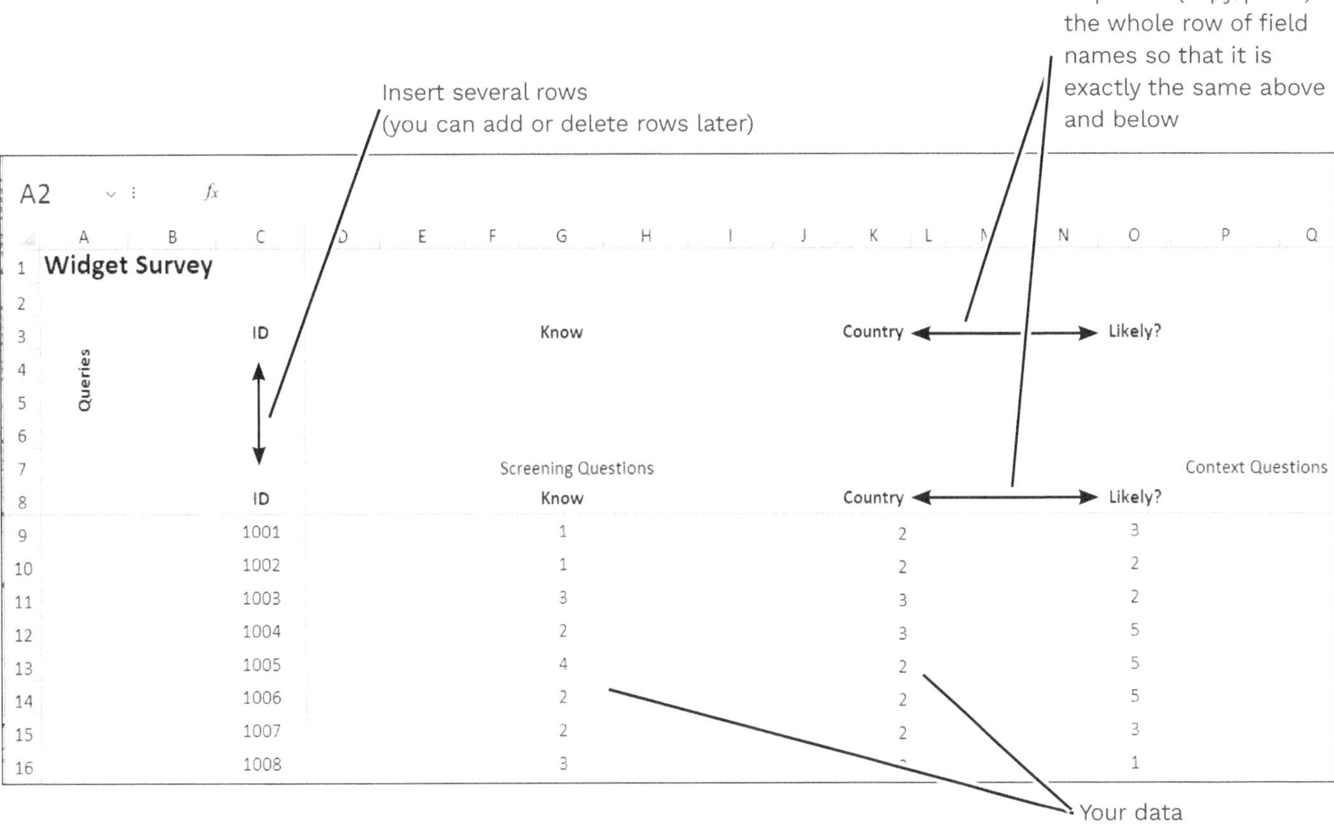

Figure 4.3: Add room for queries — don't forget to duplicate the field names up top

FREEZE WINDOW PANES

Freezing the window panes allows you to scroll in both directions and still allows the response ID numbers and the queries and field names to remain visible. See Figure 4.4.

Why bother? You will not always need to look at the rows of data, and can scroll them off screen to concentrate on creating your query and on the calculation results that the Data Dashboard produces. You will want the field names to remain visible. Similarly, your version of the Data Dashboard may be wider than your monitor. You will want the left side of the screen (ID numbers) to remain visible when you are scrolled to the right.

How-to. Position the cursor to the right of the first ID number and just below the row of field names, then go to the **(a)** View menu, **(b)** Window section of the ribbon, and pull down **(c)** Freeze Panes. Choose **(d)** Freeze Panes from the pulldown.

Said in a shorter way: *View | Window | Freeze Panes | Freeze Panes.*

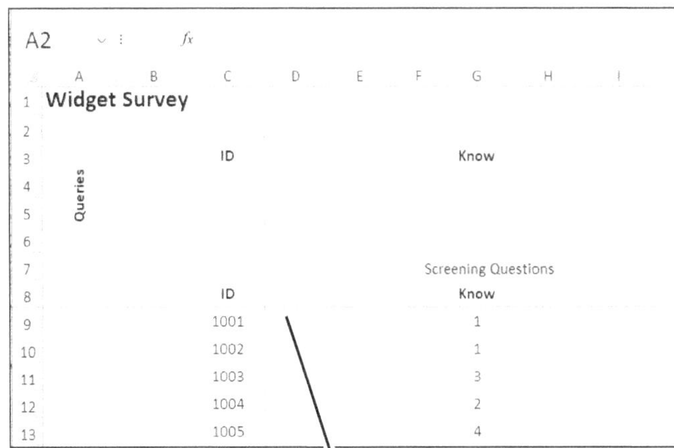

Place the spreadsheet cursor here (D9, in our case), then choose *View | Window | Freeze Panes | Freeze Panes*

Figure 4.4: Freezing the window panes in both directions

ADD BASIC STATISTICS/FULL COUNTS

Now we can begin to add some Basic Statistics to the full data set. **The Basic Statistics always refer to all the data in the column, whether that data is hidden or not.**

Data may be hidden if a query hides it.

This is our recommended set of Basic Statistics. You are free to add statistics that are meaningful to you or to delete any that are not. Figure 4.5 shows the Data Dashboard's Basic Statistics for the first three fields of the model.

Count (*COUNTA* function)

COUNTA counts the number of all non-blank cells in the field's data range (in our example model, the data ranges start on Row 9 and extend to Row 28; every field has the same number of entries from top to bottom).

Why do a count at all? By counting, we confirm that there are no records that include a blank field (cell) — and we *have* found big data sets where a single record has one blank field. You might not spot a single missing field in a big data set.

Sample Formula: (put this initially into cell **G31**)

=COUNTA(G9:G28)

COUNTA counts *non-blank cells only* (including any cells holding text). We know that there are 20 records in our tiny data set. Thus, we know that all records contain a value in the Knowledgeable field.

What to do next: Replicate that formula **across** all data fields. You can do this most easily with copy/paste because there are empty columns in between data fields that don't need a calculation.

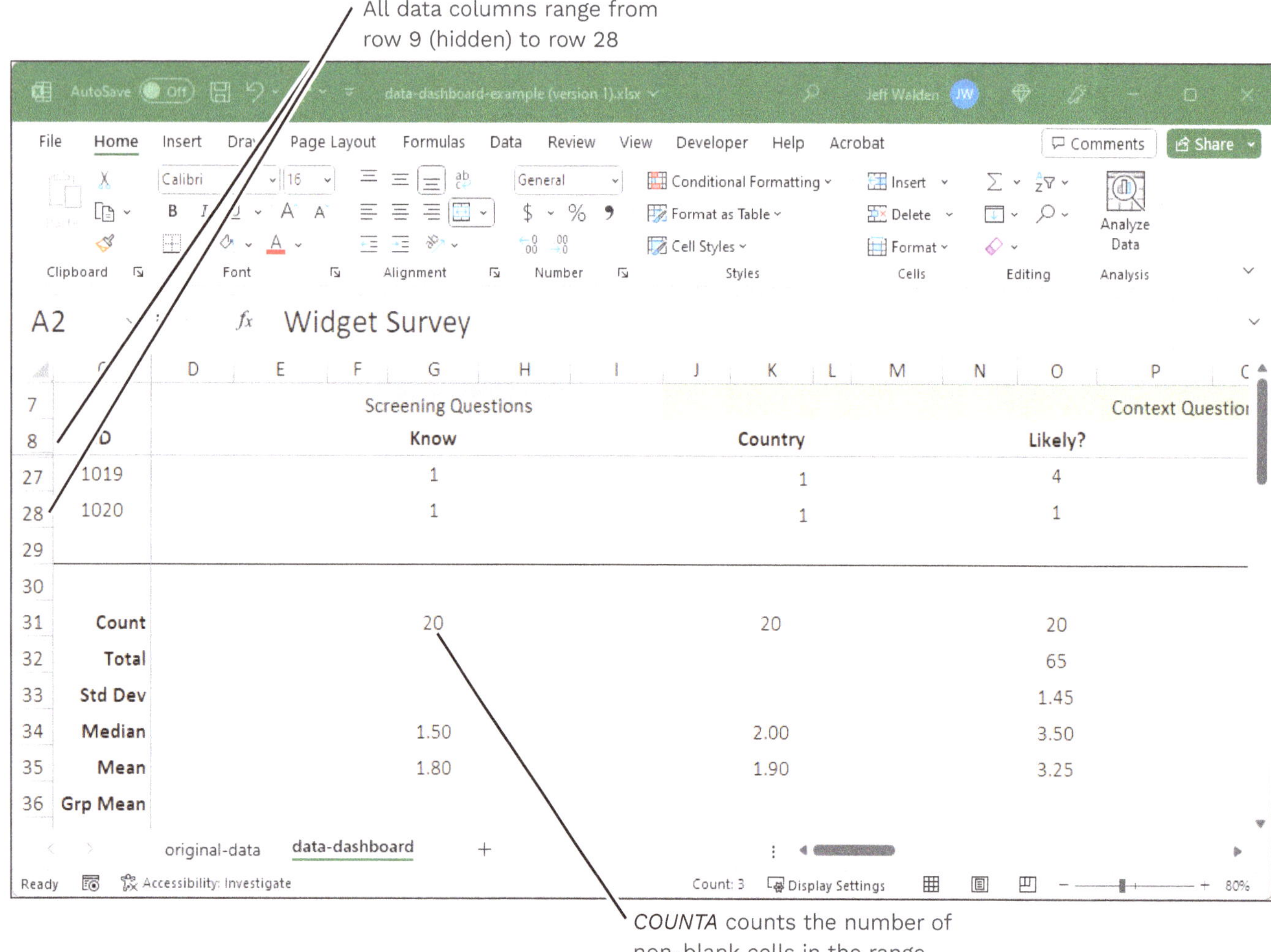

Figure 4.5: Basic Statistics, starting with the leftmost three fields

Total (*SUM* function)

SUM adds up the value of each column of entries in the data range.

How does a total help? Admittedly, Total is not pertinent to all columns (in Figure 4.5 on page 38, there is no Total value for the fields Knowledgeable or Country — it would not really *mean anything* — but we provided one for Likely).

We use Total as an *indicator*. It is useful if you want to quickly compare gross returns from two similar fields (such as in two Survey Body questions — in this use it is similar to Mean (the average) or Median (the middle). You can say that Question A has a higher (or lower) total "score" than Question B. A higher Total indicates that more respondents gave a higher-value response to Question A. The absolute value of the Total gives you a sense of *how much* higher the gross responses were.

Example: Let's say that responses range from 0 (no activity) to 5 (doing the activity well). Question A has a total of 100 (for all responses, added up). Question B has a total of 50 (for all responses). Why would responses to Question A be so different from those of Question B? It bears investigation. This is why we say that Total is an *indicator*. It was a graph of the values of Total that drew our attention to the declining scores as respondents completed the survey that we mention in the sidebar "Real World: Survey Time-to-Completion" on page 25.

Sample Formula: *SUM* adds the values in a range. Put this formula initially into cell **O32**.

=SUM(O9:O28)

What to do next: Replicate this formula across the fields for which it is meaningful. In our model, "meaningful" means all fields *other than* Knowledgeable and Country.

Standard Deviation (*STDEV.S* function)

STDEV.S shows how widely the survey values diverge from the Mean (average) when you're dealing with a *subset of a population*. Your survey responses are — by definition — a subset of a population. The Data Dashboard uses *STDEV.S* because your data is a subset. Excel can't know the full size of your population unless it's included in your range of responses (which it won't be in a survey), so Excel must guess according to an internal formula, much as it did with the sample size calculation on page 14.

This uncertainty makes the **Standard Deviation as calculated for *a sample* different from (and usually larger than) the Standard Deviation as calculated for *a full population*** (should you happen to have that data). Excel includes *STDEV.P* for use with the full-population instance.

Note: When would Excel "know" the population so that you could use *STDEV.P*? For example, if you had a "survey" of student grades and your data included every grade in the class — the *full class population*. Then Excel would "know" the population of grades. You tell it that it has the full population by using *STDEV.P*.

What does Standard Deviation tell us in a survey? A Standard Deviation value of 0 indicates that all response values are equal to the Mean (the average) — but this is highly unlikely. Standard Deviation cannot be *below* 0; thus, the *greater* the Standard Deviation:

- The *greater is the data's divergence* from the Mean value, and

- The *less meaningful* the Mean becomes as a representation for all data in the range.

The Mean is always the Mean — the arithmetic average of the scores, but if the values are widely scattered, few of the actual scores will cluster at the Mean. Table 4.1 shows the Mean and Standard Deviation for two pairs of numbers, 1–10 and 5–6. The Mean of both pairs is 5.5.

Table 4.1: Means and Standard Deviations calculated for a known population (.P) and a sample of an unknown population (.S)

	A	B	MEAN	STDEV.P	STDEV.S
Pair 1	1	10	5.5	4.5	6.36396
Pair 2	5	6	5.5	0.5	0.70711

The Mean of 1 and 10 is 5.5, but neither 1 nor 10 is close to their Mean. The Mean of 5 and 6 is also 5.5, but both values are close to their Mean. Both Means are the same, but uncertainty makes the calculation for *STDEV.S* (the sample of an unknown population) larger in both cases.

Both calculations for Standard Deviation (.P and .S) tell us that the Mean of 5 and 6 is more "accurate" or "closer to the truth" than is the Mean of 1 and 10, even though both Means are *the same value*.

Excel provides several types of Standard Deviation function; however, two have been "deprecated" (slated for eventual phase-out) and superseded by the newer *STDEV.S* and *STDEV.P*.

Sample Formula: provides the Standard Deviation for the entire range.

=STDEV.S(O9:O28)

What to do next: Replicate this formula across the fields for which it is meaningful. In our model, that means all fields other than Knowledgeable and Country.

Median (*MEDIAN* function)

MEDIAN finds the "middle" value in a range. Internally, MEDIAN arranges the data points from smallest to largest, and finds the value in the middle of the list by count. (If the number of data points is even, MEDIAN averages the middle two data points.)

How is *MEDIAN* useful in a survey? Median and Mean go hand-in-hand (Mean is the arithmetic average). See Figure 4.6 and also the discussion of Standard Deviation on page 39.

Median is the middle value by count of data points. There are as many data points above the Median as there are below the Median.

If the Mean (average) is *greater* than the Median (left side in Figure 4.6) then the data points higher than the Median are collectively high enough to tug the Mean up. This can be just a general difference or there can be major outliers.

If the Mean (average) is *less* than the Median (right side in Figure 4.6) then the data points lower than the Median are collectively low enough to

tug the Mean down. Again, this can be a general difference or there can be major outliers.

If the Mean is *equal* to the Median, then the same number of higher and lower *values* of the same higher and lower *size* lie on either side of the Median.

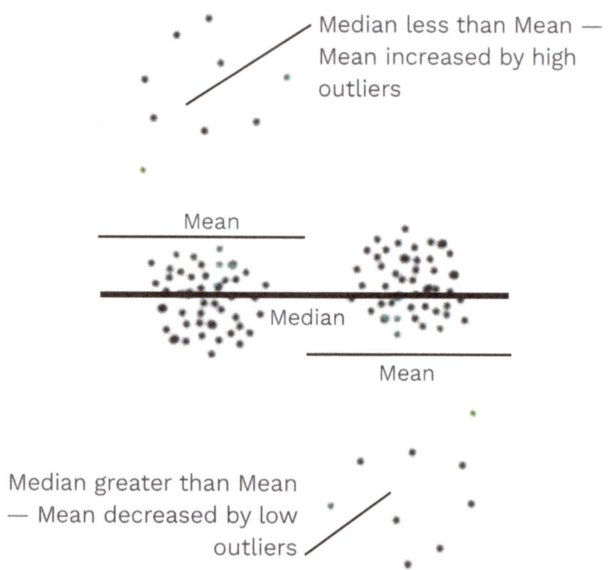

Figure 4.6:   How Median and Mean go hand-in-hand

The closer the Median and Mean are to each other, the more tightly data values cluster around the Mean, and the smaller the Standard Deviation.

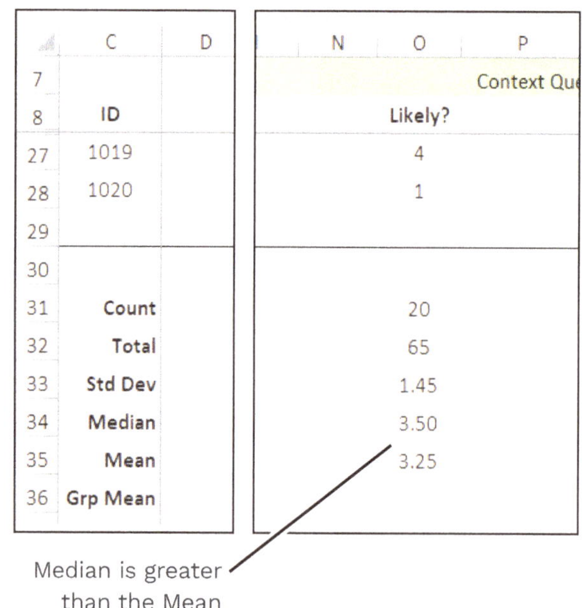

	C	D		N	O	P
7						Context Que
8	ID				Likely?	
27	1019				4	
28	1020				1	
29						
30						
31	Count				20	
32	Total				65	
33	Std Dev				1.45	
34	Median				3.50	
35	Mean				3.25	
36	Grp Mean					

Figure 4.7:   Median greater than the Mean

Figure 4.7 shows that the Mean for the Likely field is less than the Median for the Likely field. Thus, in the Likely field, the lower scores pull the Mean down from the Median. You can look at the values of the data to verify this (but hey, that's why we use statistics).

Sample Formula:

=MEDIAN(O9:O28)

What to do next: Replicate for all data columns. Median will give you a Median score for how Knowledgeable your respondents are, for example, somewhere between Knowledgeable and Very Knowledgeable.

Mean (*AVERAGE* function)

Mean is the arithmetic average of the data in a range. That is, the total of the values divided by the count of the values. For example, Figure 4.7 on page 40 shows that the Mean equals the Total (65) divided by the Count (20). This value is 3.25... which is shown correctly as the Mean. You don't have to do this calculation; Excel provides the *AVERAGE* function. The data can be widely dispersed or close; Mean is always the average.

How is having an average useful? Mean and Median go hand-in-hand (see "Median (MEDIAN function)" on page 40, and in Figure 4.6 and Figure 4.7.

Sample Formula:

=AVERAGE(O9:O28)

What to do next: Replicate the Mean across all data columns.

GROUP MEAN — HOW IT'S DIFFERENT

The Survey Body questions often are grouped by topic or category. A collective *Group Mean value* can give you "overview" insight into the topic as a whole. If you have several Survey Body groups, Group Means and Group Medians can make them easier to tabularize for reports. For example, our Widget survey asks only two sets of two questions grouped around *production* and *distribution*. Each of the production and distribution topics can have an overall Group Mean.

How is Group Mean a help in a survey? A really large survey might have five or ten such Survey Body groups, with several questions in each group. In such a case, a Group Mean (or any other group calculation you believe would be representationally useful) can be a big help in summarizing the data you gather. Because Group Mean is useful only when you are grouping responses in this way to get a value for the group as a whole, we'll put that row at the bottom of the Basic Statistics because it's not needed on most other fields. It's shown in Figure 4.8.

ID	Survey Body Group 1		Survey Body Group 2	
	Q1	Q2	Q3	Q4
1010	2	0	4	4
1011	1	1	3	3
Count	20	20	20	20
Total	66	45	59	56
Std Dev	1.65	1.70	1.72	1.81
Median	4.00	2.00	3.50	3.00
Mean	3.30	2.25	2.95	2.80
Grp Mean	2.78		2.88	

Figure 4.8: Group Mean applied to Survey Body questions when they are grouped by topic or category

Sample Group Mean Formula:

=AVERAGE (Y9:Z28)

Note that the *AVERAGE* formula for the Group Mean is the same as that for the single-column Mean, **but its range spans two columns** from top-left to bottom-right. Rather than Y9:Y28, it's Y9:Z28 (including the two columns).

If your Survey Body category had five questions or ten questions (or however many questions per category), you can do the same thing and derive a Group Mean for the entire topic by spanning all group columns with the formula.

Note: Group Mean is only an example. You can derive a Group Median (or any other group statistic you may need) in the same way — by spanning all group columns with the formula.

What to do next: The Survey Body categories comprise the only area in the Data Dashboard that requires this type of group statistic. We color the topics (and do so elsewhere in the model) to more easily distinguish the two Survey Body question groups. This helps even more when Survey Body questions and their categories begin to multiply in big industry-wide surveys.

CROSS-COUNT STATISTICS

We include cross-count statistics for the Survey Body questions (and only for the Survey Body questions) for completeness. The cross-count statistics appear in Figure 4.9.

Why do we do this? Means and Medians are the thermometers of the survey. Any individual score can be compared to a Mean or Median up and down the data column, or across columns. If your Survey Body had 50 columns (instead of our four), the cross-counts provide immediate comparison data between, say, any one Mean and the Mean of Means.

	Survey Body Group 1		Survey Body Group 2			
ID	Q1	Q2	Q3	Q4		
1010	2	0	4	4		
1011	1	1	3	3		
Count	20	20	20	20	80	Cross count
Total	66	45	59	56	56.50	Mean score
Std Dev	1.65	1.70	1.72	1.81	1.72	Mean Std Dev
Median	4.00	2.00	3.50	3.00	3.13	Median score
Mean	3.30	2.25	2.95	2.80	2.83	Mean of means
Grp Mean	2.78		2.88		2.83	Mean of groups

Figure 4.9: Cross-count statistics

Sample Formula. For the Cross-Count itself:

=SUM(Y31:AB31)

The other calculations are just *AVERAGE*s across the four columns of the Survey Body questions:

=AVERAGE (Y32:AB32)

What to do next: The Basic Statistics for the Survey Body should be complete at this point.

REVIEW DEMOGRAPHIC STATISTICS

If you've been following along with the Basic Statistics and replicating formulas across the Data Dashboard worksheet under appropriate columns, you have already added these calculations to the Demographic fields of the survey. The right-hand side of your model should look similar to Figure 4.10. (Of course, your specific values will be different if your data is different.)

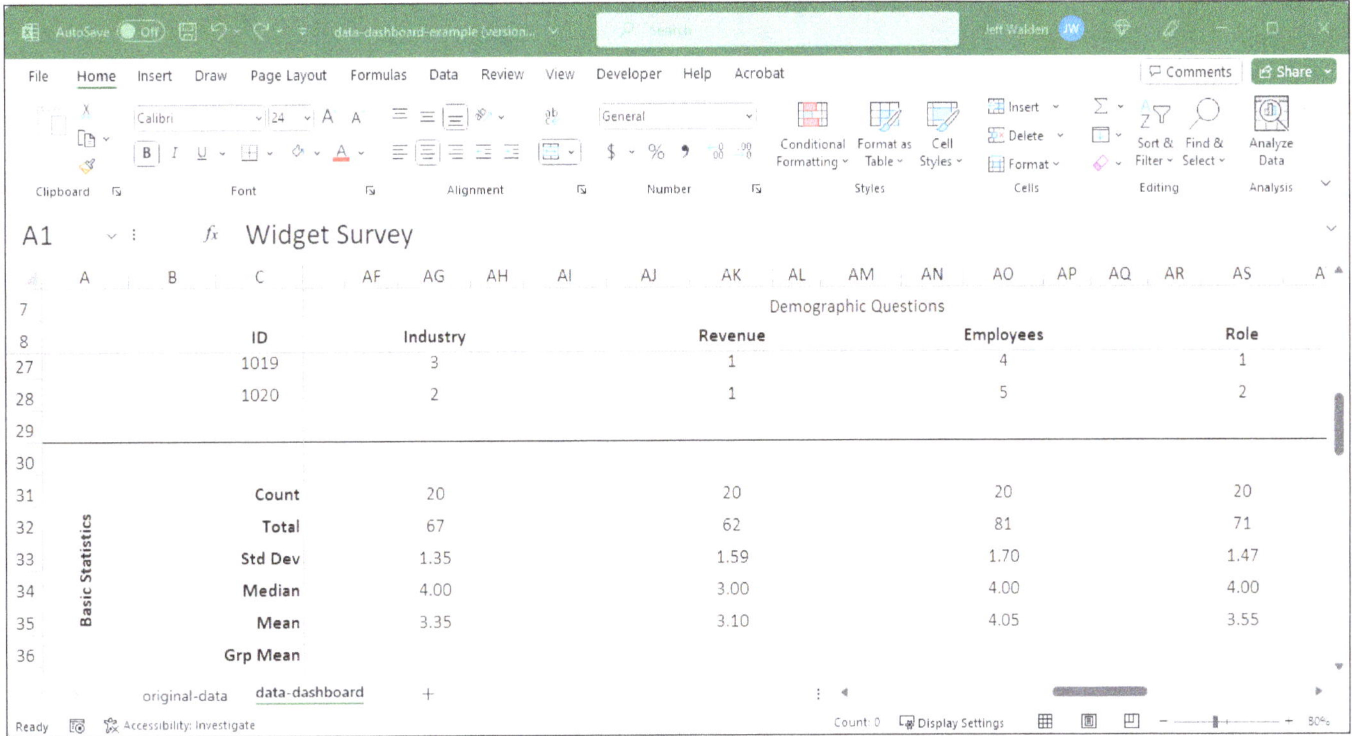

Figure 4.10: Demographic questions

COMPLETED BASIC STATISTICS

The Basic Statistics section of your Data Dashboard worksheet should look similar to Figure 4.11.

We have added color bars above the field names to aid in grouping the data.

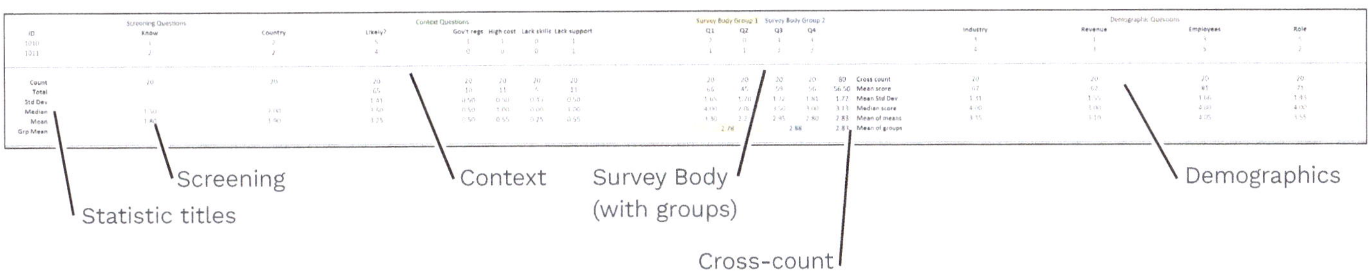

Figure 4.11: Basic Statistics, completed

RESPONSIVE COUNTS

Responsive Counts count only those values that are visible after you do a query that may hide certain rows of data based on their values. For example, when you choose to *display* only Canadian records or records of respondents with a certain number of employees, you also *hide* non-Canadian records or respondents with a different number of employees.

Responsive Counts change depending on your query. This is why we call them *responsive*.

In contrast, Basic Statistics calculate their values using the entire data set — all records, all fields, all the time — regardless of whether your query has hidden some of the records.

Figure 4.12 shows the organization of the Responsive Counts for the first three columns of data, along with their confirming totals.

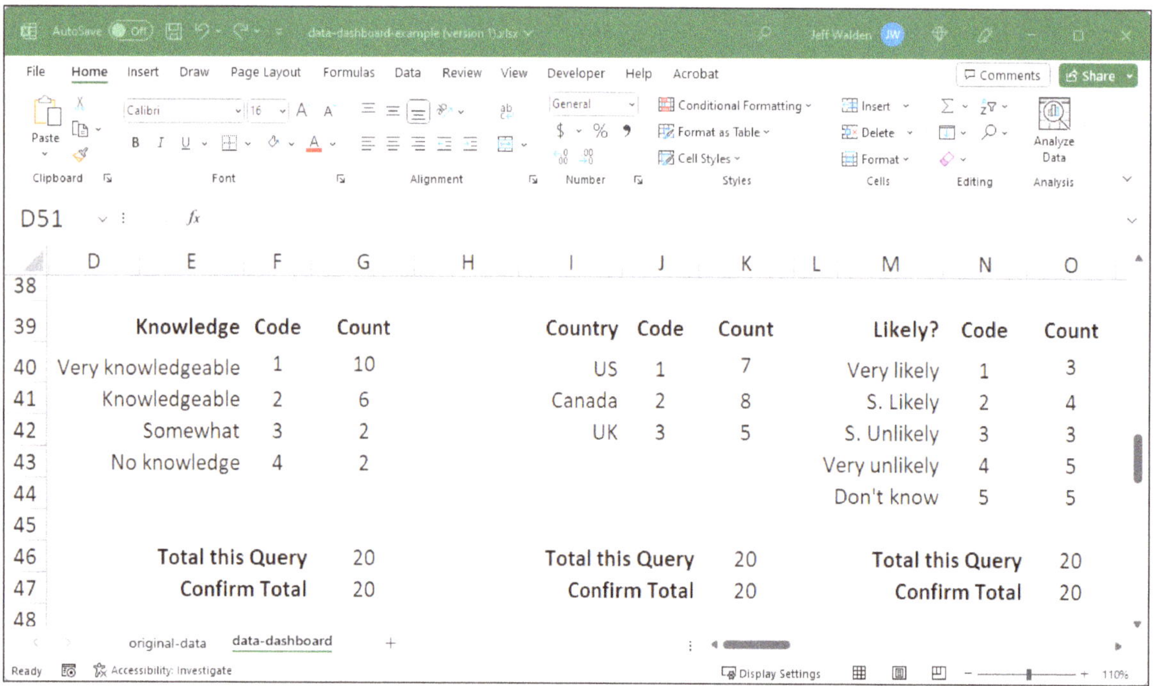

Figure 4.12: Responsive Counts for the first three columns of data — Knowledgeable, Country, and Likely

WHERE DO RESPONSIVE COUNTS GO ON THE DATA DASHBOARD WORKSHEET?

The Data Dashboard begins its Responsive Counts a few rows below the Basic Statistics, as shown in Figure 4.13.

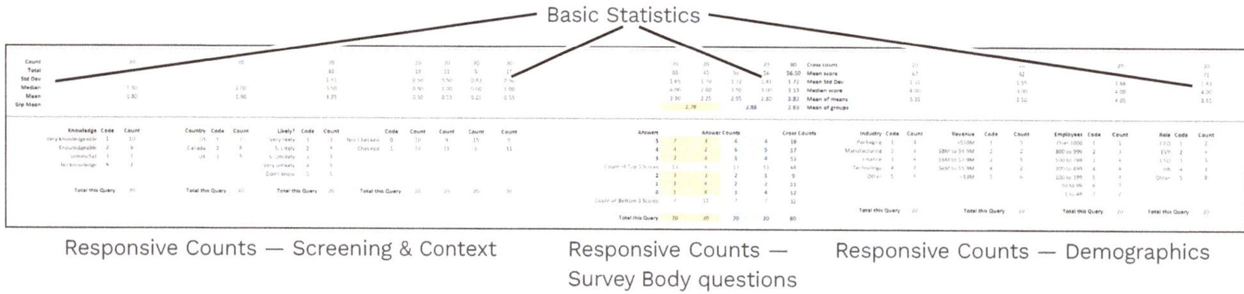

Figure 4.13: The Responsive Counts align with their data columns a few rows beneath the Basic Statistics

MAKING A COUNT RESPONSIVE

In order to make further calculations that also are responsive to subsets of the data (for example, when showing only Canadian information or only those who responded *Very Likely*) we need to *classify* and *count* responses in a way that recognizes whether data is hidden or displayed.

Once we have counts for each response value, we can do other calculations based on those counts, such as finding the percentage of each response among only the displayed records.

Think of the formula we need this way:

1. From only the displayed data (and not from any of the data that might be hidden by an Excel query)…

2. We want to count all fields that contain 1…

3. And then count all fields that contain 2…

4. And then count all fields that contain 3…

5. And then count all fields that contain 4

Thus, we must create a formula to count a value:

(a) that matches the target value, *and*
(b) that *counts only* when the data row is displayed and *does not count* when the data row is hidden.

We have found the Excel formula in Figure 4.14 to perform correctly in the context of the Data Dashboard worksheet:

=SUMPRODUCT(--(G$9:G$28=$F40) SUBTOTAL(103,OFFSET(INDEX(G$9:G$28,1), ROW(G$9:G$28)-MIN(ROW(G$9:G$28)),0)))*

Figure 4.14:   A formula that can count visible cells that match our list of values; this one comes from cell G40

It's a large and subtle formula. The operation of the formula shown in Figure 4.14 and in Figure 4.15 on page 46 is not intuitively obvious or easy to explain. It uses arrays created in Excel's memory that are not apparent (or even visible) to the user. If you're interested in how it works, please see Appendix C, "Explaining the Data Dashboard's

Most Important Formula" on page 137. If you have any interest at all in how it works, we suggest you take a look.

Although it's difficult to explain, it's relatively easy to implement.

What the formula does. The formula counts the number of *currently visible cells* in the data range but *only if the value matches* the target "Code" cell. If rows are hidden by a query, the formula does not count the cells even if they match.

What is the meaning of that double-dash in the formula's first line? The double-dash tells Excel to evaluate the arrays created by the formula as 1 or 0 rather than as TRUE or FALSE.

Look at Figure 4.15 on page 46. It shows the four responsive formulas that count the instances of the four codes for the Knowledgeable field. These formulas are (almost) identical. Each refers to the same range of data (the data for the Knowledgeable field), but each one refers to its own Code. One formula counts only 1, the next counts only 2, and so forth.

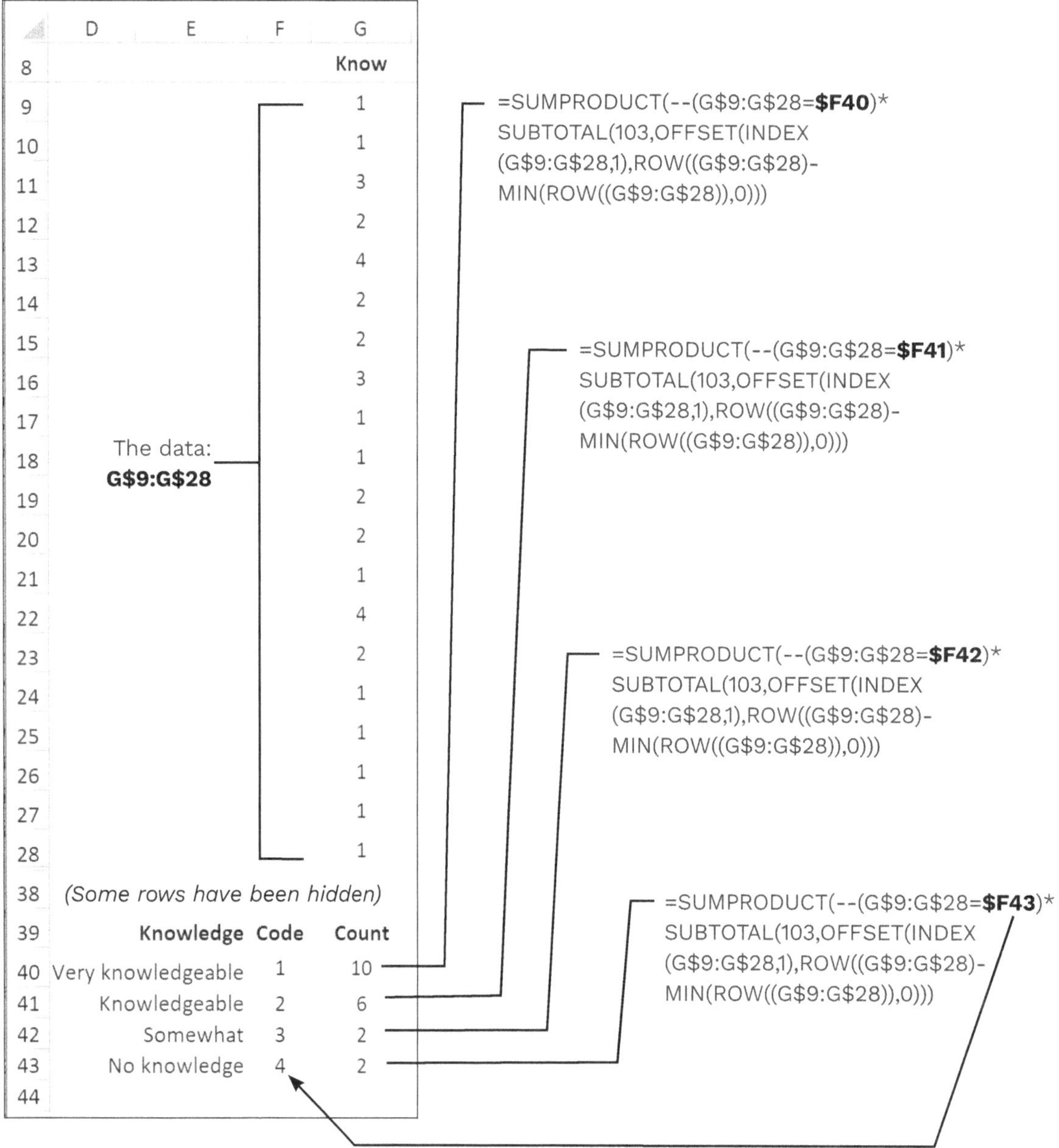

Figure 4.15: Responsive count formulas for the Knowledgeable field. All the formulas for this data range (**G$9:G$28**) are the same — except for the reference to the Code value that each is counting. You can enter this formula once in cell **G40** and then fill-down through **G41, G42,** and **G43**.

The formulas shown in Figure 4.15 are repeated over and over *across* the Data Dashboard. They vary in only two ways:

- Which column of data does the formula refer to? (In this case, the data in **G$9:G$28.**)

- Which cell holds the code value that the formula must count? (In this case, the values from **$F40** through **$F43**).

Tip: The range reference only applies the $ (absolute reference) to the row numbers of the range. **All ranges in the survey must begin and end on the same row number.** This allows you to freely copy-and-paste this formula **across** the model to use with other fields. The Code reference applies the $ to the column, which allows you to **fill-down** however many answer Codes you have set up for a given data column. **But it also means** that when you copy-and-paste the formula to count a new range, you need to correct the column of the Code reference first, and then fill-down. Can't have it both ways.

CHECKING THE TOTAL COUNT FOR THE KNOWLEDGEABLE FIELD

The *Total this Query* count adds up the records that the formula in Figure 4.15 on page 46 counted for each matched code.

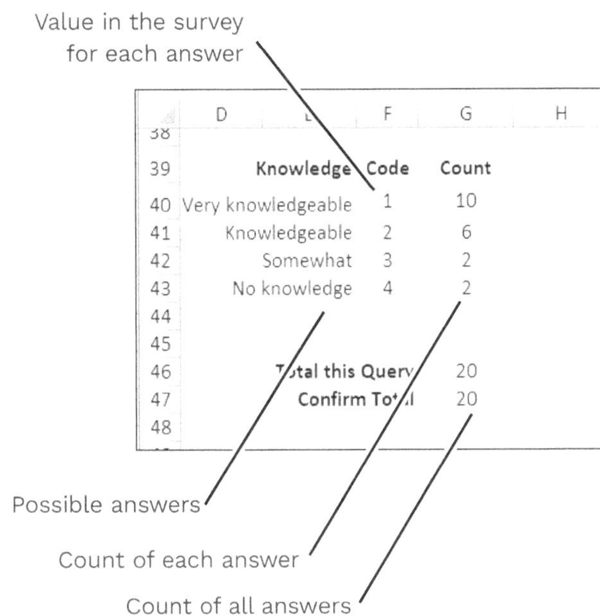

Figure 4.16: Total this Query and Confirm Total cells count up all the answers in two different ways

The formula that *Total this Query* uses (in cell **G46** in Figure 4.16) is:

=SUM(G40:G43)

But is that count correct? We've seen situations where (for example) an inappropriate 5 or 0 sneaks into a long column of data. Such an erroneous entry would not be counted by the formula in Figure 4.15 on page 46 because *neither a 0 nor a 5 is in the list of Code values* (column F).

To make sure we've counted all the visible records regardless of value, we've included a backup formula that counts the total of visible records but that does not attempt to match the specific Code values. The formula for *Confirm Total* (cell **G47** in Figure 4.16) is:

=AGGREGATE(3,5,G$9:G$28)

The number 3 tells *AGGREGATE* to count non-blank cells (internally using *COUNTA*); the number 5 tells *AGGREGATE* to ignore rows that may have

been hidden. *AGGREGATE* cannot match Code values; it only counts visible rows.

AGGREGATE is described in more detail in "AGGREGATE" on page 60, where the Data Dashboard uses several variations of this formula.

Here, *AGGREGATE* acts as an error-check on the counts we make for each Code value. **If these values don't match, there is an incorrect value somewhere in your data.**

Note: *AGGREGATE* was introduced with Excel 2010.

RESPONSIVE COUNTRY COUNTS

The setup for counting the Country data is the same as that for the Knowledgeable field.

When you copy the formula from the Knowledgeable (cell **G40**) and paste it into the first Country (cell **K40**), the **data column reference changes automatically to column K**. You need only make the adjustment for the Code reference, and change that from column F to column J, as shown in Figure 4.17.

Of course, your model using your own fields and data may use different columns and different Code values. *The underlying formula is the same.*

Figure 4.17 shows the responsive count formula for **cell K40** in Figure 4.18.

$$=SUMPRODUCT(--(K\$9:K\$28=\$J40)*$$
$$SUBTOTAL(103,OFFSET(INDEX(K\$9:K\$28,1),$$
$$ROW(K\$9:K\$28)-MIN(ROW(K\$9:K\$28)),0)))$$

Figure 4.17:   Responsive formula for Country count

Note: See Figure 4.18 for the layout of responsive counts for Country. The data range is **K9 through K28** (out of image). **Column J** holds the answer codes. Put the formula into cells **K40**, **K41**, and **K42**. Corresponding answer codes are in **J40**, **J41**, and **J42**.

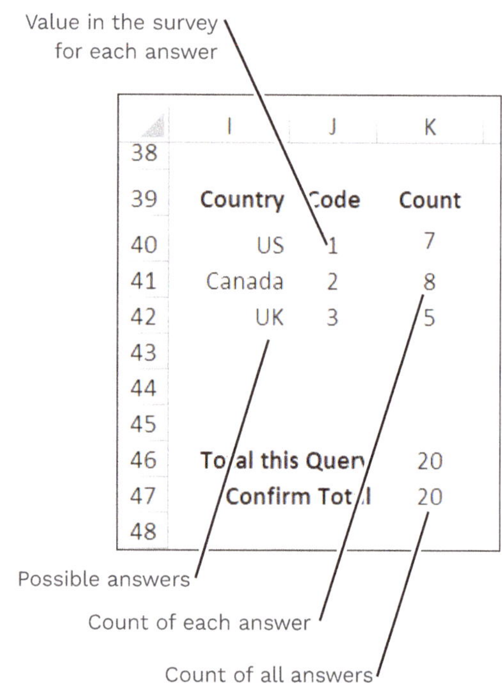

Figure 4.18:   Responsive counts for the Country data

The *Total this Query* count is likewise similar. Its formula is:

$$=SUM(K40:K42)$$

And the formula for *Confirm Total* is:

$$=AGGREGATE(3,5,K\$9:K\$28)$$

You can copy/paste these formulas also, but remember the Country range only SUMs three rows rather than four.

RESPONSIVE LIKELY COUNTS

By now you should be seeing a pattern. When you paste the responsive count formula:

(a) the data column changes (G to K, K to O),
(b) you adjust the reference to the target Code value, and then
(c) fill down.

Here is the formula (cell **O40** in Figure 4.20) that counts the data from the Likely field:

$$=SUMPRODUCT(--(O\$9:O\$28=\$N40)*$$
$$SUBTOTAL(103,OFFSET(INDEX(O\$9:O\$28,1),$$
$$ROW(O\$9:O\$28)-MIN(ROW(O\$9:O\$28)),0)))$$

Figure 4.19: Responsive formula for the Likely count

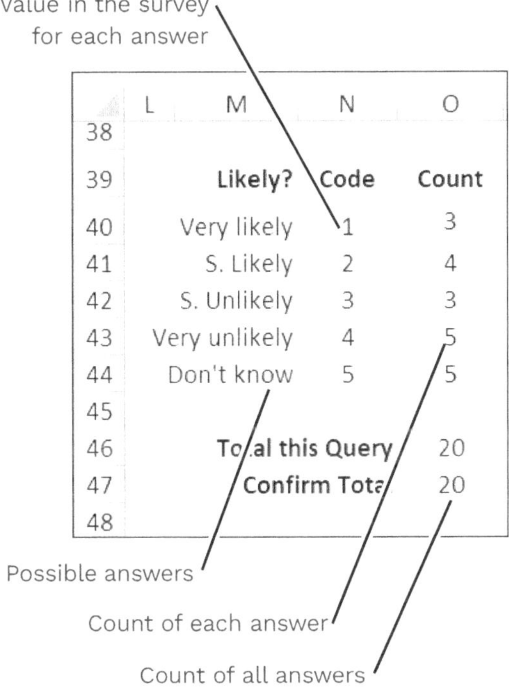

Figure 4.20: Responsive counts for the Likely data

The Likely field has *five possible* response values, so the target reference starts with **$N40** and continues with **$N41** through **$N44** as you fill down the formula in column O.

The *Total this Query* is:

$$=SUM(O40:O44)$$

And the formula for *Confirm Total* is:

$$=AGGREGATE(3,5,O\$9:O\$28)$$

Confirm Total guards against Likely data including values other than 1–5. If Total this Query and Confirm Total are different, you have an inconsistency in the data.

VARIATIONS ON A THEME

The widget survey includes a series of check-all-that-apply questions that bear on the main question *How Likely Are You To…* See the question "Which of the following reasons apply to your organization's approach to electronic widget management? (Select all that apply.)" on page 30.

There are only four such questions in our (very short) widget survey. Your survey may have more potential responses or several similar question blocs — or none at all.

For a reminde, we labeled the responses as:

- **Gov't regs** (for a "mandated conversion"),

- **High cost** (of conventional widget management)

- **Lack skills** (for a full "conversion")

- **Lack support** (for "electronic conversion")

Any or all of these questions could be checked (interpreted as 1) or left unchecked (interpreted as 0). The main difference between this set of questions and the Knowledgeable, Country, and Likely fields is that the questions of this set **have only two potential responses** and **the potential responses are the same for all questions in the set**, so they all can point at the codes in column Q for their matches.

Figure 4.21 shows what this type of question looks like with its counts in the Data Dashboard.

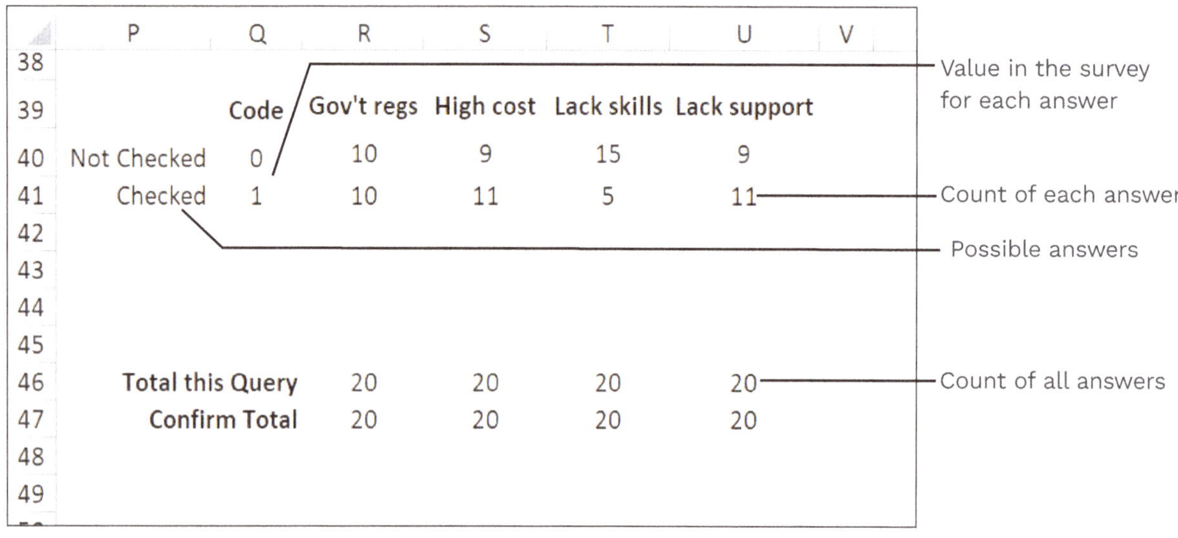

	P	Q	R	S	T	U	V
38							
39		Code	Gov't regs	High cost	Lack skills	Lack support	
40	Not Checked	0	10	9	15	9	
41	Checked	1	10	11	5	11	
42							
43							
44							
45							
46	**Total this Query**		20	20	20	20	
47	**Confirm Total**		20	20	20	20	
48							
49							

Figure 4.21:   Checked/unchecked question set

Here is the responsive formula as pasted into cell **R40**:

$$=SUMPRODUCT(--(R\$9:R\$28=\$Q40)*$$
$$SUBTOTAL(103,OFFSET(INDEX(R\$9:R\$28,1),$$
$$ROW(R\$9:R\$28)-MIN(ROW(R\$9:R\$28)),0)))$$

Here is the responsive formula as pasted into cell **U40**:

$$=SUMPRODUCT(--(U\$9:U\$28=\$Q40)*$$
$$SUBTOTAL(103,OFFSET(INDEX(U\$9:U\$28,1),$$
$$ROW(U\$9:U\$28)-MIN(ROW(U\$9:U\$28)),0)))$$

All formulas for this question on row 40 **refer to cell $Q40** for their target Code values. The main difference is which column of data (R, S, T, or U) they refer to.

Fill right from R40 to U40, and only then fill down that whole row to row 41.

The *Total this Query* for each question is the *SUM* of the Checked and Not Checked counts:

$$=SUM(R40:R41)$$

which you can fill-right from column R through

column U, and which varies only by data column, R, S, T, U — or (of course) whatever columns are appropriate to your data.

The formula for *Confirm Total* in cell **R47** is:

$$=AGGREGATE(3,5,R\$9:R\$28)$$

which you can fill-right from column R through column U.

RESPONSIVE SURVEY BODY QUESTION COUNTS

In the Data Dashboard worksheet we've created for the widget survey, respondents answer the Survey Body questions under each topic on a 0–5 scale, with 5 meaning *We're doing great!* and 0 meaning *We're sorry — no activity*. See Table 3.1 on page 31 for some typical uses for a 0–5 scale. Figure 4.22 shows how we've arranged these counts in the Data Dashboard. Yellow marks the answers for Question Group 1 and blue marks Question Group 2.

Of course, *your* survey does not need to ask its Survey Body questions on a 0–5 scale (it need not have a "Survey Body" section like this at all).

We wanted to present the Survey Body counts in this way to show:

- The numerical direction of question codes can go in either direction — up or down.

- The "top" answer for these Survey Body questions is 5; the "bottom" is 0. While in theory answers only need values that are unique, a numbering sequence (1, 2, 3, 4 or 4, 3, 2, 1) makes other calculations on these responses easier, such as Means and Medians, and produces a meaningful number.

- As with the checked/unchecked questions, because these Survey Body questions all use the same Answer Codes, the questions can be grouped visually and the responsive counting formulas all can point to the same column for their matches — in this case, column W.

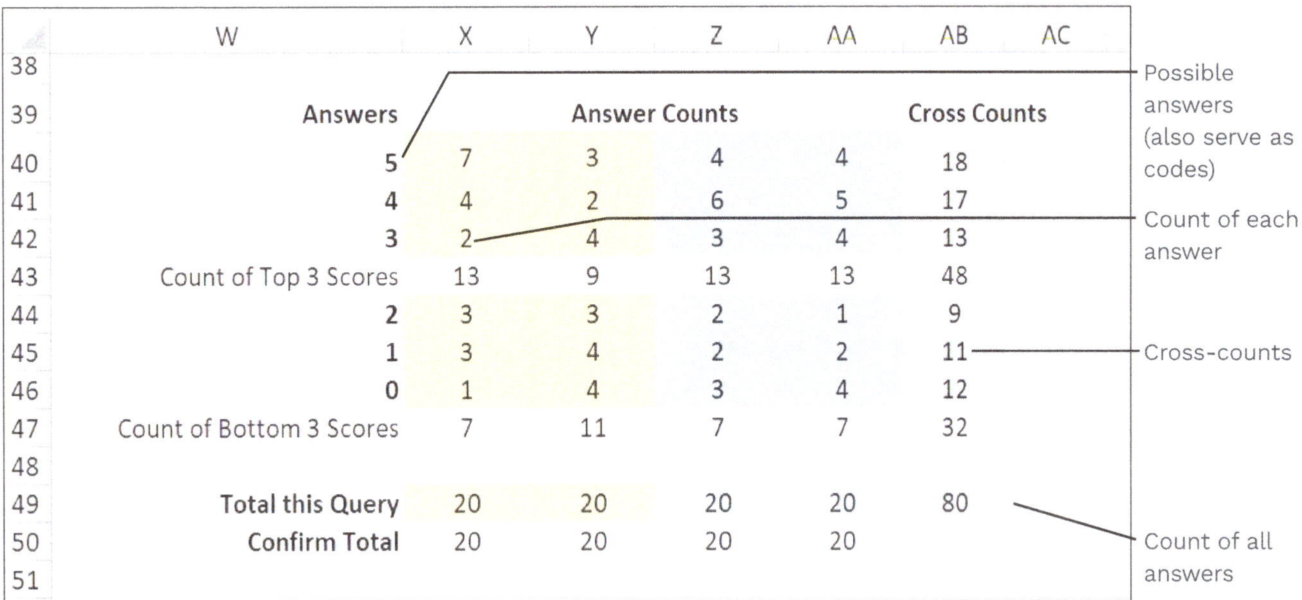

	W	X	Y	Z	AA	AB	AC
38							
39	Answers		Answer Counts			Cross Counts	
40	5	7	3	4	4	18	
41	4	4	2	6	5	17	
42	3	2	4	3	4	13	
43	Count of Top 3 Scores	13	9	13	13	48	
44	2	3	3	2	1	9	
45	1	3	4	2	2	11	
46	0	1	4	3	4	12	
47	Count of Bottom 3 Scores	7	11	7	7	32	
48							
49	Total this Query	20	20	20	20	80	
50	Confirm Total	20	20	20	20		
51							

Figure 4.22: Survey Body questions in groups

The familiar responsive counting formula **in cell X40** is:

$$=SUMPRODUCT(--(X\$9:X\$28=\$W40)*$$
$$SUBTOTAL(103,OFFSET(INDEX(X\$9:X\$28,1),$$
$$ROW(X\$9:X\$28)-MIN(ROW(X\$9:X\$28)),0)))$$

All Survey Body responses in the Data Dashboard widget example look to **column W** for their target values. You can copy and paste this formula across and then fill down.

Extra Features. To make the block of Survey Body questions easier to view and interpret, the Data Dashboard uses background color to differentiate between sets of question topics. It also creates an interim subtotal *between* 5-4-3 and 2-1-0, and also *after* 2-1-0. We interpret 5-4-3 as "top scores" and 2-1-0 as "bottom scores," but — as should be obvious by now — you don't have to break the counts at all, or can break them in any other way that you find useful, such as grouping them **0–1 | 2–3 | 4–5**, or **0-1-2 | 3 | 4-5** — whatever way you feel would be most helpful to interpret your survey.

The formula for "Count of Top 3 Scores" in cell **X43** is:

$$=SUM(X40:X42)$$

The count of the "Bottom 3 Scores" in cell **X47** is the SUM of the three cells above it:

$$=SUM(X44:X46).$$

The query totals at the bottom of each column are either:

$$=SUM(X40:X42)+SUM(X44:X46)$$
or...
$$=X43+X47$$

the second of which we find simpler and easier to understand.

To confirm the totals, we've added the *Confirm Total* formula:

$$=AGGREGATE(3,5,X\$9:X\$28)$$

which you can use to fill-right across the bottom of the Survey Body columns.

Cross counts. As yet another check on counts, the Data Dashboard worksheet does cross-counts for the Survey Body questions. The cross-counts are SUMs across the columns in a single row. For example, the cross count in **cell AB40** is:

$$=SUM(X40:AA40)$$

We find that the cross-count of the top three scores is 48 and the cross-count of the bottom three scores is 32. They total 80. The total of the individual four Survey Body columns is also 80.
It checks.

Real World: Cross-Counts

Cross-counts and totals help you spot inconsistencies in the data that may be there even after eagle-eyed review. In the real world, after several iterations of this model on substantial data, we still found that a set of checked/unchecked questions (which should only hold 0s and 1s) somehow also contained a couple of records with a 2 and a 3...

RESPONSIVE DEMOGRAPHIC COUNTS

The four Demographic questions (Figure 4.23) are handled by the same responsive formula we've been using. For example, for *Industry* data, the formula in **cell AG40** is:

$$=SUMPRODUCT(--(AG\$9{:}AG\$28=\$AF40)*$$
$$SUBTOTAL(103,OFFSET(INDEX$$
$$(AG\$9{:}AG\$28,1),$$
$$ROW(AG\$9{:}AG\$28)-$$
$$MIN(ROW(AG\$9{:}AG\$28)),0)))$$

The range for the Industry data column is **AG\$9:AG\$28**, and the first target value (Packaging/Code 1) is located in **cell \$AF40**.

Copy the responsive count formula from AG40 to AK40, AO40, and AS40.

Adjust the target cell references for each column (\$AF40, \$AJ40, \$AN40, \$AR40).

Fill down as appropriate for each column.

Add the *Total this Query* and *Confirm Total* calculations.

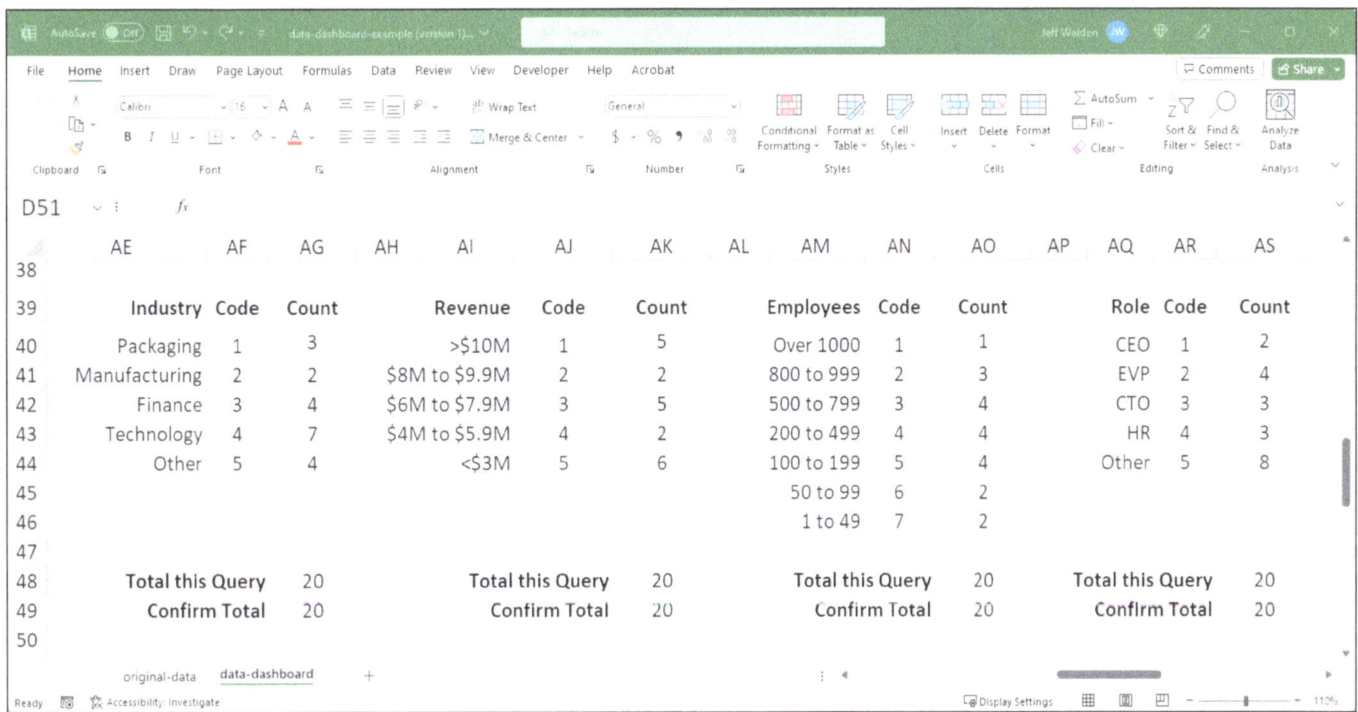

Industry	Code	Count		Revenue	Code	Count		Employees	Code	Count		Role	Code	Count
Packaging	1	3		>$10M	1	5		Over 1000	1	1		CEO	1	2
Manufacturing	2	2		$8M to $9.9M	2	2		800 to 999	2	3		EVP	2	4
Finance	3	4		$6M to $7.9M	3	5		500 to 799	3	4		CTO	3	3
Technology	4	7		$4M to $5.9M	4	2		200 to 499	4	4		HR	4	3
Other	5	4		<$3M	5	6		100 to 199	5	4		Other	5	8
								50 to 99	6	2				
								1 to 49	7	2				
Total this Query	20			Total this Query	20			Total this Query	20			Total this Query	20	
Confirm Total	20			Confirm Total	20			Confirm Total	20			Confirm Total	20	

Figure 4.23: The widget survey's four Demographic questions

DERIVING RESPONSIVE PERCENTAGES FROM COUNTS

The whole purpose of creating query-responsive counts of the various values in the data is so that we can make other calculations that also respond to queries... but without needing such large, cumbersome formulas to do them. Figure 4.24 shows an overview of the Responsive Percentages area.

Screening   Context   Survey Body   Demographics

Figure 4.24: Overview of layout for Responsive Percentages

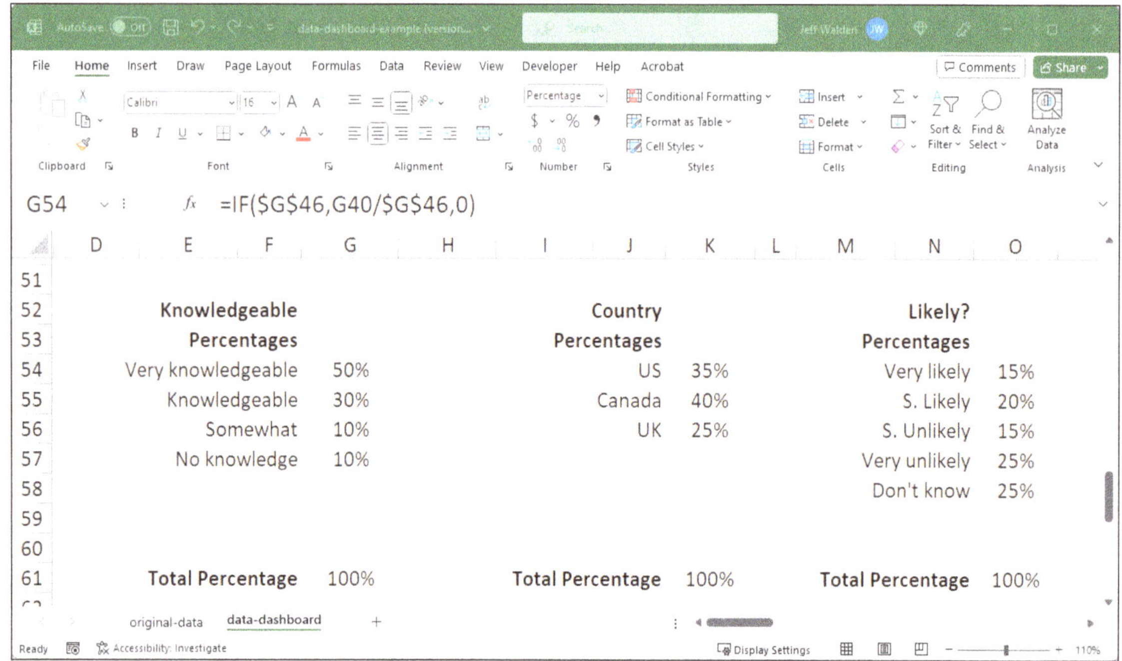

Figure 4.25: Responsive Percentages for the first three data columns, Knowledgeable, Country, and Likely

Figure 4.25 shows the Responsive Percentages for the first three data columns of the widget survey — Knowledgeable, Country, and Likely. The percentages are derived by dividing the Responsive Count by the Total Count.

Figure 4.27 on page 55 shows the responsive counts and percentages focusing on just the Knowledgeable field.

Underlying the calculation is simple division formatted as a percent. Figure 4.26 shows the method for calculating the percentage Knowledgeable field:

Count for Very Knowledgeable

Total Count this Query

Figure 4.26: Divide one field count by the count for all responses and make it a percentage — simple, right?

Um... However. Occasionally — not often, but often enough — a query can produce 0 records that correspond to your criteria. The smaller your data set (and the widget survey is small indeed) or the more demanding your criteria, the more likely you are to produce a 0 count.

Suddenly, you find that your model is dividing by 0. Excel does not like this.

You must fortify your formulas against division by 0.

Luckily, this is easy.

DON'T FORGET YOUR UMBRELLA!

In Figure 4.27, you can see that a normal percentage calculation for Very Knowledgeable in cell **G54** *would be*:

=G40/$G$46

BUT, you must wrap this otherwise simple formula in divide-by-zero protection (below is the revised cell **G54**):

=IF($G$46,G40/$G$46,0)

The revised **G54** above is an IF-THEN-ELSE statement. It means:

- **IF** the value in **$G$46** (*Total this Query*) evaluates to a non-zero number, the value is *TRUE*; that is, the formula in *Total this Query* has counted more than 0 records. If *$G$46* evaluates to 0, the value is *FALSE*.

- If the first term is *TRUE*, the formula says, **THEN** execute the second term (the division that we want to do, **G40/$G$46**). This means that you're *dividing by something* and it's Okay to do the calculation.

- If the first term is *FALSE* (which it is if **$G$46** evaluates to 0), **ELSE** execute the third term (a plain **0**). Rather than perform any calculation, the formula simply delivers 0 as its answer.

Wrapping the original **G40/$G$46** division formula in the IF-THEN-ELSE prevents Excel from returning a division-by-0 error. Instead, the formula just returns 0% when the Total this Query count is 0.

Once you create the first calculation (for example, **in the revised G54**), you can **fill down**. All the Responsive Percentages require this same protection from division by 0. **Don't forget your umbrella.** Later, we'll find other calculations

that need this protection, too, and for the same reason — the Responsive Count now can be 0 if your query does not find any matches and all your percentages will still work.

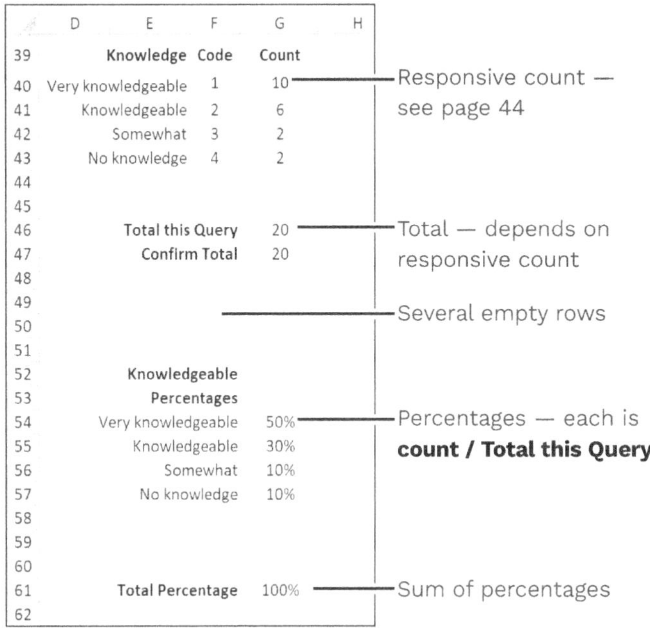

Figure 4.27 text (spreadsheet):

	D	E	F	G	H	
39		Knowledge	Code	Count		
40	Very knowledgeable		1	10		Responsive count — see page 44
41	Knowledgeable		2	6		
42	Somewhat		3	2		
43	No knowledge		4	2		
44						
45						
46		Total this Query		20		Total — depends on responsive count
47		Confirm Total		20		
48						
49						Several empty rows
50						
51						
52		Knowledgeable				
53		Percentages				
54	Very knowledgeable			50%		Percentages — each is **count / Total this Query**
55	Knowledgeable			30%		
56	Somewhat			10%		
57	No knowledge			10%		
58						
59						
60						
61		Total Percentage		100%		Sum of percentages
62						

Figure 4.27: Position percentages below the corresponding responsive counts

Note: Be sure to format cells **G54** through **G57** as percentages.

Why bother with Responsive Percentages? While you might make-do with the bare responsive counts, most people who use the decimal system tend to think in percentages. If we tell you that Knowledgeable people make up 6 of 20 respondents... the first thing you're likely to ask is, "What percentage is that?" (30%) Percentages are easier to compare than are "plain" numbers. And we've already done the heavy lifting formula-wise (at least for the Data Dashboard) by obtaining the Responsive Counts.

Do the Responsive Percentages for the Country and Likely fields using the same simple division (plus the umbrella wrapper) as you did for the Knowledgeable field. (See Figure 4.28 on page 56.)

Country (cell **K54**):

 =IF($K$46,K40/$K$46,0)

Then fill down.

Likely? (cell **O54**):

 =IF($O$46,O40/$O$46,0)

Then fill down.

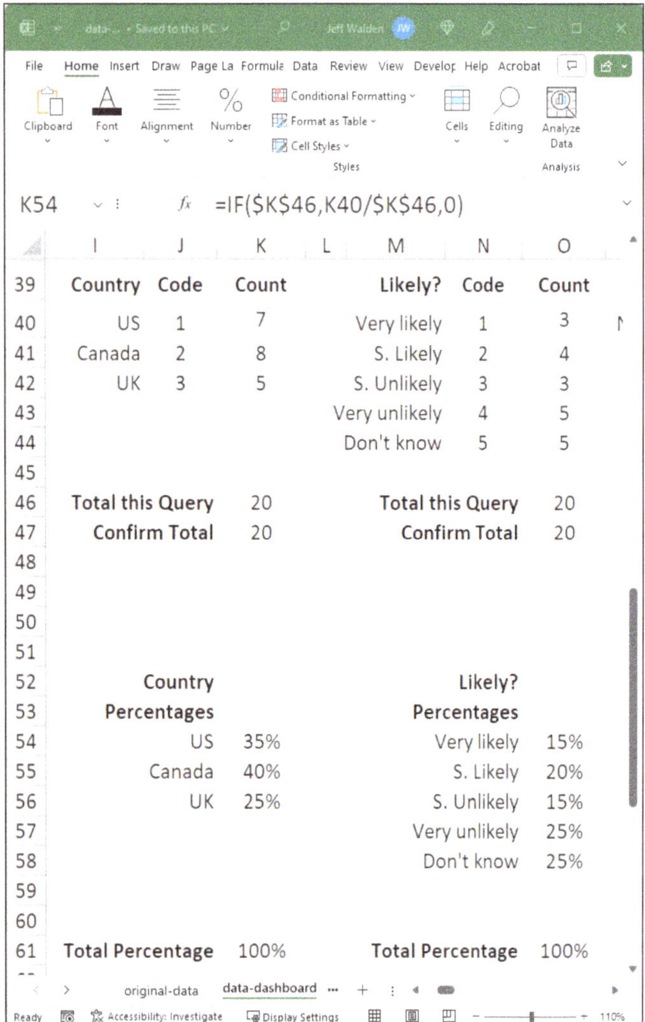

Figure 4.28: Percentages for Country and Likely fields

Note: Remember that references to the ***Total this Query*** cell must be **absolute** (dollar signs) — $K$46 and $O$46 respectively. This makes it easy to fill down.

SUM up percentages for each field, as shown in Figure 4.27 and Figure 4.28.

RESPONSIVE PERCENTAGES — CHECKED-AND-NOT-CHECKED

Responsive Percentages for the checked-and-not-checked fields (see Figure 4.29) are repeats of the **simple division**, **umbrella**, and **percent formatting** we've been doing on the previous percentage fields.

For example, in Figure 4.29, the formula for **cell R54** is:

 =IF(R$46,R40/R$46,0)

Because we intend to fill-right across the checked-not-checked fields, we left off the $ symbol from the R40 in the numerator. That way, the column increments automatically as the formula replicates rightwards.

This is different from the responsive count formulas in **row 40**, all of which point to the same target value, cell **$Q$40**.

	P	Q	R	S	T	U	V
		Code	Gov't regs	High cost	Lack skills	Lack support	
39							
40	Not Checked	0	10	9	15	9	
41	Checked	1	10	11	5	11	
42							
43							
44							
45							
46	Total this Query	20	20	20	20		
47	Confirm Total	20	20	20	20		
48							
49							
50							
51							
52							
53	Percentages	Gov't regs	High cost	Lack skills	Lack support		
54	Not Checked	50%	45%	75%	45%		
55	Checked	50%	55%	25%	55%		
56							
57							
58							
59							
60							
61	Total Percentage	100%	100%	100%	100%		
62							

Figure 4.29: Checked and not-checked fields

In cell **R61**, the formula SUMs the percentages:

 =SUM(R54:R55)

You can fill-right for the checked-not-checked columns across row 61 with that formula.

RESPONSIVE SURVEY BODY PERCENTAGES

After creating the formula for cell **X54**:

=IF(X$49,X40/X$49,0)

...you should be able to
(a) fill-right and then
(b) fill-down for all the Survey Body percentage cells, including the Cross-Percents. They all refer back to their own column-specific value from **Total this Query** in **row 49**. See Figure 4.30.

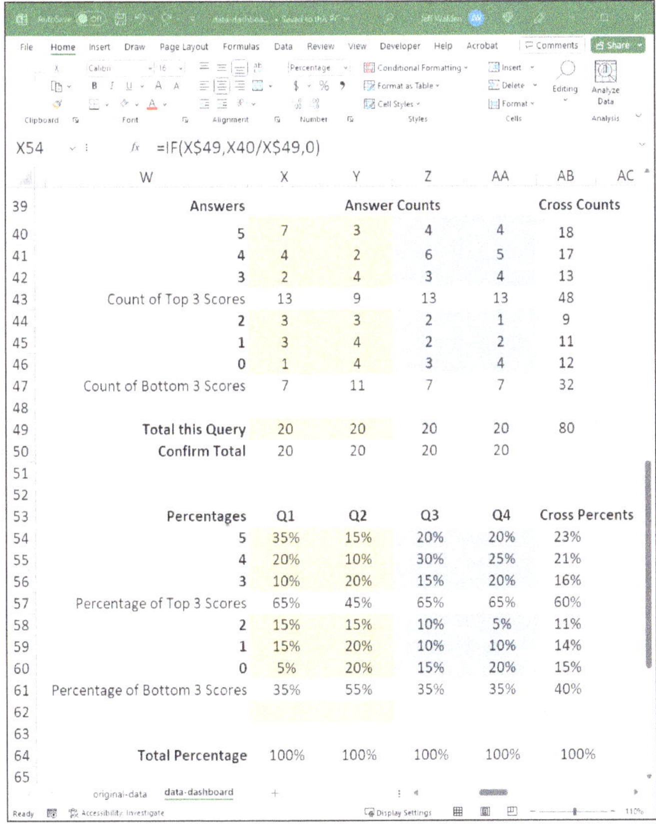

Figure 4.30: Survey Body percentages

The formula for Total Percentage in cell **X64** is:

=X57+X61

Fill-right to replicate the formula in **X64** across the Survey Body columns.

POLISHING OFF RESPONSIVE PERCENTAGES WITH DEMOGRAPHIC FIELDS

The Responsive Percentages of all the Demographic fields — as with the fields that went before them — are created with simple division, the IF-THEN-ELSE umbrella, and formatting as a percentage.

Note: We've tried to keep the rows of ***Total this Query*** and ***Total Percentage*** the same across fields, even though the numbers of the counts above them have varied. This is so we can copy/paste the same formula with minimal modification. It also tends to keep the overall worksheet looking neater. You can see this at work in Figure 4.31, where *Total this Query* and *Total Percentage* line up even though the number of codes varies.

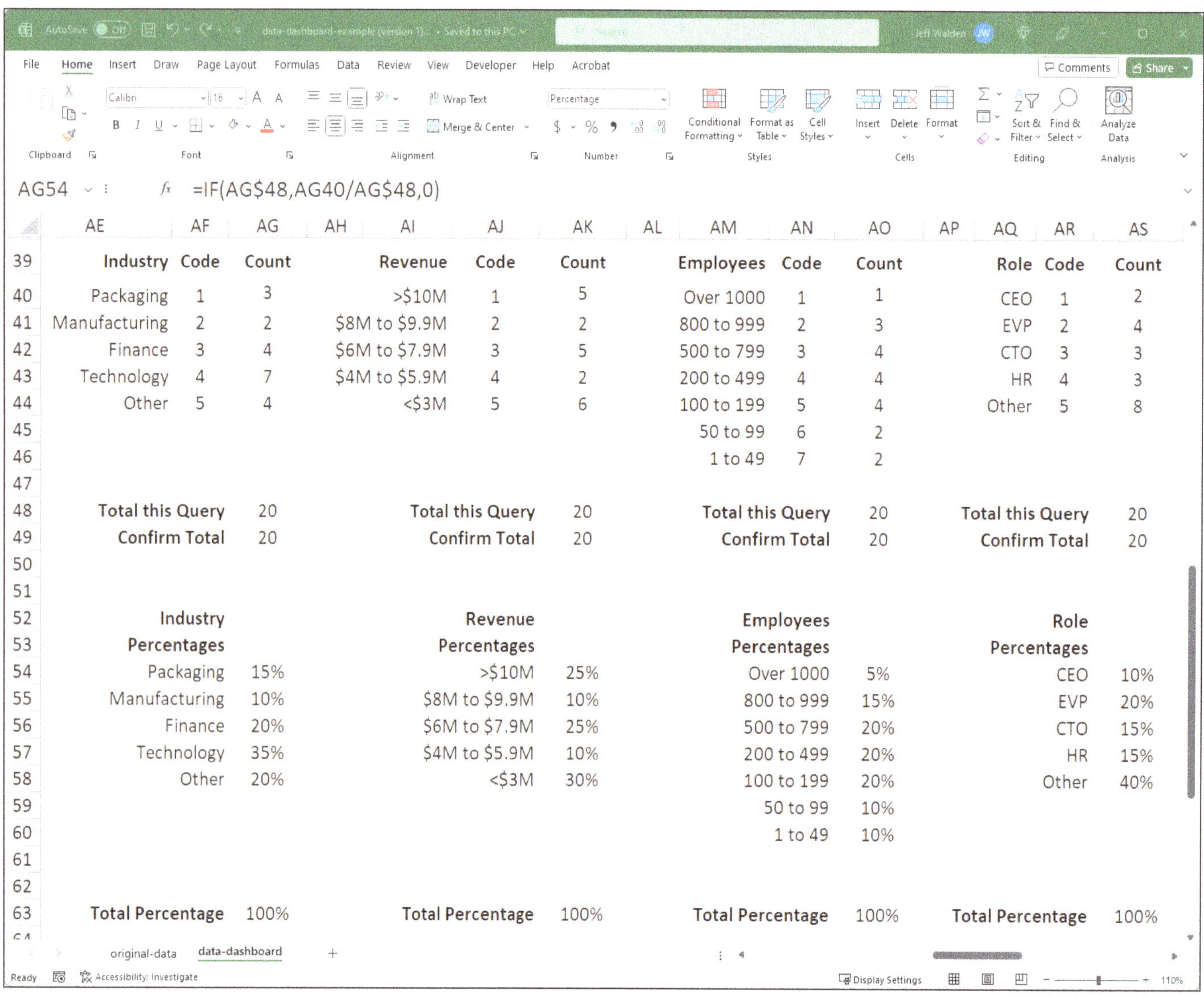

The spreadsheet formula bar shows cell **AG54** with formula `=IF(AG$48,AG40/AG$48,0)`.

	Industry Code	Count		Revenue	Code	Count		Employees	Code	Count		Role	Code	Count
40	Packaging	1	3	>$10M	1	5		Over 1000	1	1		CEO	1	2
41	Manufacturing	2	2	$8M to $9.9M	2	2		800 to 999	2	3		EVP	2	4
42	Finance	3	4	$6M to $7.9M	3	5		500 to 799	3	4		CTO	3	3
43	Technology	4	7	$4M to $5.9M	4	2		200 to 499	4	4		HR	4	3
44	Other	5	4	<$3M	5	6		100 to 199	5	4		Other	5	8
45								50 to 99	6	2				
46								1 to 49	7	2				
47														
48	Total this Query		20	Total this Query		20		Total this Query		20		Total this Query		20
49	Confirm Total		20	Confirm Total		20		Confirm Total		20		Confirm Total		20

	Industry Percentages			Revenue Percentages			Employees Percentages			Role Percentages	
54	Packaging	15%		>$10M	25%		Over 1000	5%		CEO	10%
55	Manufacturing	10%		$8M to $9.9M	10%		800 to 999	15%		EVP	20%
56	Finance	20%		$6M to $7.9M	25%		500 to 799	20%		CTO	15%
57	Technology	35%		$4M to $5.9M	10%		200 to 499	20%		HR	15%
58	Other	20%		<$3M	30%		100 to 199	20%		Other	40%
59							50 to 99	10%			
60							1 to 49	10%			
63	Total Percentage	100%		Total Percentage	100%		Total Percentage	100%		Total Percentage	100%

Figure 4.31: Responsive percentages for Demographic fields

RESPONSIVE STATISTICS

Along the bottom of the Data Dashboard, we've added **Responsive Statistics** for most fields. Providing such statistics for the Knowledgeable data or the Country data is near-meaningless. Calculating a Country Mean of 1.90 for all data (and we did — just to try it) tells you only the average of the Country counts in the data column not their significance, since they are not "scores." You can, of course, calculate it or any other statistic if you wish. You already know the relative percentages that the three Country values have in the data mix because of Responsive Counts and Percentages.

However, knowing the Responsive Statistics can be valuable when comparing them to the *other* fields of the Data Dashboard.

The Data Dashboard places the Responsive Statistics below the rows of Responsive Percentages, as in Figure 4.32.

O70 =IF($O$46,(AGGREGATE(1,5,O9:O28)),0)

	Likely?		Gov't regs	High cost	Lack skills	Lack support
Mean this Query	3.25	Mean this Query	0.50	0.55	0.25	0.55
Median this Query	3.50	Median this Query	0.50	1.00	0.00	1.00
St Dev this Query	1.45	St Dev this Query	0.51	0.51	0.44	0.51
Min this Query	1	Min this Query	0.00	0.00	0.00	0.00
Max this Query	5	Max this Query	1.00	1.00	1.00	1.00

	Survey Body Group 1		Survey Body Group 2		Cross Stats	
	Q1	Q2	Q3	Q4		
Group Mean	2.78		2.88		2.83	Mean
Mean this Query	3.30	2.25	2.95	2.80	2.83	Mean
Median this Query	4.00	2.00	3.50	3.00	3.13	Median
St Dev this Query	1.69	1.74	1.76	1.85	1.76	Std Dev
Min this Query	0	0	0	0	0	Min
Max this Query	5	5	5	5	5	Max

	Industry	Revenue	Employees	Role
Mean this Query	3.35	3.10	4.05	3.55
Median this Query	4.00	3.00	4.00	4.00
St Dev this Query	1.35	1.59	1.70	1.47
Min this Query	1	1	1	1
Max this Query	5	5	7	5

Figure 4.32: Responsive Statistics (for meaningful fields)

Figure 4.33 shows Responsive Statistics for the Likely field and the following Yes/No fields

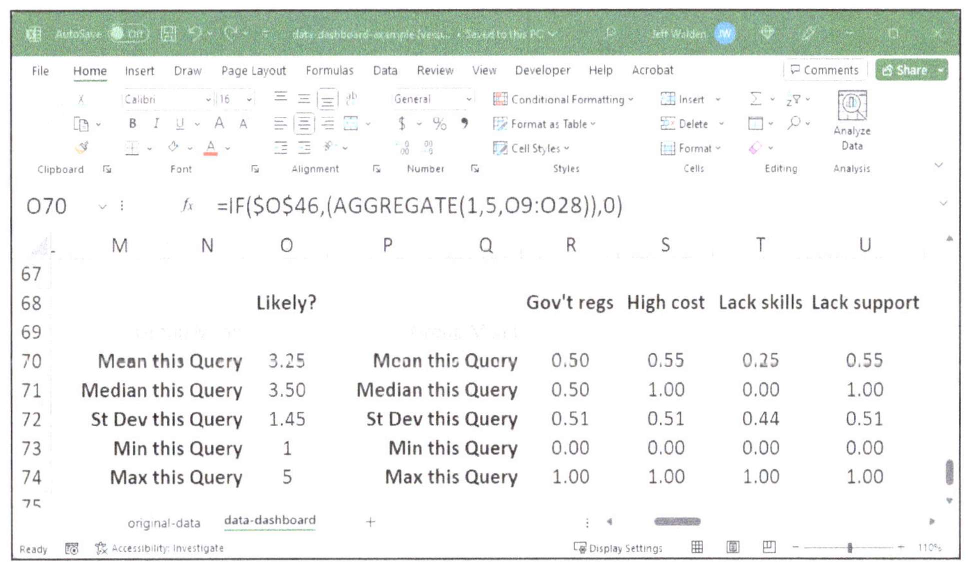

Figure 4.33: Responsive Statistics for Likely and the Yes/No fields

SO, WHAT STATISTICS DO YOU WANT?

For the Data Dashboard, we've selected the following set of statistics to respond to the changing counts for each query. All the statistics apply to data **only from the current query** (or all data if you have not run a query). We discuss how to run queries in the next chapter, "Running Advanced Filter Queries" on page 67.

Group Mean

Mean

Median

Standard Deviation

Min

Max

These statistics do not depend on the *count* of individual field values (Very Likely, Somewhat Likely, etc...), only on the *records that are visible* for the current query. **They are responsive to the data in the query, not to the counts.**

The statistics include Group Mean for the benefit of the Survey Body questions that are grouped by topic. If your survey does not group Survey Body questions by topic (or if you have no Survey Body questions separate from Context questions) there is no need for a Group Mean.

AGGREGATE

For the Responsive Statistics, we use Excel's *AGGREGATE* function. ***AGGREGATE* can pay attention to whether a record is displayed or hidden.** *AGGREGATE* lets you pick the function you want to perform and control if it ignores hidden rows or not. It enables you to add more than our small example set of calculations and statistics, if you wish.

You'll recall from Responsive Percentages (calculated using division) that the percentage calculation had to be protected against a condition of 0 data records (because you can't divide by zero).

Not all of *AGGREGATE*'s functions involve division, but some of its functions produce errors other than Division-by-Zero that also need protection when they encounter the condition of having no data to work with (no values for a field returned by a query). The umbrella technique works to protect against these errors, too.

Table 4.2 show the functions of *AGGREGATE,* which *AGGREGATE* functions require umbrella protection against a 0 count of data, and the errors that they produce if they don't receive it.

AGGREGATE and its functions are fully documented in Excel Help, but we'll summarize in case you want to vary your set of Responsive Statistics.

Its syntax is:

AGGREGATE*(function,option,ref1[,ref2])*

where *function* is a number from Table 4.2, *option* is a number from Table 4.3 on page 61, and *ref1* is the data range for the field you're calculating (for example, O9:O28). **(*Ref2* is an optional reference used by functions 14–19; they produce a Value error if ref2 is *not* present.)**

Table 4.2: Functions of AGGREGATE, which require the umbrella, and the error produced if they're not protected

NUMBER	FUNCTION	UMBRELLA?	ERROR ON 0
1	AVERAGE	Yes	Div 0
2	COUNT	No	NO ERROR
3	COUNTA	No	NO ERROR
4	MAX	No	NO ERROR
5	MIN	No	NO ERROR
6	PRODUCT	No	NO ERROR
7	STDEV.S (sample)	Yes	Div 0
8	STDEV.P (population)	Yes	Div 0
9	SUM	No	NO ERROR
10	VAR.S (sample)	Yes	Div 0
11	VAR.P (population)	Yes	Div 0
12	MEDIAN	Yes	Num
13	MODE.SNGL	Yes	N/A
14	LARGE	N/A	Value
15	SMALL	N/A	Value
16	PERCENTILE. INC	N/A	Value
17	QUARTILE. INC	N/A	Value
18	PERCENTILE. EXC	N/A	Value
19	QUARTILE. EXC	N/A	Value

Note: >*AGGREGATE* functions 14–19 require a *second reference* and produce a Value error if one is not present.

>*AGGREGATE* does not react to hide/show *when used with a horizontal range (only when used in a column).*

>The "errors" it ignores (options 3, 6, and 7 in Table 4.3 on page 61) refer to errors that may appear in its reference data range — not to an error caused by the lack of data (0 records as result of a query).

Table 4.3: AGGREGATE Options

OPTION	BEHAVIOR
0	Ignore nested *SUBTOTAL* and *AGGREGATE* functions (may be omitted)
1	Ignore hidden rows, nested *SUBTOTAL* and *AGGREGATE* functions
2	Ignore error values, nested *SUBTOTAL* and *AGGREGATE* functions
3	Ignore hidden rows, error values, nested *SUBTOTAL* and *AGGREGATE* functions
4	Ignore nothing
5	Ignore hidden rows
6	Ignore error values
7	Ignore hidden rows and error values

For the *AGGREGATE* function as used in the Responsive Statistics:

Each *AGGREGATE* formula is the same *ACROSS* columns. It varies only in that the data range designates different columns. For example, the Likely data is in the range O9:O28 and the Gov't regs data is in the range R9:R28. **The *AGGREGATE* functions do not in themselves check the *Total Count* value provided by the Data Dashboard. They perform their own internal count of visible records.** However, they still need to be protected against the condition of finding no records, and the way to do that is to use an IF THEN ELSE umbrella that *DOES* refer to the *Total Count* value, as shown in the sample formulas of Table 4.4.

Each *AGGREGATE* formula is *different* FROM ROW TO ROW. The formula for Mean uses a different *AGGREGATE* function (and a different function number to represent it) from the formula for Median or Standard Deviation. *AGGREGATE* *must* specify the function it calculates.

Table 4.4 shows the formulas used across the Responsive Statistics section.

Table 4.4: Sample formulas for functions that vary with the query (Group Mean spans the Q1-Q2 data columns)

FUNCTION	FORMULA
Group Mean	=IF(Y49+Z49,(AGGREGATE (1,5,Y9:Z38)),0) used only in Survey Body columns. Note the multiple-column range as well as adding together the *Total this Query* values for Q1 and Q2 so as not to calculate the Group Mean if the total of both fields returned are 0.
Mean	=IF($O$46,AGGREGATE (1,5,O9:O28)),0)
Median	=IF($O$46,AGGREGATE (12,5,O9:O28)),0
St. Dev.	=IF($O$46,AGGREGATE (7,5,O9:O28)),0) (we use .S the sample version, function 7 from Table 4.2)
Min	=IF($O$46,AGGREGATE (5,5,O9:O28)),0)
Max	=IF($O$46,AGGREGATE (4,5,O9:O28)),0)

Figure 4.34 on page 62 shows the Responsive Statistics for the *Likely* field and the four checked-not-checked reasons-for fields.

Again, using the *AGGREGATE* function, you can add other Responsive Statistics that are meaningful for your survey.

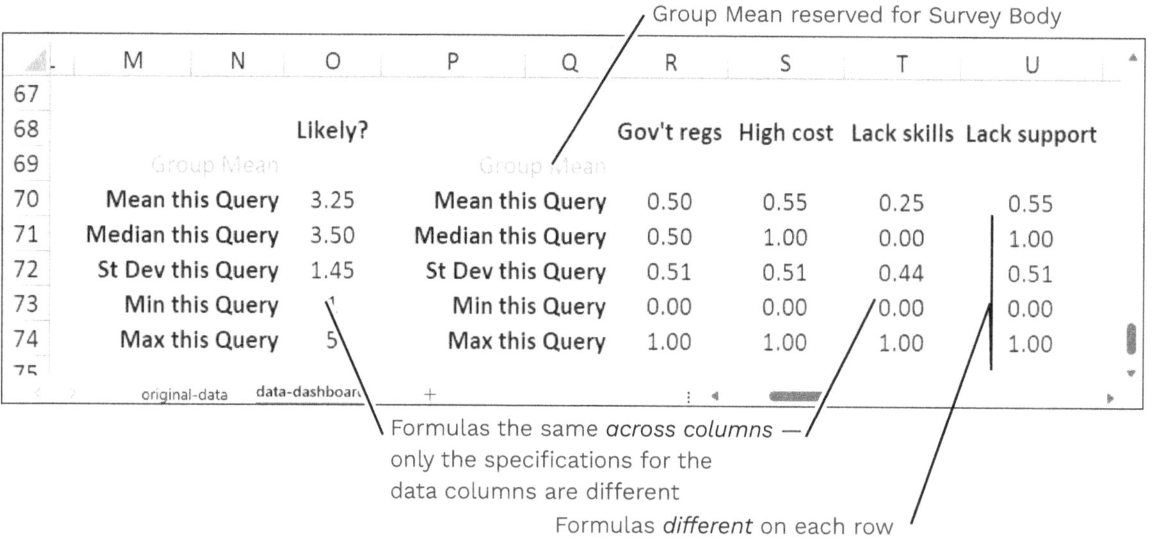

Figure 4.34: Responsive Statistics for Likely field and for the checked-not-checked questions

SURVEY BODY STATISTICS

The formulas for the Survey Body statistics are similar to those shown in Table 4.4 on page 61. Only the data range must be adjusted — which happens automatically when you fill-right.

Tip: Create all the formulas in column X, select **X70** through **X74**, and then **fill-right** to and including column AA. The Group Mean should be created separately — but you can use the Group Mean to fill-right for several sets of Survey Body topic Group Means if you have them.

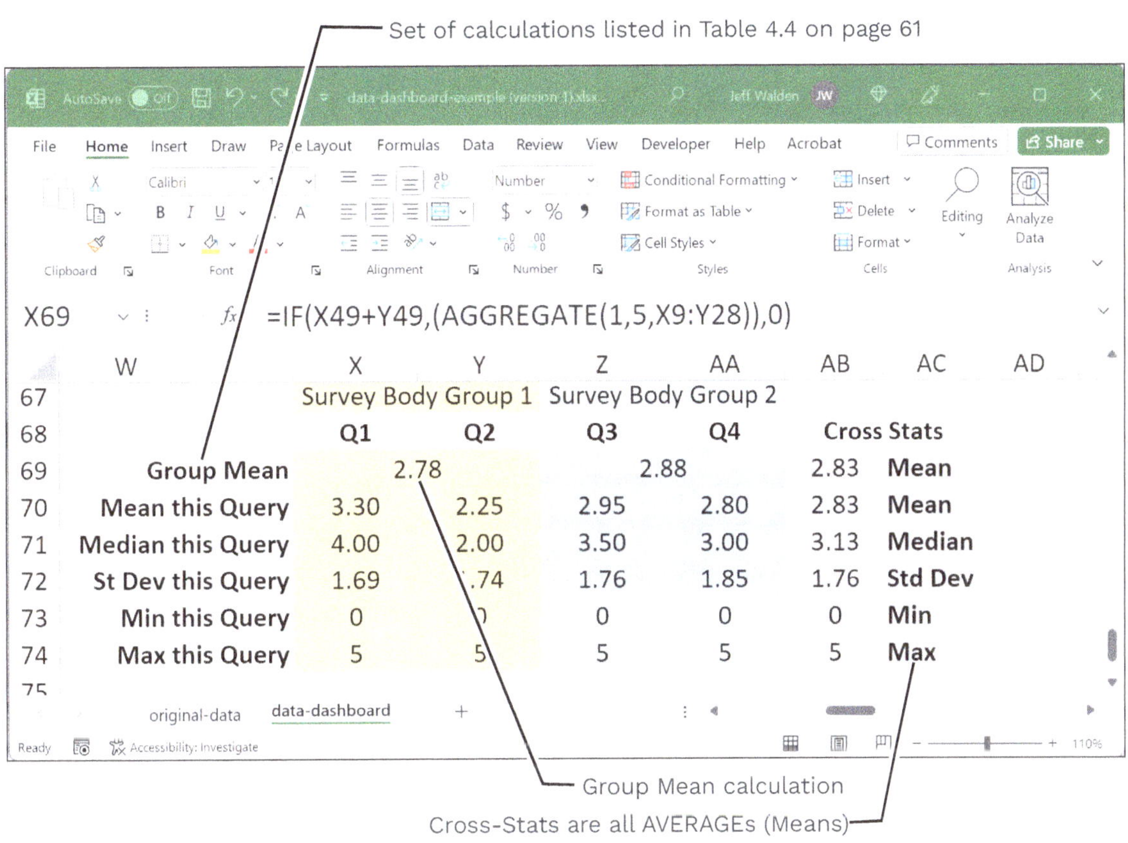

Figure 4.35:   Survey Body Responsive Statistics

The Group Mean calculations that combine columns **X** and **Y**, and columns **Z** and **AA** refer to multiple columns (we show two such combinations, you may have several more if you're grouping answers like this). A sample formula for these columns appears in the formula bar in Figure 4.35 and in Table 4.4 on page 61.

Column **AB** holds cross-statistics for the Survey Body. The formula for each of the cross-statistics is the Mean (*AVERAGE*) of the four Survey Body cells in each row. Note the use of the range:

=AVERAGE(Y69:AB69)

You might have 10, 20, or 30 columns in your Survey Body questions; but the cross-statistics average them all.

DEMOGRAPHIC STATISTICS

Spreadsheet calculations are awfully repetitive, and the Data Dashboard is no exception.

The Responsive Statistics for the Demographic fields are the same as those used for the Context fields and the Survey Body fields. Only the designation of the data column varies.

You can find the formulas in Table 4.4 on page 61.

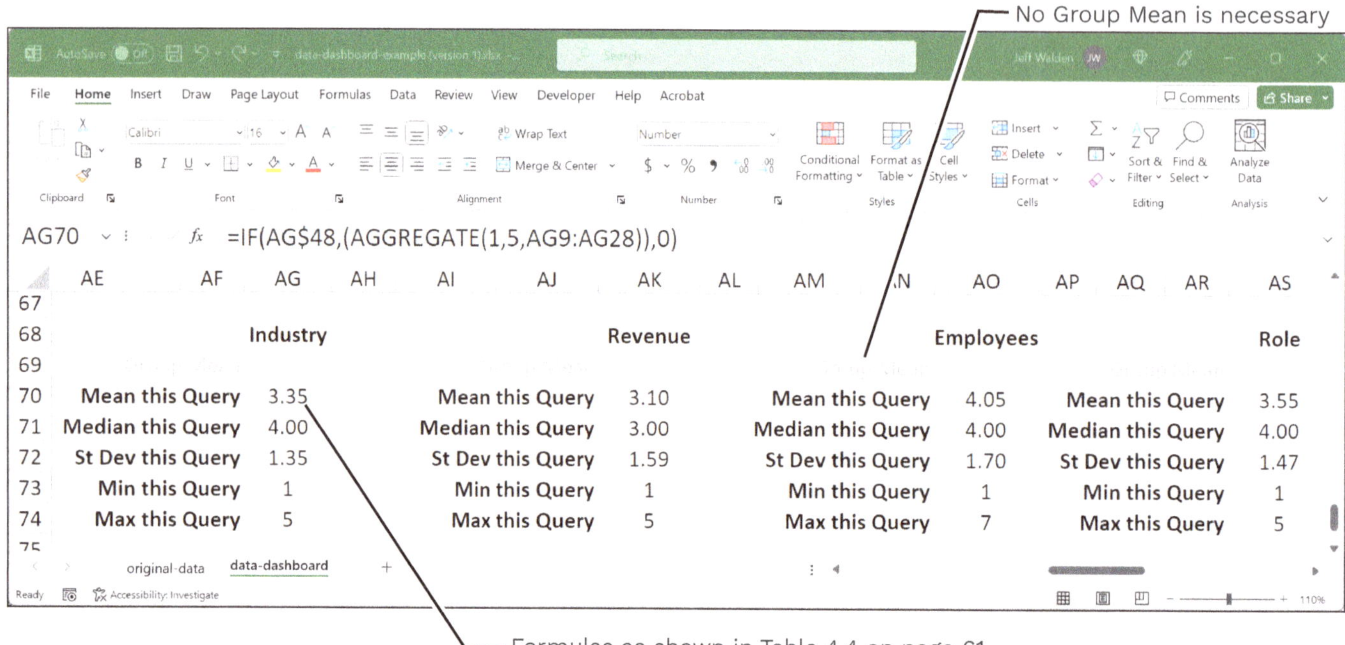

Figure 4.36: Responsive statistics for the Demographic fields

We strongly encourage you to save your spreadsheet model at this point. You wouldn't want all this work to go to waste!

SUMMARY

Section by section, we have built the Data Dashboard — the first step in analysis. The Data Dashboard allows you to see the differences between various subsets of your data, and provides you with information that you can graph or tabularize.

Now, you will be able to see what's going on.

Figure 4.37 shows an overview of the completed Data Dashboard. Yours may look different depending on the number of fields you have and what kind of data they hold. The differences make it flexible and able to accommodate different surveys.

The chapter "Running Advanced Filter Queries" on page 67 shows how to query the Data Dashboard.

Figure 4.37:   An overview of the completed Data Dashboard

Figure 4.37 labels the parts of the Data Dashboard:

1. **Query area**, where you tell the Data Dashboard which records to display and which to hide.

2. **Data area.** The widget survey only contains 20 records. Your data may contain hundreds of records. Usually, you will scroll these records off-screen.

3. **Basic Statistics.** These are reference statistics for the entire data set. The Basic Statistics do not change when a query shows or hides records. You can always compare the statistics from a given query to the Basic Statistics.

4. **Responsive Counts.** A key aspect of the model. Each group of answers — the 1s, the 2s, the 3s — are counted. These counts naturally vary with the query.

5. **Responsive Percentages.** This section calculates the percentage that comprises each responsive group of answers *after* the query. Thus, while the UK may comprise 25% of the original data, it may comprise 50% of the visible data after a specific query, or may comprise 100% if your query is to display UK data only. This is why we call the percentages *responsive*.

6. **Responsive Statistics.** While similar to the Basic Statistics that operate on all data in the data set, Responsive Statistics operate only on those records that are visible after a query.

Chapter 5

Running Advanced Filter Queries

Excel's *Advanced Filter query* is a formalized way to display a subset of information from the data set. Essentially, a query hides and shows records according to the criteria you enter, allowing the Responsive Counts, Responsive Percentages, and Responsive Statistics in the Data Dashboard to reflect the changes made by your criteria.

You can also extract sets of data for use elsewhere in tables and graphs.

Dashboard queries are not very complex, but they are specific about how you must format your criteria. Once you have made your query, *information* begins to emerge from mere *data*. This chapter describes how to create and run an Advanced Filter query in the Data Dashboard.

You already may be familiar with Microsoft Excel's **Basic Filters** (see Figure 5.1).

With Basic Filters, you can highlight a block of data that includes column names, choose *Data / Sort & Filter / Filter*, and Excel displays pulldown arrows at the top of each column that allow you to sort and select records according to the values in one or more of the columns of data.

While this approach works — more or less — in the Data Dashboard worksheet, it has disadvantages that are overcome by Excel's Advanced filters.

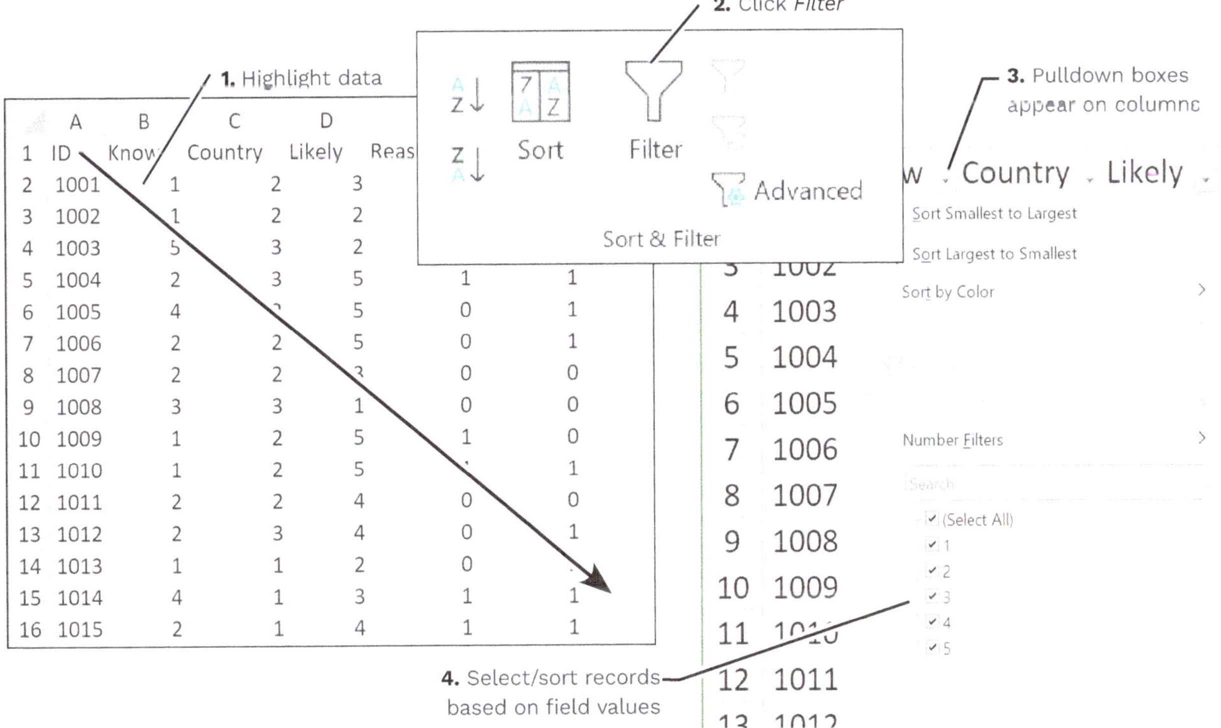

Figure 5.1:   You may have used Excel's Basic Filters

RULES? YES, WE HAVE RULES

Figure 5.2 shows where we placed the query area (called the Criteria range) on the Data Dashboard. You may recall that the first thing we did with the Data Dashboard after spreading out the original data was to insert several rows at the top of the worksheet and copy and paste the field names **EXACTLY**. (See page 37.) We put those field names near the top of the worksheet with several blank rows beneath them to be ready for query criteria. You can add or delete query rows later as needed without adjusting the formulas of the model below them.

You can review how we added these rows in "Add Rows for Queries Up Top" on page 36.

There are other (and some pretty neat) ways you can form and use Excel's Advanced Filter queries, and other places you can put query criteria. We explain these in Appendix B, "Become a Query Ninja" on page 119. The current chapter explains how to query the Data Dashboard model specifically.

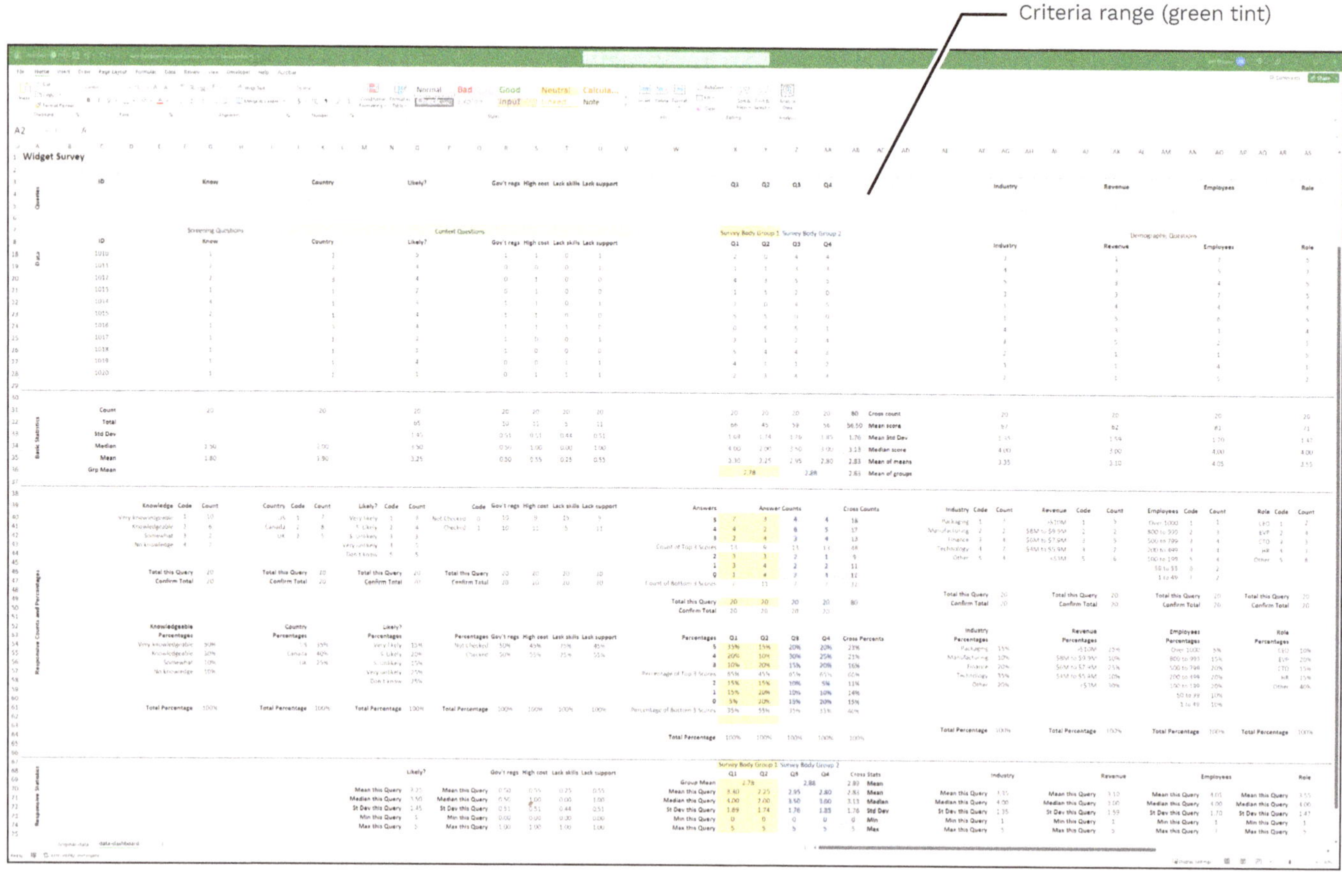

Figure 5.2: The full Data Dashboard worksheet in Excel, highlighting the Criteria range of the query area

---

There Are Queries and Then There Are *Queries*

There is an important difference between Excel's Advanced filters (that we are calling *queries*) and a true database query language such as SQL (Structured Query Language). Even Excel's Advanced filters only select, copy, or hide and display data for you according to your criteria. In themselves, they cannot transform, update, or delete the data. You can do such tasks — even in Excel — either manually or by using Excel's built-in Power Query Editor. The Power Query Editor operates on data coming into Excel or on data in a worksheet. SQL is available for Excel using add-ins such as Python, a programming language, Excel can be connected to an SQL server, or you can use Microsoft Query, but SQL is not natively available in Excel without some add-in. You can also use Visual Basic for Applications (VBA), which is built into Excel. This book describes how to create two VBA macros for running specific *ad hoc* Advanced Filter queries; other than that, the Power Query Editor, SQL, and VBA programming techniques are beyond the scope of this book.

A TALE OF TWO RANGES: *LIST* AND *CRITERIA*

There are two main ranges used in Data Dashboard queries: the List range and the Criteria range, each of which are user-definable. These are shown in Figure 5.3 on page 70.

- **List range:** The List range includes all data columns and their headers (the column names), as well as any empty columns that may lie between the data columns.

  - The List range is *contiguous,* top left to bottom right, with no gaps.
  - The List range includes the ID numbers we've given our records.
  - In the Data Dashboard model, the List range includes the headers on row 8 from column C through column AS, and the data in rows 9 through 28 for all data columns, **even including the empty and unnamed empty columns** between the columns that hold actual data.
  - The headers on row 8 are *frozen*; the ID column is also *frozen*. You can select them anyway.

- **Criteria range:** The criteria range includes

  - **(a)** the copy of the data column headers you placed in row 3 (remember — you duplicated them there) and
  - **(b)** ONLY as many rows below those headers as you need to enclose the query criteria **BUT NO EMPTY ROWS *WITHIN* THE CRITERIA RANGE**.
  - There must be at least one criterion within the range on each row of the range you define. You can have additional criteria on that same row.
  - There MUST BE AT LEAST ONE EMPTY ROW **BELOW** THE CRITERIA RANGE to separate it from the List range.

This sounds complex, but we think that Figure 5.3 on page 70 will help simplify it.

You will define these ranges later, during the Advanced Filter query process, but it's good to know about them now.

There is a third range called **Copy To:** to use when copying data for use in a table or graph. The field for this range is live only when you are copying data to a location and not when you are hiding and showing records. We cover that case in Appendix B, "Become a Query Ninja" on page 119.

Note: If you inadvertently include an empty row in your Criteria range, the query does not execute and does not produce an error to tell you that anything is wrong. It can be puzzling until you figure that out.

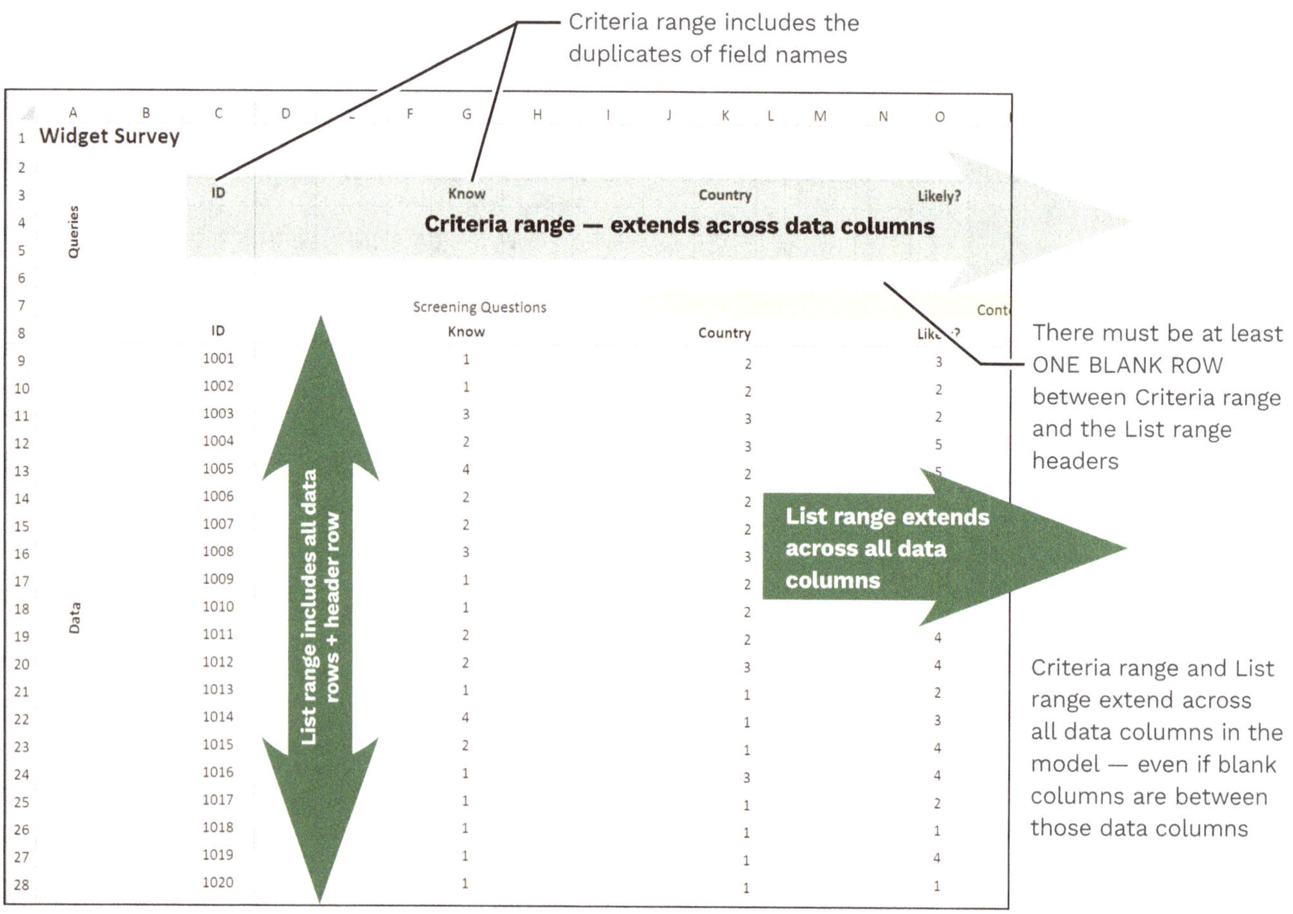

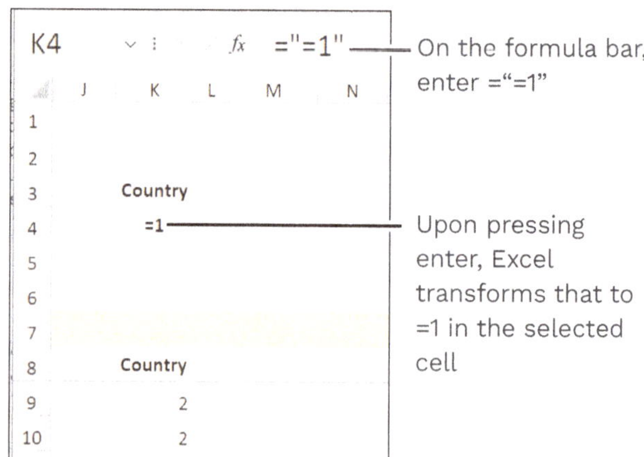

Figure 5.3 shows a Widget Survey spreadsheet illustrating the List range (for data) and Criteria range (for query).

ID	Know	Country	Likely?
1001	1	2	3
1002	1	2	2
1003	3	3	2
1004	2	3	5
1005	4	2	5
1006	2	2	
1007	2	2	
1008	3	3	
1009	1	2	
1010	1	2	
1011	2	2	4
1012	2	3	4
1013	1	1	2
1014	4	1	3
1015	2	1	4
1016	1	3	4
1017	1	1	2
1018	1	1	1
1019	1	1	4
1020	1	1	1

Figure 5.3: List range (for data) and Criteria range (for query)

HOW TO SPECIFY
WHAT YOU'RE LOOKING FOR

To specify a criterion, enter it into a cell beneath the appropriate field name in the Criteria range.

Microsoft describes the method in Figure 5.4 that shows entering a criterion into the Excel formula bar for a query. By using the quotation marks, you assure that =1 appears in the cell, not just 1 (Excel's formulas all begin with =).

Figure 5.4: Microsoft's method for entering a criterion into a query

Whatever you put inside the quotation marks is what the query tries to match. For example, if you want to find all records from the US, and you know that the Country code for the US is 1, put **=1** between quotation marks in the formula bar following the specific method shown in Figure 5.4.

Um... However. While Microsoft's method is unquestionably valid (we've used it often), it is not the only way. We've found that you can also **just type** directly into a Criteria range cell without the extra **=** and quotes. For example, these all appear to be equivalent:

1   =1   <>1

We think that's a lot plainer.

> **Note:** *Caution.* You may find an instance where you **must** use Microsoft's quote method to get the query to work to your requirements or to get it to work at all. **It is necessary to know Microsoft's recommended method.** Our experience indicates that it may not always be required, especially with criteria expressed as numbers, but it is Microsoft's specified method.

USING OPERATORS

Life is not made up of exact matches. Excel's queries can use operators to look for various kinds of matches, as shown in Table 5.1.

Table 5.1: How different operators affect how a query criterion matches the data set 1, 2, 3, 4, 5

OPERATOR	EXAMPLE
= (equal)	**="=1"** or **=1** or **1** looks for records where the data is equal to 1 (finds 1 from the set 1, 2, 3, 4, 5)
> (greater than)	**=">2"** or **>2** looks for records where the data is greater than 2 (finds 3, 4, 5)
< (less than)	**="<3"** or **<3** looks for records where the data is less than 3 (finds 1, 2)
>= (greater than or equal to)	**=">=3"** or **>=3** looks for records where the data is greater than or equal to 3 (finds 3, 4, 5)
<= (less than or equal to)	**="<=3"** or **<=3** looks for records where the data is less than or equal to 3 (finds 1, 2, 3)
<> (not equal to)	**="<>3"** or **<>3** looks for records where the data is not 3 (finds 1, 2, 4, 5)

> **Note:** **There are no text fields in the Data Dashboard widget example**, and no potential text responses in the widget survey. However, if you have such text-containing fields, you can use familiar wildcards such as * (any number of characters) and ? (any single character) as text criteria:
>
> ="widget" (finds *widget*)
> ="widget*" (finds widget or *widgetmaster*)
> ="widget?" (finds *widgetx*, *widgety*, and *widgetz*.
>
> This is an instance of the Microsoft criteria entry method with quotation marks applied to text. **With text, we recommend this method.**
>
> For more about handling fields that include text values, see Chapter 6, "Handling Text Fields in Surveys" on page 97.

QUERIES USING AND / OR

The advantage of Advanced Filter queries over Basic Filter is that you can use the row position of the criteria to create **AND** and **OR** combinations, which the basic by-the-column filters cannot do. Basic Filters only add criteria together (equivalent to AND).

The concept of AND and *OR is just as logical as* you might think.

AND. "Show me the data where field value A **AND** field value B match my criteria." (Both fields A and B must match criteria.)

Or. "Show me the data where **either** field value A **OR** field value B matches my criteria." (Either field A or B must match criteria; both do not have to match, but may.)

Together, AND and OR allow you to create a query that can find records that match this example criteria statement:

UK OR Canada
OR
Highly Likely AND Packaging Industry

See Figure 5.5 through Figure 5.7 to see how AND and OR work together.

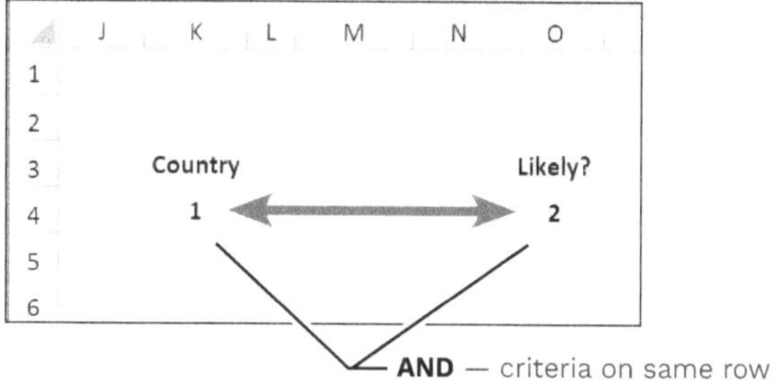

Figure 5.5: AND — place **AND** criteria on the **same row**: Country =1 **AND** Likely =2

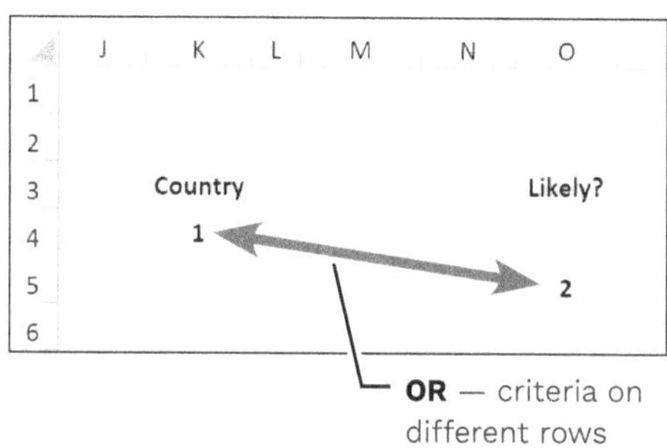

Figure 5.6: OR — place **OR** criteria on **different rows**: Country = 1 **OR** Likely = 2

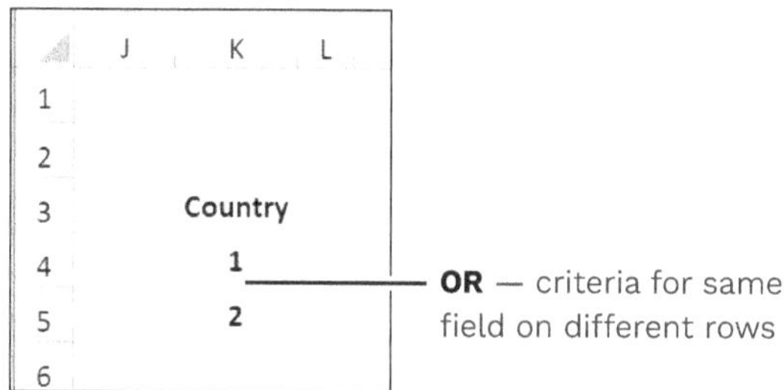

Figure 5.7: OR — place **OR** criteria for the **same field on different rows**: Country = 1 **OR** Country = 2 (you can also say Country <>3)

The Inevitable Rules and Guidelines

Overall Rule of Thumb: For any given data set, the more criteria you specify, the **less likely** it is that you'll turn up a record that matches all criteria.

In operating the Data Dashboard, your real aim is **to see what effect one selection (or small sets of selections) have on other responses.** "Those who said it was likely that they would institute electronic widget management also said…" and "Respondents from the Packaging industry said…" and "Organizations with greater than \$10M revenue answered the Survey Body questions like this…" and "What is the profile of a top widget producer?"

Use a minimum number of rows for your criteria. You can add (or delete) Criteria range rows as needed as your queries grow and shrink.

NO BLANK ROWS are allowed within the Criteria range above or between rows that contain criteria.

There MUST be at least one blank row between the bottom of the Criteria range and the header row of the List range.

Complex queries will always give you what you ask for — but whether that's what you expected or needed is a different question.

AT LONG LAST WE DO A QUERY

Let's take a look at the Responsive Counts, Percentages, and Statistics in the Data Dashboard for the set of **all responses** (Figure 5.8 following, through Figure 5.11 on page 76), and then look at the same fields after a query. Initially, all values for Country are represented, as are all values for the other fields.

As a reminder, there are 20 records in the widget survey data.

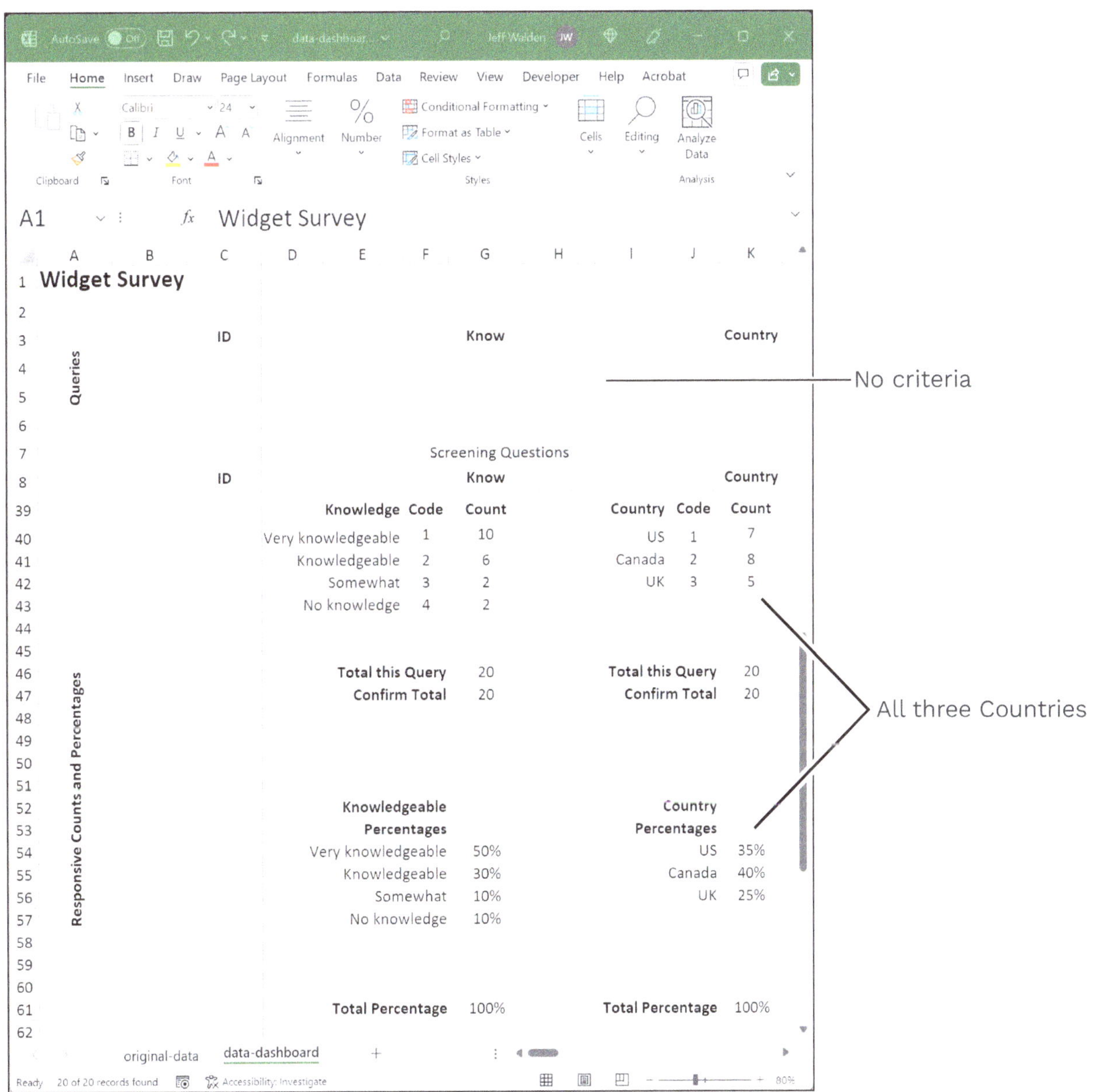

Figure 5.8: Responsive Counts and Percentages for all responses in the data set (no criteria); there are no Responsive Statistics for these two fields — just counts and percentages

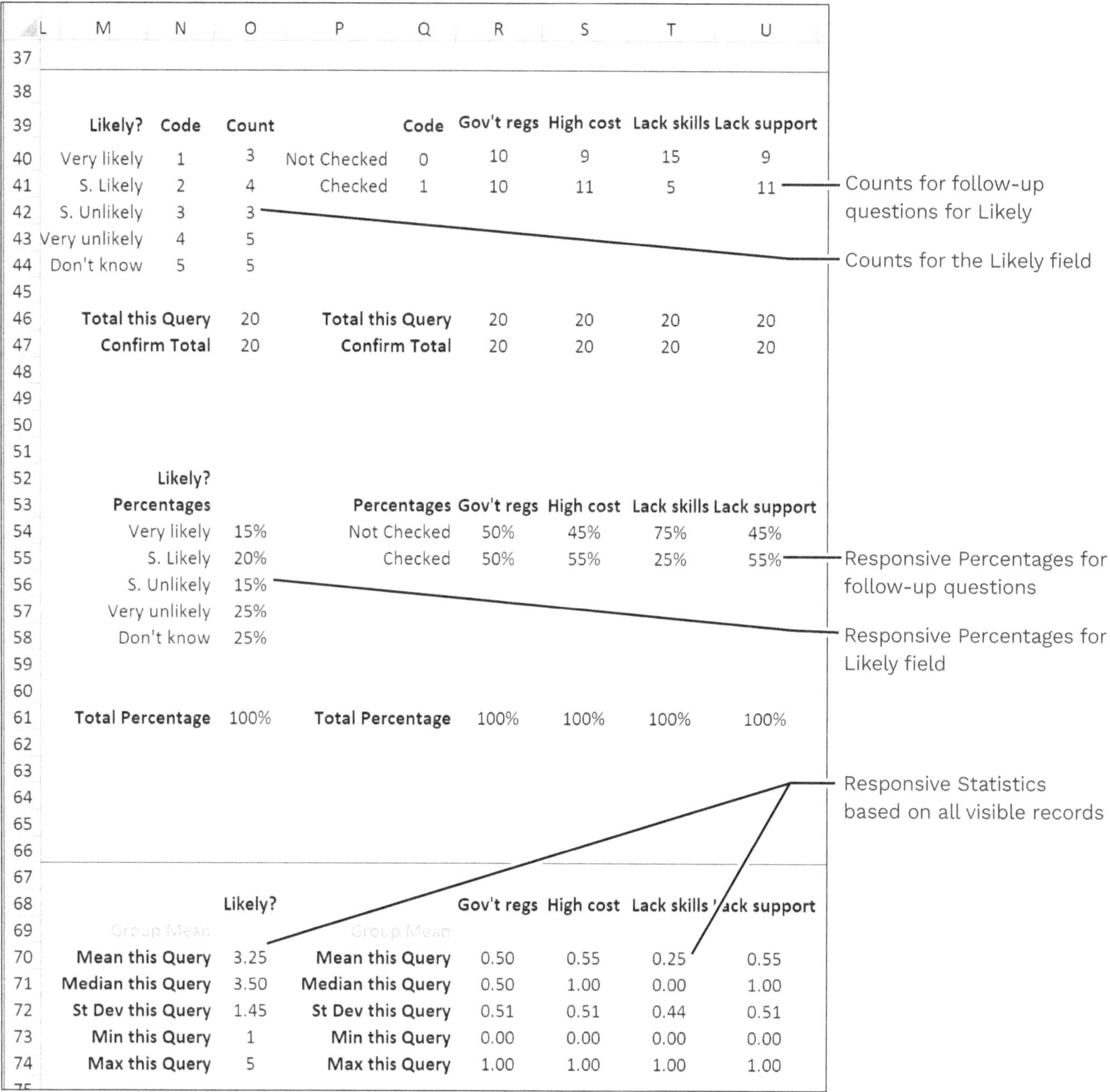

Figure 5.9: The Likely field and its follow-up questions, their Responsive Counts and Responsive Percentages, and the Responsive Statistics (no criteria, all records)

Note: Before looking through the Responsive Statistics, you may want to review Standard Deviation, Mean, and Median, beginning on page 39. Min and Max are self-explanatory: the smallest and largest values (respectively) for the field in the data.

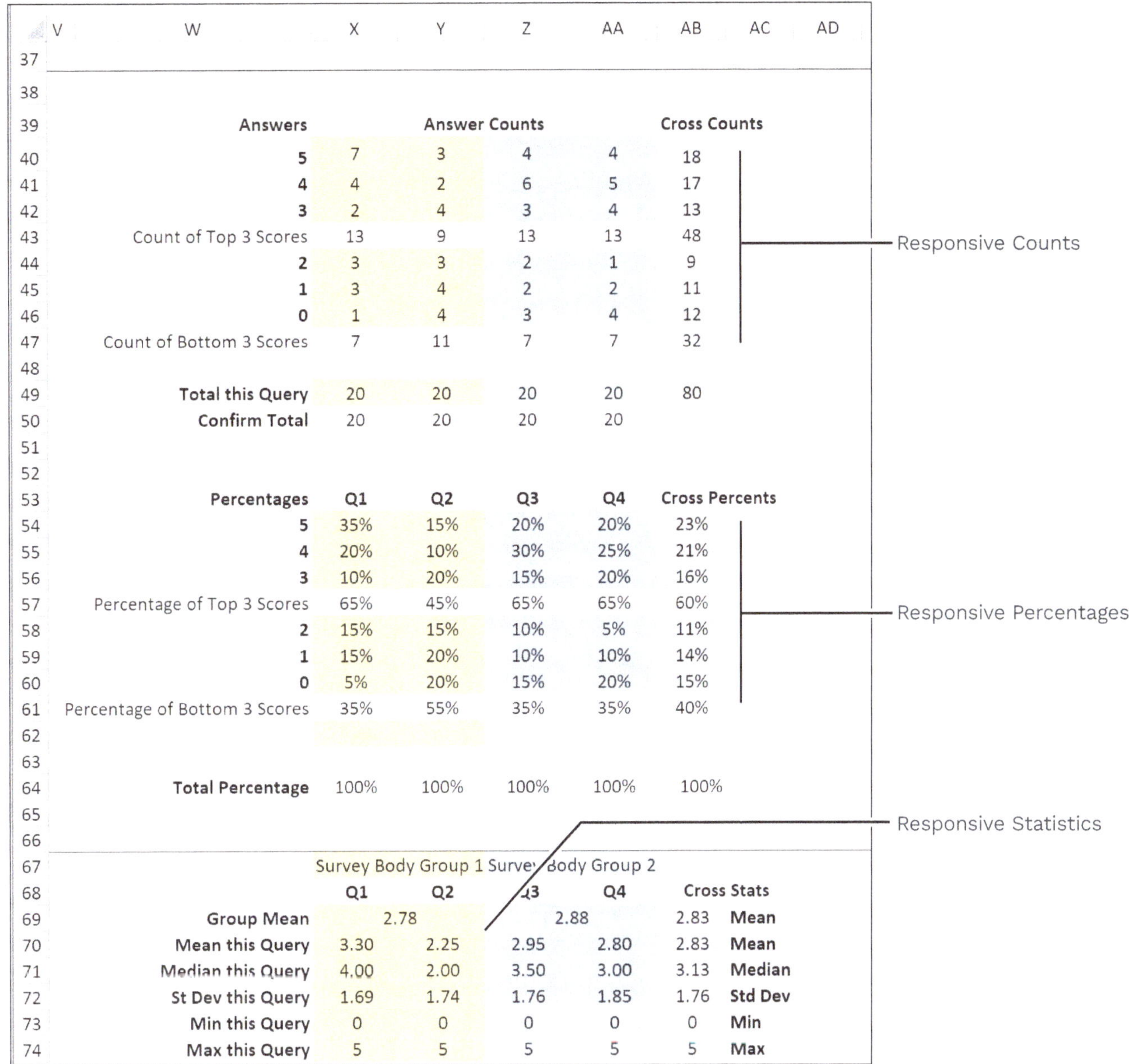

	V	W	X	Y	Z	AA	AB	AC	AD
37									
38									
39		Answers		Answer Counts			Cross Counts		
40		5	7	3	4	4	18		
41		4	4	2	6	5	17		
42		3	2	4	3	4	13		
43		Count of Top 3 Scores	13	9	13	13	48		
44		2	3	3	2	1	9		
45		1	3	4	2	2	11		
46		0	1	4	3	4	12		
47		Count of Bottom 3 Scores	7	11	7	7	32		
48									
49		Total this Query	20	20	20	20	80		
50		Confirm Total	20	20	20	20			
51									
52									
53		Percentages	Q1	Q2	Q3	Q4	Cross Percents		
54		5	35%	15%	20%	20%	23%		
55		4	20%	10%	30%	25%	21%		
56		3	10%	20%	15%	20%	16%		
57		Percentage of Top 3 Scores	65%	45%	65%	65%	60%		
58		2	15%	15%	10%	5%	11%		
59		1	15%	20%	10%	10%	14%		
60		0	5%	20%	15%	20%	15%		
61		Percentage of Bottom 3 Scores	35%	55%	35%	35%	40%		
62									
63									
64		Total Percentage	100%	100%	100%	100%	100%		
65									
66									
67			Survey Body Group 1		Survey Body Group 2				
68			Q1	Q2	Q3	Q4	Cross Stats		
69		Group Mean	2.78		2.88		2.83	Mean	
70		Mean this Query	3.30	2.25	2.95	2.80	2.83	Mean	
71		Median this Query	4.00	2.00	3.50	3.00	3.13	Median	
72		St Dev this Query	1.69	1.74	1.76	1.85	1.76	Std Dev	
73		Min this Query	0	0	0	0	0	Min	
74		Max this Query	5	5	5	5	5	Max	

Figure 5.10: Counts, Percentages, and Responsive Stats for all the Survey Body questions (all responses, no query)

	AE	AF	AG	AH	AI	AJ	AK	AL	AM	AN	AO	AP	AQ	AR	AS
37															
38															
39	Industry	Code	Count		Revenue	Code	Count		Employees	Code	Count		Role	Code	Count
40	Packaging	1	3		>$10M	1	5		Over 1000	1	1		CEO	1	2
41	Manufacturing	2	2		$8M to $9.9M	2	2		800 to 999	2	3		EVP	2	4
42	Finance	3	4		$6M to $7.9M	3	5		500 to 799	3	4		CTO	3	3
43	Technology	4	7		$4M to $5.9M	4	2		200 to 499	4	4		HR	4	3
44	Other	5	4		<$3M	5	6		100 to 199	5	4		Other	5	8
45									50 to 99	6	2				
46									1 to 49	7	2				
47															
48	Total this Query		20		Total this Query		20		Total this Query		20		Total this Query		20
49	Confirm Total		20		Confirm Total		20		Confirm Total		20		Confirm Total		20
50															
51															
52	Industry				Revenue				Employees				Role		
53	Percentages				Percentages				Percentages				Percentages		
54	Packaging	15%			>$10M	25%			Over 1000	5%			CEO	10%	
55	Manufacturing	10%			$8M to $9.9M	10%			800 to 999	15%			EVP	20%	
56	Finance	20%			$6M to $7.9M	25%			500 to 799	20%			CTO	15%	
57	Technology	35%			$4M to $5.9M	10%			200 to 499	20%			HR	15%	
58	Other	20%			<$3M	30%			100 to 199	20%			Other	40%	
59									50 to 99	10%					
60									1 to 49	10%					
61															
62															
63	Total Percentage	100%			Total Percentage	100%			Total Percentage	100%			Total Percentage	100%	
64															
65															
66															
67															
68	Industry				Revenue				Employees				Role		
69															
70	Mean this Query	3.35			Mean this Query	3.10			Mean this Query	4.05			Mean this Query	3.55	
71	Median this Query	4.00			Median this Query	3.00			Median this Query	4.00			Median this Query	4.00	
72	St Dev this Query	1.35			St Dev this Query	1.59			St Dev this Query	1.70			St Dev this Query	1.47	
73	Min this Query	1			Min this Query	1			Min this Query	1			Min this Query	1	
74	Max this Query	5			Max this Query	5			Max this Query	7			Max this Query	5	
75															

Figure 5.11: Demographic questions, Responsive Counts, Percentages, and Statistics (all responses, no query)

ENTER A QUERY

For the following steps, we use the widget survey data and the example Data Dashboard worksheet. If you've built your Data Dashboard using your own data, of course the fields and field values will be different.

1. Enter **1** immediately beneath the Country header in the Criteria range (in the widget Dashboard, this is several rows above the headers for the data set itself). **See Figure 5.12** on the right.

   We've found that you can enter a number directly, or use the Microsoft method described on page 70.

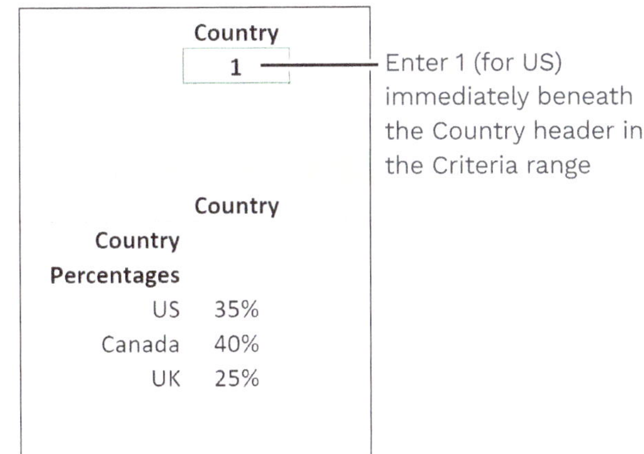

Figure 5.12: Enter 1 under Country in the Criteria range

2. Choose *Data | Sort & Filter | Advanced*. (That is, on the Data menu, click Advanced in the Sort & Filter area, Figure 5.13).

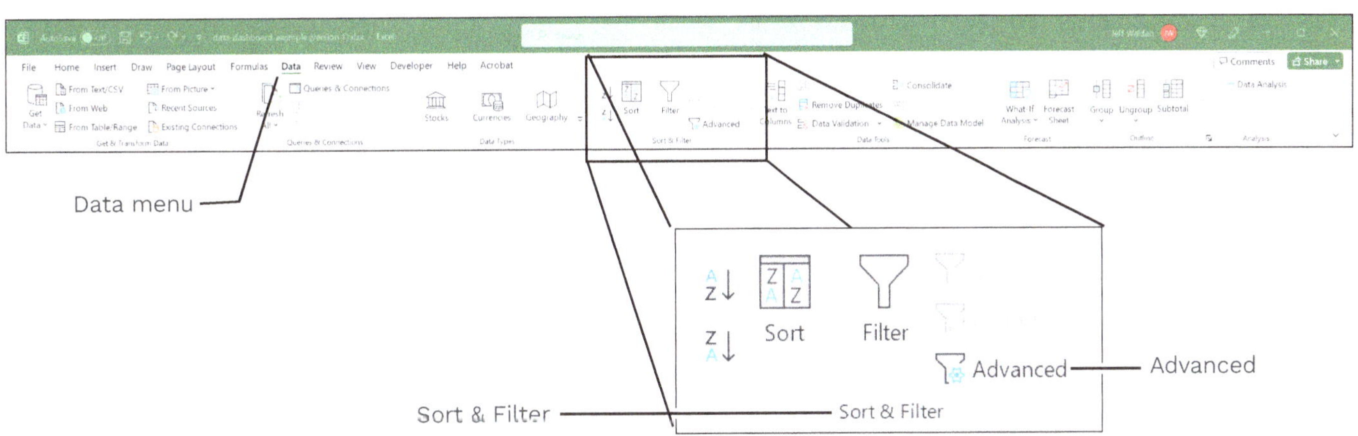

Figure 5.13: *Data | Sort & Filter | Advanced*

Excel displays the Advanced Filter dialog box (Figure 5.14). Make sure that you have selected **Filter the list in place** in the Advanced Filter dialog box.

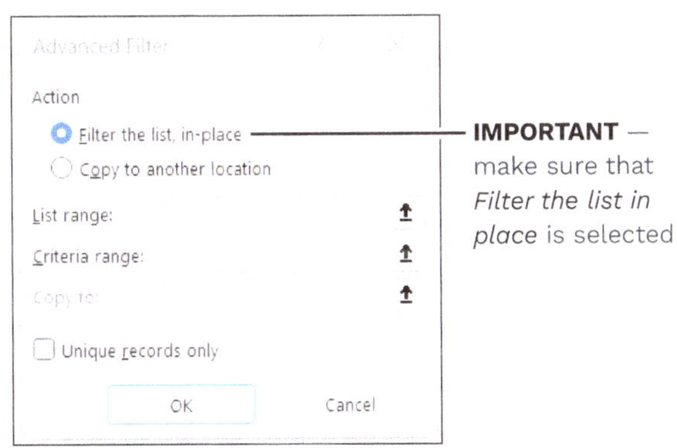

Figure 5.14: Advanced Filter dialog

3. In the Advanced Filter box, **click within the List range field**, then highlight the List range, including the field names. This range extends from the ID column header across the spreadsheet to the Role column on the far right, as shown in Figure 5.15 on page 78. By selecting it, you enter the range into the List range field. You can also type the range directly into the List range field.

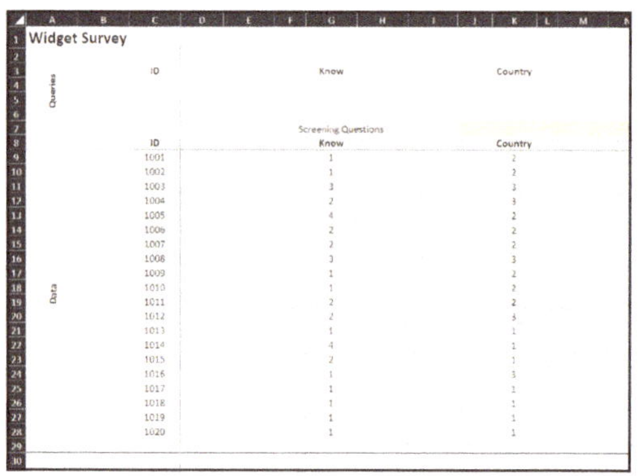 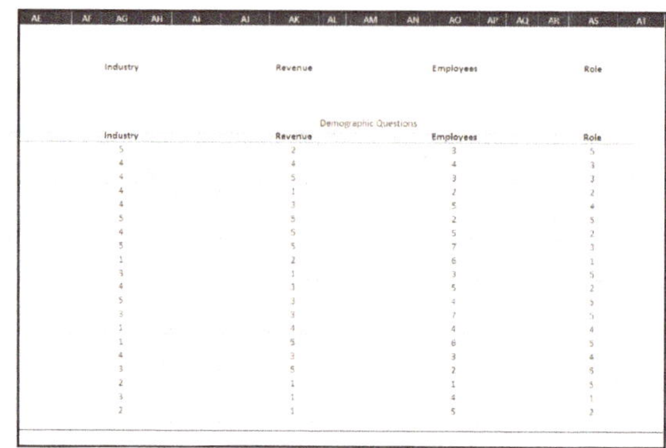

Figure 5.15: Highlight the List range, all rows plus header, from ID through the Role column

4. In the Advanced Filter dialog box, **click within the Criteria range field**, then highlight the Criteria range at the top of the Data Dashboard, including the Criteria range field names, for all columns across the Data Dashboard (green tinted box at the top of Figure 5.16). The range appears in the Criteria range field on the Advanced Filter dialog box. You can also type the range directly.

Note: **Remember the Criteria range rules:** The Criteria range must cover only the field names and the row(s) that contain criteria. No empty rows above or within the criteria. Also: leave at least one empty row between the Criteria range and the headers of the List range.

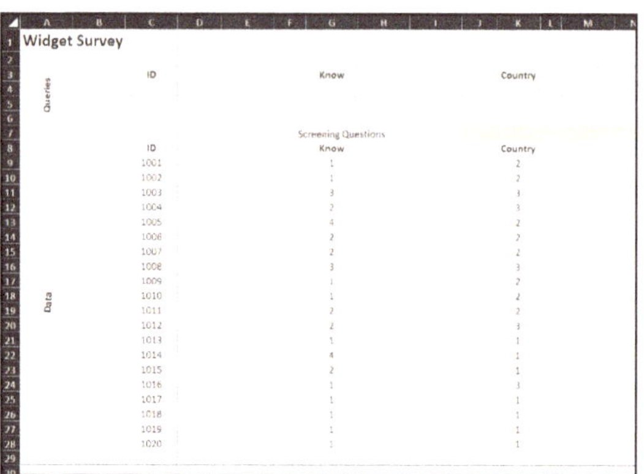 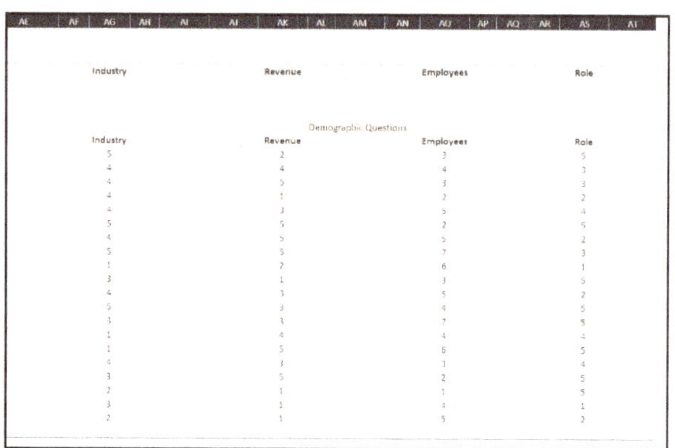

Figure 5.16: Highlighting the Criteria range, left to right

5. With criteria defined and the ranges in place (Figure 5.17 on page 79), click OK on the Advanced Filter dialog box.

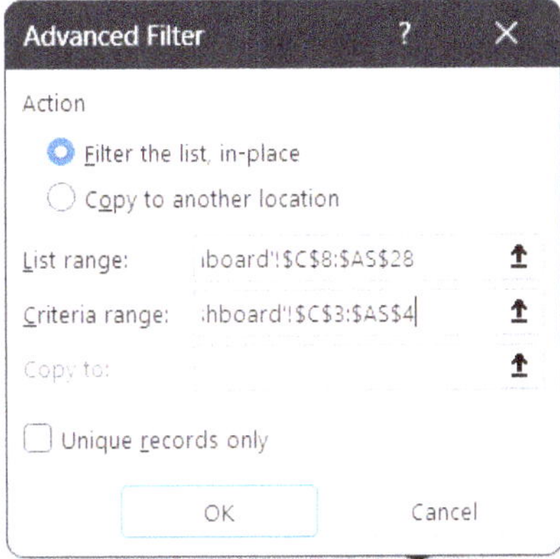

Figure 5.17: Click OK on the Advanced Filter dialog box

When you click OK on the Advanced Filter dialog box, Excel:

- Closes the Advanced Filter dialog.

- Hides and shows data rows according to your criteria. (You may have scrolled the data rows off-screen.)

The Data Dashboard worksheet:

- Performs a Responsive Count.

- Calculates new Responsive Percentages according to the Responsive Counts.

- Calculates Responsive Statistics based on the rows that the Data Dashboard displays after the query.

Note: Did you have a problem? See "Troubleshoot the Query" on page 84.

CHANGES TO THE DASHBOARD'S CALCULATIONS

Even the simple query that restricts the data only to US respondents makes a dramatic change to information on the Data Dashboard (see Figure 5.18 below through Figure 5.21 on page 83 and compare them to the equivalent figures beginning with Figure 5.8 on page 73).

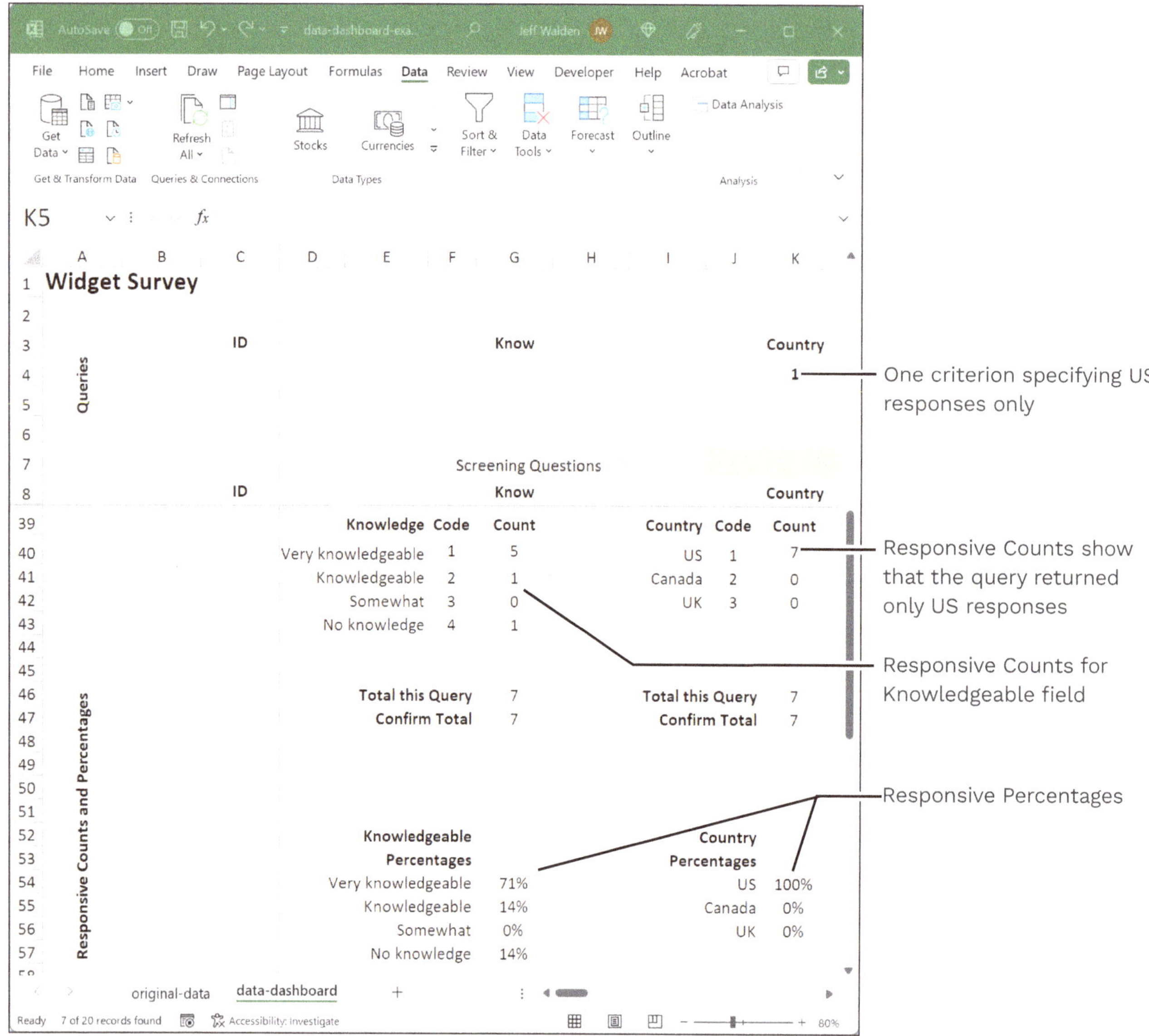

Figure 5.18: Changes to the Data Dashboard after you do a query (compare to Figure 5.8 on page 73); there are no Responsive Statistics for these two fields. Country Percentages show that 100% of the responses are from the US.

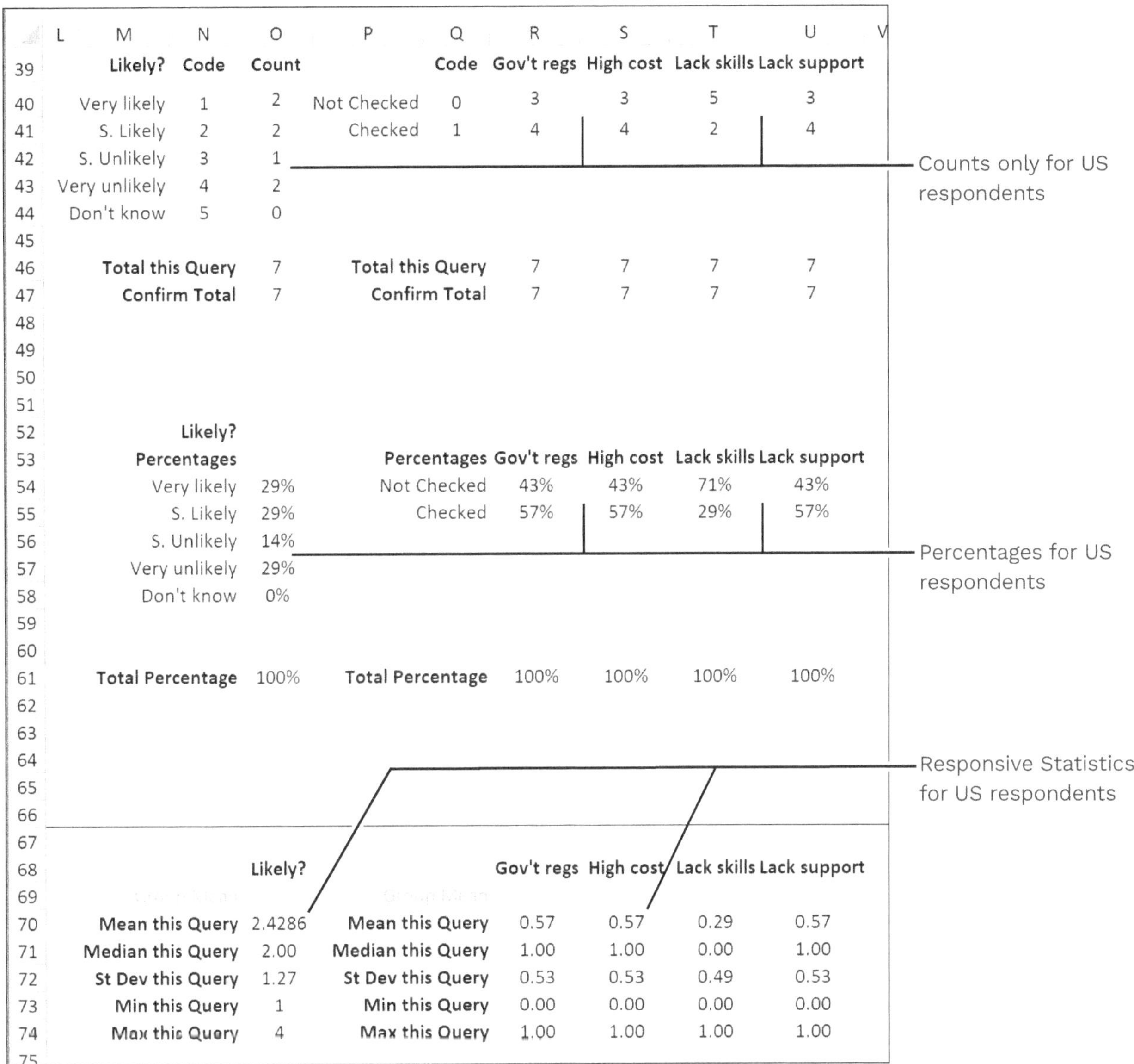

	L	M	N	O	P	Q	R	S	T	U	V
39		Likely?	Code	Count		Code	Gov't regs	High cost	Lack skills	Lack support	
40		Very likely	1	2	Not Checked	0	3	3	5	3	
41		S. Likely	2	2	Checked	1	4	4	2	4	
42		S. Unlikely	3	1							
43		Very unlikely	4	2							
44		Don't know	5	0							
45											
46		Total this Query		7	Total this Query		7	7	7	7	
47		Confirm Total		7	Confirm Total		7	7	7	7	
48											
49											
50											
51											
52			Likely?								
53		Percentages			Percentages	Gov't regs	High cost	Lack skills	Lack support		
54		Very likely	29%		Not Checked	43%	43%	71%	43%		
55		S. Likely	29%		Checked	57%	57%	29%	57%		
56		S. Unlikely	14%								
57		Very unlikely	29%								
58		Don't know	0%								
59											
60											
61		Total Percentage	100%		Total Percentage	100%	100%	100%	100%		
62											
63											
64											
65											
66											
67											
68			Likely?				Gov't regs	High cost	Lack skills	Lack support	
69											
70		Mean this Query	2.4286		Mean this Query		0.57	0.57	0.29	0.57	
71		Median this Query	2.00		Median this Query		1.00	1.00	0.00	1.00	
72		St Dev this Query	1.27		St Dev this Query		0.53	0.53	0.49	0.53	
73		Min this Query	1		Min this Query		0.00	0.00	0.00	0.00	
74		Max this Query	4		Max this Query		1.00	1.00	1.00	1.00	
75											

Figure 5.19: The Likely field and its follow-up questions, their Responsive Counts and Responsive Percentages; and the Responsive Statistics (only US records); compare to Figure 5.9 on page 74

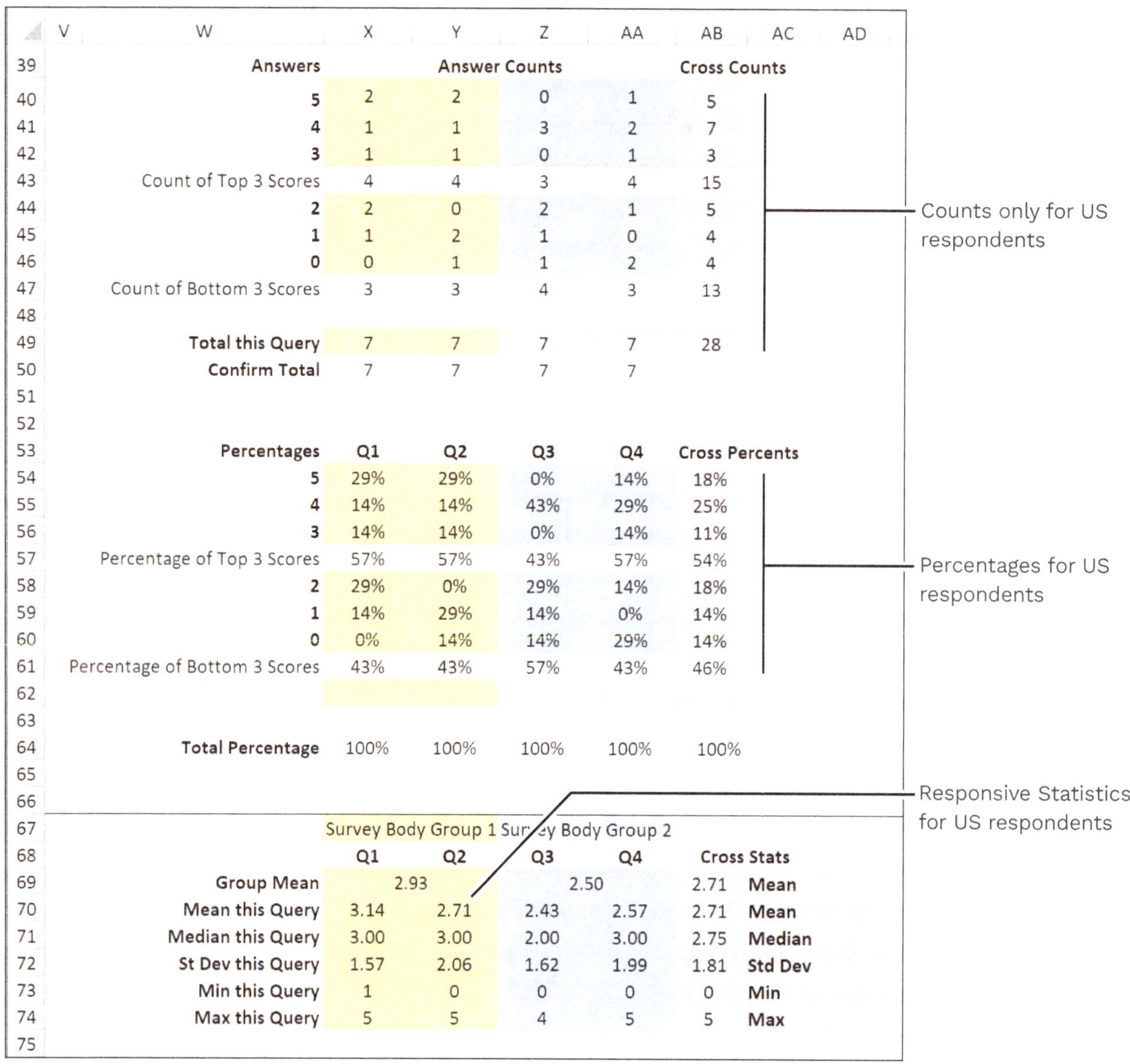

	V	W	X	Y	Z	AA	AB	AC	AD
39		Answers	Answer Counts				Cross Counts		
40		5	2	2	0	1	5		
41		4	1	1	3	2	7		
42		3	1	1	0	1	3		
43		Count of Top 3 Scores	4	4	3	4	15		
44		2	2	0	2	1	5		
45		1	1	2	1	0	4		
46		0	0	1	1	2	4		
47		Count of Bottom 3 Scores	3	3	4	3	13		
48									
49		Total this Query	7	7	7	7	28		
50		Confirm Total	7	7	7	7			
51									
52									
53		Percentages	Q1	Q2	Q3	Q4	Cross Percents		
54		5	29%	29%	0%	14%	18%		
55		4	14%	14%	43%	29%	25%		
56		3	14%	14%	0%	14%	11%		
57		Percentage of Top 3 Scores	57%	57%	43%	57%	54%		
58		2	29%	0%	29%	14%	18%		
59		1	14%	29%	14%	0%	14%		
60		0	0%	14%	14%	29%	14%		
61		Percentage of Bottom 3 Scores	43%	43%	57%	43%	46%		
62									
63									
64		Total Percentage	100%	100%	100%	100%	100%		
65									
66									
67			Survey Body Group 1		Survey Body Group 2				
68			Q1	Q2	Q3	Q4	Cross Stats		
69		Group Mean	2.93		2.50		2.71	Mean	
70		Mean this Query	3.14	2.71	2.43	2.57	2.71	Mean	
71		Median this Query	3.00	3.00	2.00	3.00	2.75	Median	
72		St Dev this Query	1.57	2.06	1.62	1.99	1.81	Std Dev	
73		Min this Query	1	0	0	0	0	Min	
74		Max this Query	5	5	4	5	5	Max	
75									

Figure 5.20: The Survey Body responses, their Responsive Counts, Responsive Percentages, and Responsive Statistics (only US records; compare to Figure 5.10 on page 75

	AE	AF	AG	AH	AI	AJ	AK	AL	AM	AN	AO	AP	AQ	AR	AS
39	Industry	Code	Count		Revenue	Code	Count		Employees	Code	Count		Role	Code	Count
40	Packaging	1	2		>$10M	1	3		Over 1000	1	1		CEO	1	1
41	Manufacturing	2	2		$8M to $9.9M	2	0		800 to 999	2	1		EVP	2	1
42	Finance	3	3		$6M to $7.9M	3	1		500 to 799	3	0		CTO	3	0
43	Technology	4	0		$4M to $5.9M	4	1		200 to 499	4	2		HR	4	1
44	Other	5	0		<$3M	5	2		100 to 199	5	1		Other	5	4
45									50 to 99	6	1				
46									1 to 49	7	1				
47															
48	Total this Query		7		Total this Query		7		Total this Query		7		Total this Query		7
49	Confirm Total		7		Confirm Total		7		Confirm Total		7		Confirm Total		7
50															
51															
52	Industry				Revenue				Employees				Role		
53	Percentages				Percentages				Percentages				Percentages		
54	Packaging	29%			>$10M	43%			Over 1000	14%			CEO	14%	
55	Manufacturing	29%			$8M to $9.9M	0%			800 to 999	14%			EVP	14%	
56	Finance	43%			$6M to $7.9M	14%			500 to 799	0%			CTO	0%	
57	Technology	0%			$4M to $5.9M	14%			200 to 499	29%			HR	14%	
58	Other	0%			<$3M	29%			100 to 199	14%			Other	57%	
59									50 to 99	14%					
60									1 to 49	14%					
61															
62															
63	Total Percentage	100%			Total Percentage	100%			Total Percentage	100%			Total Percentage	100%	
64															
65															
66															
67															
68	Industry				Revenue				Employees				Role		
69															
70	Mean this Query	2.14			Mean this Query	2.86			Mean this Query	4.14			Mean this Query	3.86	
71	Median this Query	2.00			Median this Query	3.00			Median this Query	4.00			Median this Query	5.00	
72	St Dev this Query	0.90			St Dev this Query	1.86			St Dev this Query	2.12			St Dev this Query	1.68	
73	Min this Query	1			Min this Query	1			Min this Query	1			Min this Query	1	
74	Max this Query	3			Max this Query	5			Max this Query	7			Max this Query	5	
75															

Figure 5.21: Demographic questions, their Responsive Counts, Responsive Percentages, and Responsive Statistics for US only. Note that there are no returns in the Industry field for Technology (4) and Other (5), so that the percentages also are 0%, and Max this Query shows a value of 3 (meaning there are no 4s or 5s). Compare to Figure 5.11 on page 76.

WHAT NEXT?

Try additional queries. The quick and easy way of changing the query — from Country 1 to Country 3, for example — is simply to type a **3** into the Criteria range cell currently holding the **1**, and then re-run the query.

To re-run the query: choose *Data | Sort & Filter | Advanced.* The Advanced filter "remembers" the List range and Criteria range from your previous query (as long as you don't Clear first). Click OK and the new query executes.

You can Clear the existing query before a new query. See Figure 5.22 on page 84. Clear **(a)** restores all previously hidden data to the List range and **(b)** removes the previous List range definition from the Advanced Filter dialog — just in case you wish to re-define it. Clear leaves the previous Criteria range in place. (We find this behavior a minor annoyance when working with an unchanging set of data but with a set of criteria that frequently may change in size.)

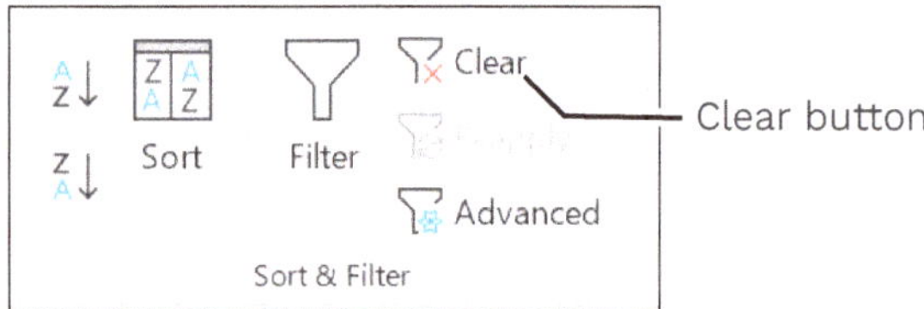

Figure 5.22:   Clearing an existing query

TRY AN *OR* QUERY

As explained in "Queries Using AND / OR" on page 72, you can OR between criteria by putting them on separate sequential rows within the Criteria range.

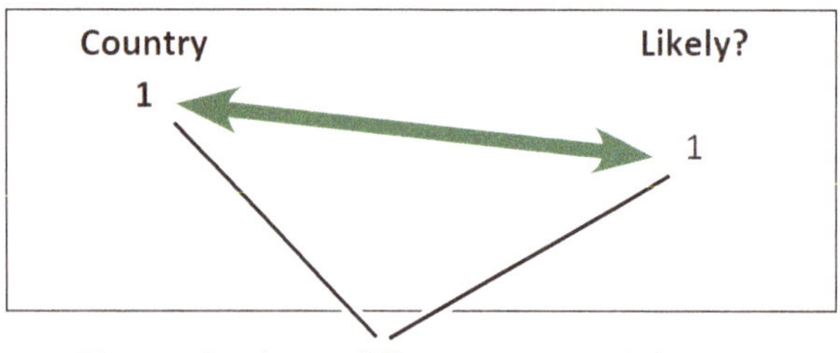

Place criteria on different sequential rows
(no blank rows between them)

Figure 5.23:   An OR query for Country 1 OR Very Likely

At first, the results of the OR query (Figure 5.24) may seem confusing — didn't we specify US respondents only? Why do we have one UK respondent?

We did specify US respondents (Code 1), but we also specified those who answered *Very Likely* (also Code 1) to *How likely are you to institute electronic widget management?* Some US respondents may have been other than *Very Likely* (but we got them in the returns because they are from the US), and one *Very Likely* respondent was from the UK rather than the US. Note that in both cases, we returned 8 respondents; that is, the OR query returned 8 records — 7 from the US and 1 from the UK.

Country	Code	Count		Likely?	Code	Count
US	1	7		Very likely	1	3
Canada	2	0		S. Likely	2	2
UK	3	1		S. Unlikely	3	1
				Very unlikely	4	2
				Don't know	5	0
Total this Query		8		**Total this Query**		8

Figure 5.24:   Results of the OR query in Figure 5.23

TROUBLESHOOT THE QUERY

The query didn't happen? Nothing seemed to change? Odd things occurred? Here are a few conditions to check:

If things are truly fouled up...

- If things have become completely, totally, and unimaginably confusing, **before you do anything else,** type Control-Z (Windows undo) or Command-Z (Macintosh undo). This *should* restore your widget model to its condition before you executed the query. Keep typing undo... slowly... slowly... checking between tries, until you get back to some condition that you recognize.

If things are not all that bad...

- *Did things **really** not change?* Are you sure? With a small data set (like that in the widget survey), changes can be almost instantaneous. They will be slower with a big data set. With 800 or 1000 records and 50 fields or so, you can watch the model count for almost 3 seconds! Scroll up and look at the actual list of widget responses. Are all 20 there? If they are, then something else may be wrong; if they are not all there, your query has been successful — at least in part. **How to fix: You can always click Clear and try again.**

- *Advanced Filter does not like blank rows.* Is there an extra blank row between the **Criteria range** headers and your criteria? Did you leave a blank line somewhere within the Criteria range? Did you include an extra blank line within the Criteria range but under your criteria? **How to fix: Click Advanced for the Advanced Filter dialog box and re-define the Criteria range.**

- *Forgotten mandatory blank row.* Did you remember to leave at least one unselected and mandatory blank row **between** the Criteria range and the headers for the List range? **How to fix: Re-define the Criteria range.** You may need to add a new row to the Criteria area — the Data Dashboard will move everything down to accommodate this and the formulas in the worksheet will still work.

- *Are the ranges correct?* Does your List range include **all data rows and all data columns**, including the ID header and column, all the way to the far right data header and column (which on our widget model is *Role*)? Did your List range stop short for some reason? **How to fix: You can click Clear and try again.**

- **Leaving out a column** from the List range can be *less of a problem* than **leaving out one or more rows** from the List range. **Why?** The Data Dashboard works by hiding and showing **entire** worksheet rows. If you accidentally leave out a column (often the leftmost or rightmost column) from a List range definition, *the Data Dashboard may still hide and show the correct rows* — as long as you're not leaving out a column you've used for a criterion. But, if you miss including a row or two (often the top or bottom row(s) in the List range), the Data Dashboard does not filter them. It leaves them untouched and in place — *just as you told it to do*. See Figure 5.25.

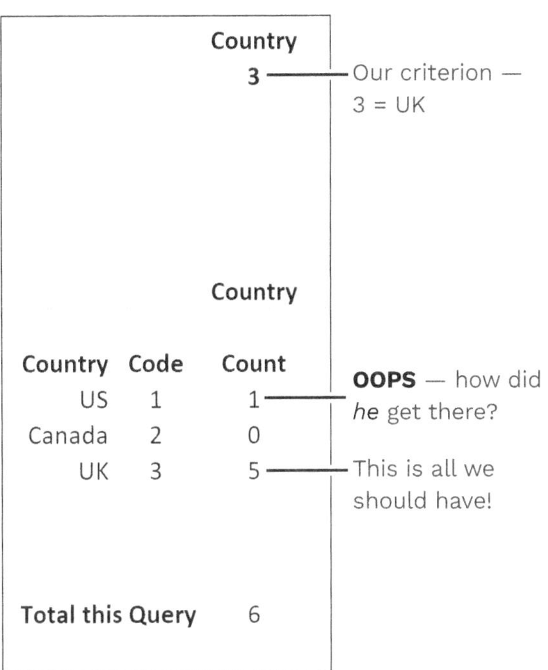

Figure 5.25: *OOPS — the List range did not include that one last record line...*

This is an instance where the responsive counts can help you diagnose what happened. If you're only looking for UK respondents and a US record pops up (or, more accurately, was not hidden as it should have been) — it should be obvious that *Something Is Wrong* with the List range.

How to solve the row-left-out problem. Click Clear to display all rows and try again. (See Figure 5.22 on page 84 for the Clear button.) Be sure to include all rows and all columns in the List range.

WHAT QUERIES LIKE THIS CAN TELL YOU

You have all the data. The Data Dashboard does statistical calculations for you. If you need the Standard Deviation or the Mean, it's there. Why bother to slice and dice the data using Advanced Filter queries?

Queries help you to see where differences and similarities lie.

If you have 800 or 1,000 responses in your survey, it's humanly impossible simply to look at a blinding array of rows and columns of numbers and discern a pattern.

Unfortunately, the widget survey is fictional and very small. But let's pretend that the data is for a real industry.

The first query you're likely to make is by location (if your data includes such a field).

The next query might be to view survey answers by Revenue or Role in the organization — to see how the biggest organizations responded or find out what the CEOs or CTOs said.

But what's next?

Here's a possible scenario.

PROFILING DEMOGRAPHICS BY RESPONDENT ANSWERS

In the widget survey, answers to the Survey Body questions are on a 0–5 scale, where 0 means (essentially) "We don't do that," and 5 means "We're doing that all the time and get great results."

What we want to do is see how the most successful (or, sometimes, least unsuccessful) responses are reflected in the Demographic statistics. How large are those organizations? Where are they located? How many people do they employ?

This is the reverse of asking "How does a large company answer our questions?" or "How do people from Canada answer our questions?" which is valuable in itself. Here, we know the answers we'd like to get (all high scores) — now, what kind of respondent answers that way?

So we ask: *How many people answered the Survey Body questions with all fives?*

It's only a little survey; there are few top performers. Alas, we queried the widget data looking for respondents who answered 5 to all four Survey Body questions.

There were none. (See Figure 5.26.)

This is an **AND** query — any returned records must answer ALL questions with 5s.

Was this a "successful query" even though it found nothing? *Yes.* It told us something that we didn't know: Not one organization who responded to the survey answered every Survey Body question with a "top score."

Life is hard in the widget industry, evidently.

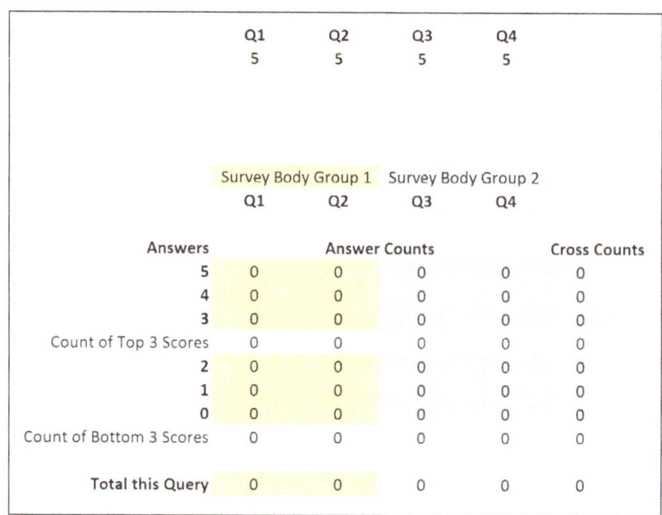

	Q1	Q2	Q3	Q4
	5	5	5	5

	Survey Body Group 1		Survey Body Group 2	
	Q1	Q2	Q3	Q4

Answers	Answer Counts				Cross Counts
5	0	0	0	0	0
4	0	0	0	0	0
3	0	0	0	0	0
Count of Top 3 Scores	0	0	0	0	0
2	0	0	0	0	0
1	0	0	0	0	0
0	0	0	0	0	0
Count of Bottom 3 Scores	0	0	0	0	0
Total this Query	0	0	0	0	0

Figure 5.26: No top performers in the widget query

Note: Notice that ***Total this Query*** returned 0 records. This is *EXACTLY* why we added the divide-by-zero IF-THEN-ELSE umbrella described in "Don't Forget Your Umbrella!" on page 55. Because of that provision, the Data Dashboard does not fill with divide-by-zero errors when this happens.

If we can't find a record with *ALL* 5s, what about records with *ANY* 5s? To find respondents who answered 5 to any of the Survey Body questions, we did an **OR** query, as shown in Figure 5.27 on page 87. We inserted rows to make room for the criteria, and then entered a 5 (each criterion on a separate row).

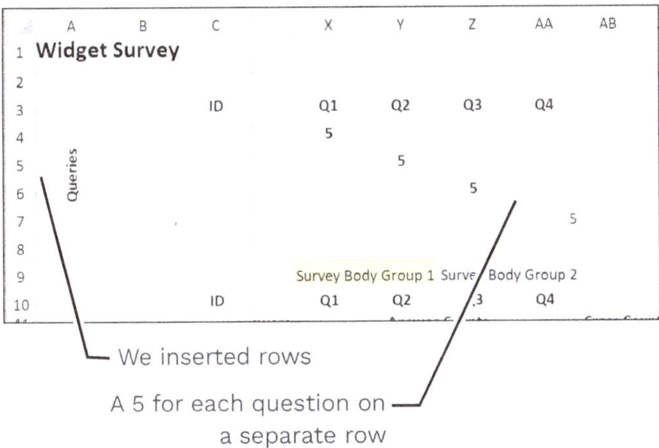

Figure 5.27: An OR query designed to find respondents who answered 5 to *any* of the Body Survey questions

The OR query was successful. It found 13 responses *that answered 5 to any* of the Survey Body questions, see Figure 5.28 on page 88.

There are 13 respondents who answered 5 to *at least one question*. This breaks down as:

> **7** of 13 answered 5 to Q1
>
> **3** of 13 answered 5 to Q2
>
> **4** of 13 answered 5 to Q3
>
> **4** of 13 answered 5 to Q4
>
> or *18 answers of 5* among the 13.

Medians are higher than Means for each question (see the Responsive Statistics at the bottom of Figure 5.28). When this happens, lower values have drawn downward the average (Mean) below the middle value (Median). See "Median (MEDIAN function)" on page 40.

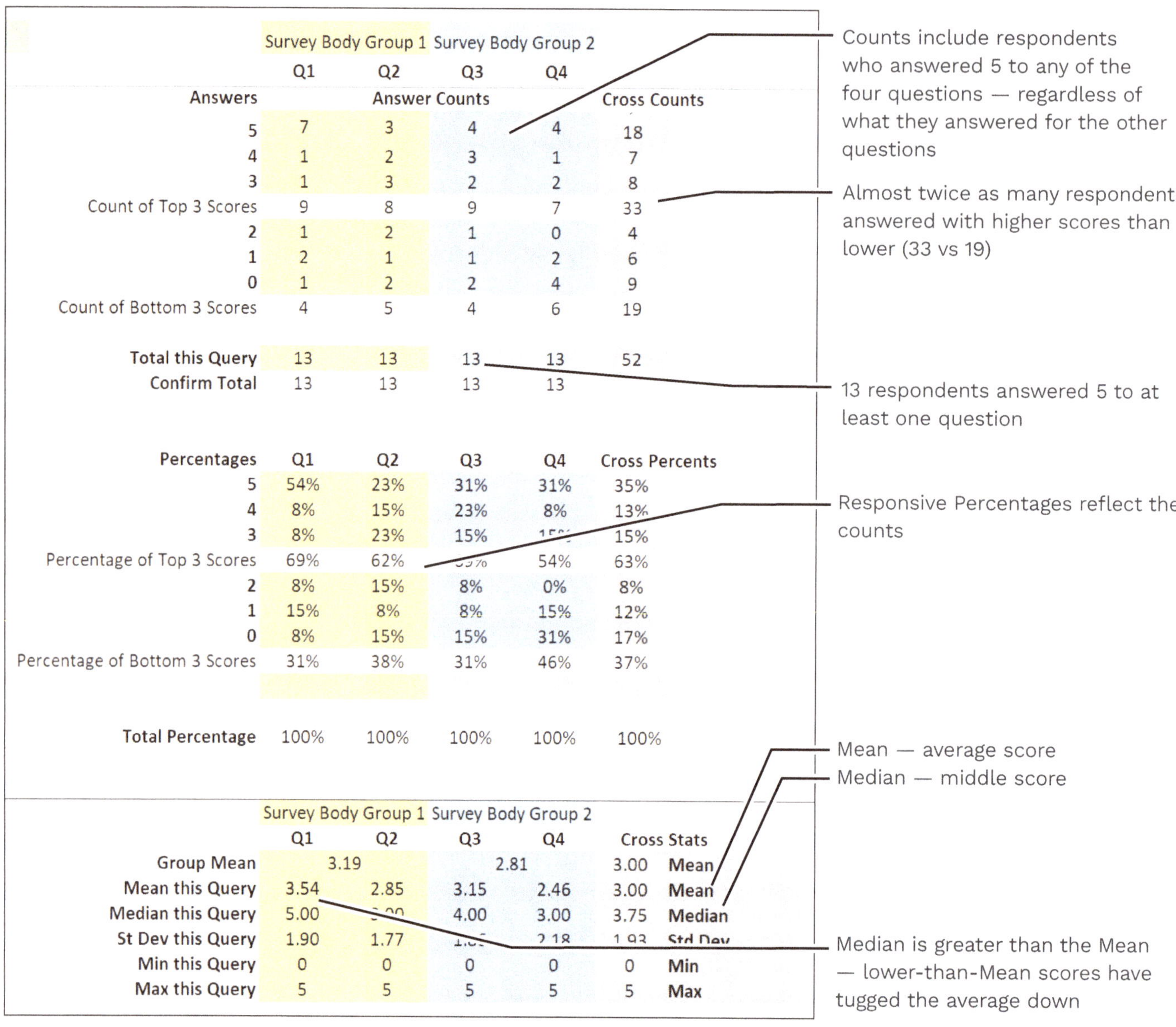

Answers	Survey Body Group 1		Survey Body Group 2		
	Q1	Q2	Q3	Q4	
Answers		Answer Counts			Cross Counts
5	7	3	4	4	18
4	1	2	3	1	7
3	1	3	2	2	8
Count of Top 3 Scores	9	8	9	7	33
2	1	2	1	0	4
1	2	1	1	2	6
0	1	2	2	4	9
Count of Bottom 3 Scores	4	5	4	6	19
Total this Query	13	13	13	13	52
Confirm Total	13	13	13	13	

Percentages	Q1	Q2	Q3	Q4	Cross Percents
5	54%	23%	31%	31%	35%
4	8%	15%	23%	8%	13%
3	8%	23%	15%	15%	15%
Percentage of Top 3 Scores	69%	62%	[illegible]%	54%	63%
2	8%	15%	8%	0%	8%
1	15%	8%	8%	15%	12%
0	8%	15%	15%	31%	17%
Percentage of Bottom 3 Scores	31%	38%	31%	46%	37%
Total Percentage	100%	100%	100%	100%	100%

	Survey Body Group 1		Survey Body Group 2			
	Q1	Q2	Q3	Q4	Cross Stats	
Group Mean		3.19		2.81	3.00	Mean
Mean this Query	3.54	2.85	3.15	2.46	3.00	Mean
Median this Query	5.00	[illegible]	4.00	3.00	3.75	Median
St Dev this Query	1.90	1.77	[illegible]	2.18	1.93	Std Dev
Min this Query	0	0	0	0	0	Min
Max this Query	5	5	5	5	5	Max

Figure 5.28: The OR query found 13 respondents who answered 5 to any of the four Survey Body questions.

Who are the organizations that answered with 5s? From Figure 5.29, we can see that 61% of responses come from the Packaging and Tech industries. Oddly, the values for Revenue seem to cluster at the lower end, while Employee counts appear to be divided evenly (again, more-or-less). Perhaps the biggest surprise is the Other percentage for Role in the organization — 38% of respondents say they don't fit into the set of roles we proposed. In future surveys, we'll have to expand this list. Role might have been a candidate to be a write-in field so that we can have our respondents tell us who they are. While that is a text field, we can sort through those responses and classify them for any reports. They're not "open-ended."

We may have to do another survey!

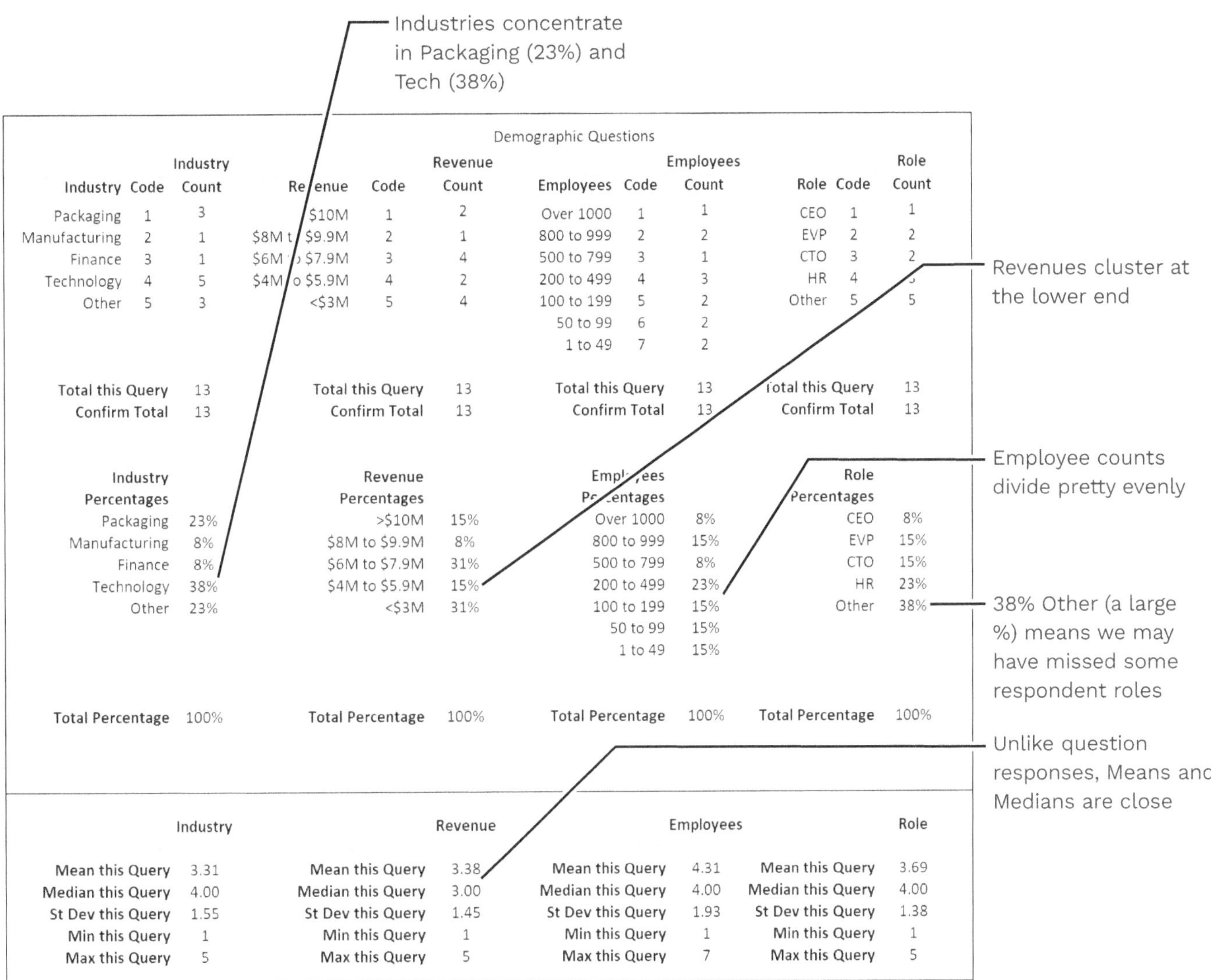

Industry	Code	Industry Count		Revenue	Code	Revenue Count		Employees	Code	Employees Count		Role	Code	Role Count
Packaging	1	3		>$10M	1	2		Over 1000	1	1		CEO	1	1
Manufacturing	2	1		$8M to $9.9M	2	1		800 to 999	2	2		EVP	2	2
Finance	3	1		$6M to $7.9M	3	4		500 to 799	3	1		CTO	3	2
Technology	4	5		$4M to $5.9M	4	2		200 to 499	4	3		HR	4	3
Other	5	3		<$3M	5	4		100 to 199	5	2		Other	5	5
								50 to 99	6	2				
								1 to 49	7	2				
Total this Query		13		Total this Query		13		Total this Query		13		Total this Query		13
Confirm Total		13		Confirm Total		13		Confirm Total		13		Confirm Total		13

Industry Percentages			Revenue Percentages			Employees Percentages			Role Percentages	
Packaging	23%		>$10M	15%		Over 1000	8%		CEO	8%
Manufacturing	8%		$8M to $9.9M	8%		800 to 999	15%		EVP	15%
Finance	8%		$6M to $7.9M	31%		500 to 799	8%		CTO	15%
Technology	38%		$4M to $5.9M	15%		200 to 499	23%		HR	23%
Other	23%		<$3M	31%		100 to 199	15%		Other	38%
						50 to 99	15%			
						1 to 49	15%			
Total Percentage	100%		Total Percentage	100%		Total Percentage	100%		Total Percentage	100%

Industry			Revenue			Employees			Role	
Mean this Query	3.31		Mean this Query	3.38		Mean this Query	4.31		Mean this Query	3.69
Median this Query	4.00		Median this Query	3.00		Median this Query	4.00		Median this Query	4.00
St Dev this Query	1.55		St Dev this Query	1.45		St Dev this Query	1.93		St Dev this Query	1.38
Min this Query	1		Min this Query	1		Min this Query	1		Min this Query	1
Max this Query	5		Max this Query	5		Max this Query	7		Max this Query	5

Figure 5.29: The Demographic identity of the respondents that answered with 5s to the Survey Body questions

What is the location of these 13 respondents?
By scrolling back to the Country field, we see how the 13 respondents are distributed. They appear to be as equally divided as any group of 13 respondents can be; see Figure 5.30.

Country	Code	Country Count
US	1	4
Canada	2	5
UK	3	4
Total this Query		13
Confirm Total		13

	Country Percentages
US	31%
Canada	38%
UK	31%
Total Percentage	100%

Figure 5.30: Country distribution of the 13 respondents who answered any of the Survey Body questions with 5

From here, we can do additional queries to see a further demographic breakdown of respondents from any of the individual three Countries who answered 5 to any of the Survey Body questions. We can even look at the ID numbers of these responses and examine each of them individually (remember — they are anonymous).

OTHER ANALYSES USING THE DATA DASHBOARD AND WIDGET DATA

Who responded to our widget survey?

There are several ways we can answer this question, but probably the best way is **according to various aspects of the Demographics data**. That's the answer we'd be most interested in initially.

With any query cleared so that **all records are included once again** in the responsive counts, we can look at the values for **Role** (in the company) for *everyone*, as in Figure 5.31. We've already — *ahem* — discovered that our survey data is a little biased towards "Other" (see Figure 5.29 on page 89).

This overall information is a good start. But how would we want to tabularize the information? Most probably by **Country** and **Role**, as shown in Figure 5.32.

Role	All		US		Canada		UK	
	#	%	#	%	#	%	#	%
CEO								
EVP								
CTO								
HR								
OTHER								
Total								

Figure 5.32: Table of Role versus Country, created in a Microsoft Word document

Fill in the All column from the data in Figure 5.31, which shows both the count and the percentage for each Role of respondent. It's logical to include both the count and the percentage — but this is your call. For example, CEO is a count of 2 and makes up 10% of the total — so 2 and 10%.

Query the three Countries separately. Enter their data in the table. Figure 5.33 on page 92 shows a query for Canada information.

Successive queries produce information for each of the three Countries. See Figure 5.34 on page 92.

You can assemble such a "who responded" table in a few minutes from counts and percentages provided by querying the Data Dashboard.

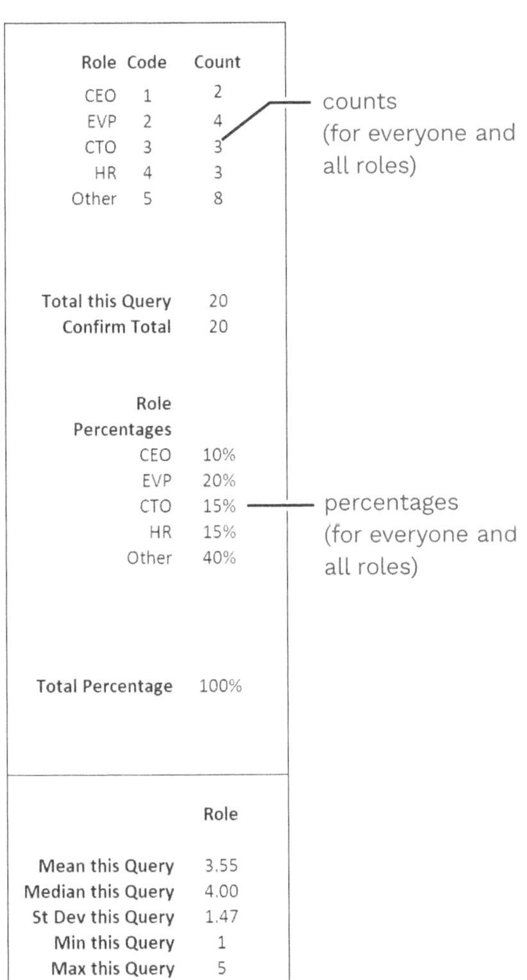

Figure 5.31: Counts by company role for all respondents

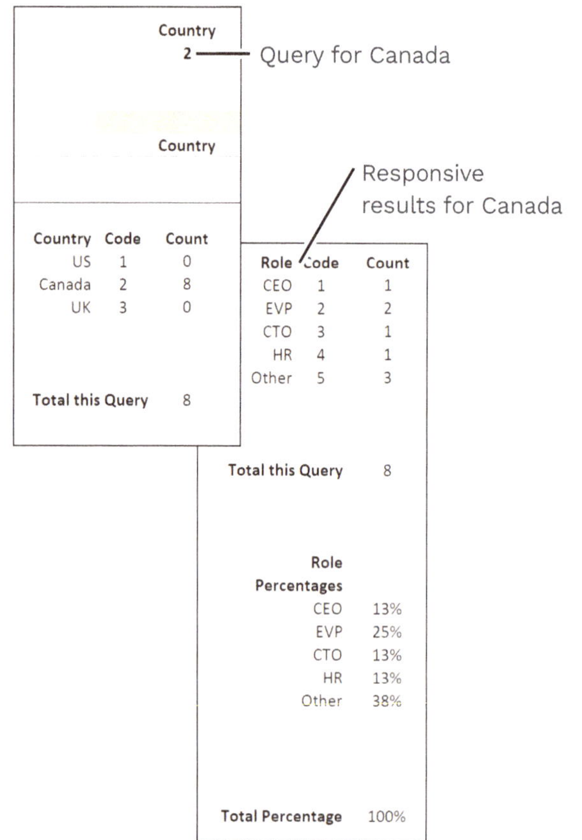

Figure 5.33: Query for Canada information

Role	All		US		Canada		UK	
	#	%	#	%	#	%	#	%
CEO	2	10	1	14	1	13	0	0
EVP	4	20	1	14	2	25	1	20
CTO	3	15	0	0	1	13	1	20
HR	3	15	1	14	1	13	1	20
OTHER	8	40	4	57	3	38	1	20
Total	20	100	7		8		5	

Figure 5.34: Who responded table

ORGANIZE SURVEY BODY GROUP MEANS BY COUNTRY

The Survey Body questions on the Data Dashboard have been grouped by topic. Admittedly, we have only two topics — but you might have several, each of which may contain several questions. Each of the Survey Body groups has its own Group Mean (the average of all its responses).

We want to create a table like that in Figure 5.35, which shows the Mean value for each Survey Body group organized by Country. The widget survey is small — with such a small number of questions, you may want to show the actual

values for each of the four questions, and you can; but consider how big a similar table of 30 or 40 questions in six groups would grow. This is why the Data Dashboard calculates a Group Mean.

Topic	All	US	Can	UK
Survey Body Grp 1	2.78	2.93	2.31	3.30
Survey Body Grp 2	2.88	2.50	2.94	3.30
Average	2.83	2.71	2.63	3.30

Figure 5.35: Survey Body questions, Group Means by Country

As with the table in Figure 5.34, start with All. Clear any existing query from the Data Dashboard, then scroll to the statistics for the Survey Body questions, as in Figure 5.36.

	Survey Body Group 1		Survey Body Group 2			
	Q1	Q2	Q3	Q4	Cross Stats	
Group Mean	2.78		2.88		2.83	Mean
Mean this Query	3.30	2.25	2.95	2.80	2.83	Mean
Median this Query	4.00	2.00	3.50	3.00	3.13	Median
St Dev this Query	1.69	1.74	1.76	1.85	1.76	Std Dev
Min this Query	0	0	0	0	0	Min
Max this Query	5	5	5	5	5	Max

Figure 5.36: Survey Body question statistics for All

Copy the Group Means for Survey Body Group 1 and Group 2 (and their Cross Stat). Then paste them into the table. You can include the Cross Stat because it becomes the Average line at the bottom of Figure 5.35.

Tip: Do you find yourself **copying sideways *but* want to paste vertically**? You can. After copying, choose *Home | Paste | Paste Special* and then click *Transpose | OK*. Excel changes the direction of the paste from horizontal to vertical or vertical to horizontal. It's a big time-saver.

Do a query for the US (Code 1). The Data Dashboard shows the Survey Body statistics just for the US, as in Figure 5.37 on page 93. Immediately, you can see they are different from the statistics for All. For one thing, the minimum value for Q1 is not 0, but 1, and the maximum value for Q3 is 4.

	Survey Body Group 1		Survey Body Group 2		Cross Stats	
	Q1	Q2	Q3	Q4		
Group Mean	2.93		2.50		2.71	Mean
Mean this Query	3.14	2.71	2.43	2.57	2.71	Mean
Median this Query	3.00	3.00	2.00	3.00	2.75	Median
St Dev this Query	1.57	2.06	1.62	1.99	1.81	Std Dev
Min this Query	1	0	0	0	0	Min
Max this Query	5	5	4	5	5	Max

Figure 5.37: US-only Survey Body statistics

Sequential queries provide Group Means by Country. You can assemble the table shown previously in Figure 5.35 on page 92.

ORGANIZE SURVEY BODY GROUP MEANS BY INDUSTRY TYPE

Organizing data by Country (Location — City, State, Province — however your data is organized) is natural. You can organize the same data by the Industry of your respondents, by their Revenue, or Number of Employees — which may be even more interesting to your marketing efforts.

Using a similar technique of querying one-by-one by Industry Type, Revenue level, or Number of Employees, you can obtain Group Means for the Body Survey questions by whatever category of answer you please, as in Figure 5.38.

You will almost assuredly find that the Group Means by Country are different from the Group Means when organized by anything else.

Topic	All	Pack'g	Mfg	Finance	Tech	Other
Survey Body Grp 1	2.78	3.00	3.50	2.13	2.79	2.88
Survey Body Grp 2	2.88	2.50	3.75	2.38	2.93	3.13
Average	2.83	2.75	3.63	2.25	2.86	3.00

Figure 5.38: Survey Body Group Means organized by Industry

RESPONDENTS WHO SAID *THIS*, ALSO SAID *THAT*...

You may recall that in the widget survey itself, we asked the following question:

- **How likely are you to institute the new practice of electronic widget management within the next 12 months?**

  - Very Likely (1)
  - Somewhat Likely (2)
  - Somewhat Unlikely (3)
  - Very Unlikely (4)
  - Don't know (5)

After that, the survey offered some potential reasons our respondents could choose regarding how they had answered the original question. They chose these answers by checking the appropriate responses. There were four potential responses. Each one can be checked or left unchecked to indicate its relevance.

- **Which of the following reasons apply to your organization's approach to electronic widget management? (Select all that apply.)**

  - Government regulation has mandated a conversion to electronic widget management in our region.
  - We are concerned about the high cost of conventional widget management, and want to reduce costs by going electronic.
  - We lack internal skills to convert to full electronic widget management at this time.
  - We lack internal support for electronic conversion.

The *Likely* field poses a dimension problem. Consider: For each value of *Very Likely* through *Don't know*, there is a percentage of respondents who answered Question 1, 2, 3, or 4 as Yes (1) or No (0). In addition, some respondents are from the US, Canada, or the UK, some are from Technology companies or Financial companies, some have high Revenue values and some have lower.

Because tables in reports only come in two dimensions, we must decide which information is most relevant to our widget survey.

For our table, we decided *Likely* was the most important guide and that we would create a table of All respondents. You might decide differently. Perhaps discovering how respondents from the Packaging industry feel about new widget technology is most important to you regardless of its *Likely*-ness. You may want to take the time to develop several such tables and compare them. That's all part of "analyzing a simple survey."

Let's talk about how we pulled together the table in Figure 5.39.

Comments	ALL		V Likely		S Likely		S Unlikely		V Unlikely		Don't Know	
	Yes	No	Yes	No	Yes	No	Yes	No	Yes	No	Yes	No
Government regulation has mandated a conversion to electronic widget management in our region.	50%	50%	33%	67%	75%	25%	33%	67%	40%	60%	60%	40%
We are concerned about the high cost of conventional widget management and want to reduce costs by going electronic.	55%	45%	33%	67%	50%	50%	33%	67%	60%	40%	80%	20%
We lack internal skills to convert to full electronic widget management at this time.	25%	75%	33%	67%	0%	100%	33%	67%	40%	60%	20%	80%
We lack internal support for electronic conversion.	55%	45%	33%	67%	75%	25%	67%	33%	60%	60%	60%	40%

Figure 5.39: Likely table with response percentages

Clear any previous query. This gives us the data for *All* — all locations, all Demographics, and so forth.

Query by each *Likely* value in turn. (1–5) The Data Dashboard shows you the counts and percentages of how people answered for that specific *Likely* value. See Figure 5.40 on page 95.

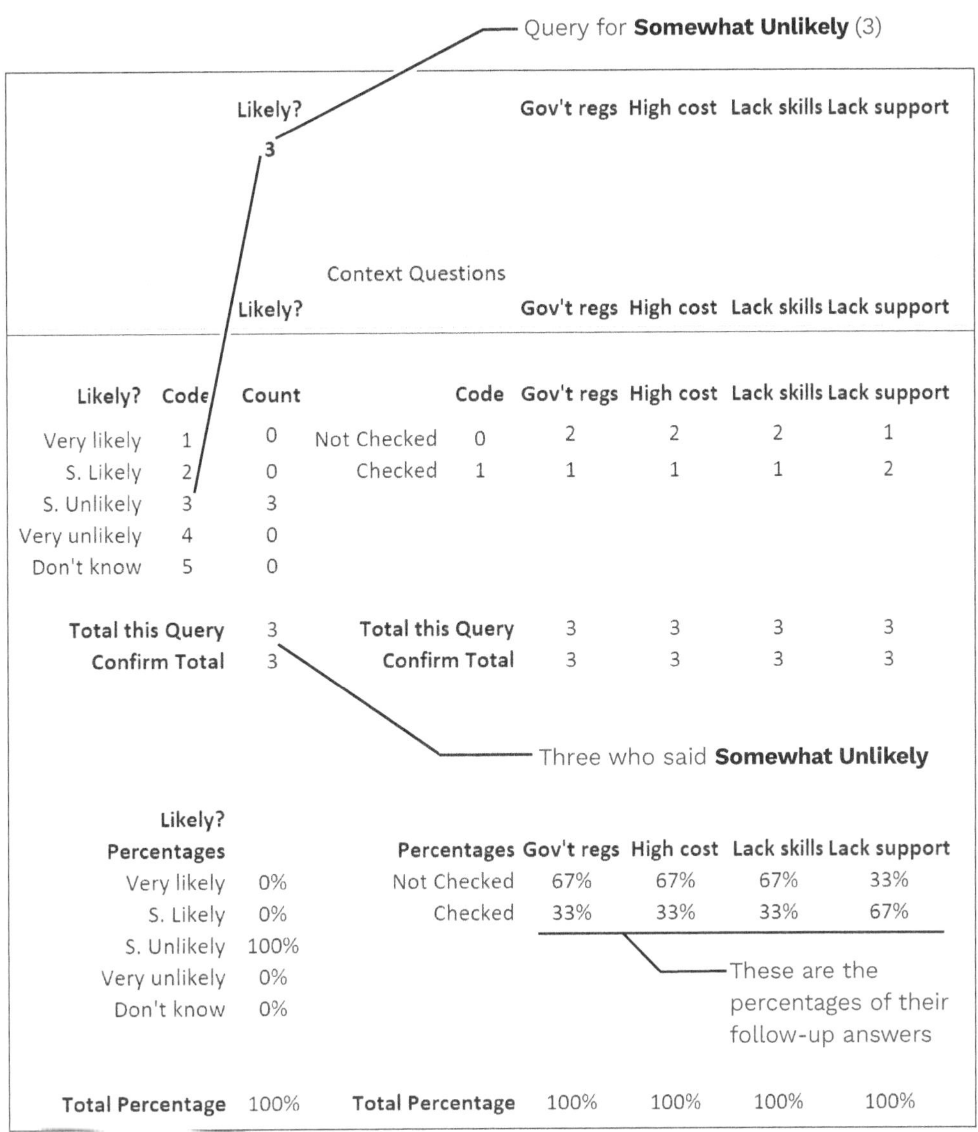

Figure 5.40: Query by the list of "Likely" values and see the percentages of how people answered the follow-up questions

What does the table in Figure 5.39 on page 94 tell us? Well... People who are *Very Likely* to implement electronic widget management appear to be less concerned with governmental mandates to do so than are people who are only *Somewhat Likely*. This may be reasonable: If you're going to implement electronic management anyway, what does it matter if there is a mandate? The question then becomes, *Did the mandate* make *them Very Likely...?*

Similarly, **no one** who is *Somewhat Likely* to implement electronic widget management tells us that they lack the internal skills to convert. Therefore, their hesitation comes from another source.

Of course, this information is all fictional and bears no relationship to anything that appears in the real world. There are no "widgets." The point is that taking a statement of fact — **How likely are you to...?** and comparing those values to what people select as meaningful reasons for their responses can give you tremendous insight into your responding population.

Every field has a relationship to every other field. Any query may turn up interesting information about any set of fields. The Data Dashboard does not restrict you to the relationship between *How Likely* and its potential reasons. For example, Figure 5.41 shows how people who responded *Very Likely* answered the four Survey Body questions. Is there a cause-and-effect relationship? Probably not in the widget survey, but in *your* survey there very well might be!

Scores	Q1	Q2	Q3	Q4	Averages
5	33%	0%	0%	33%	17%
4	0%	67%	67%	33%	42%
3	33%	33%	0%	33%	25%
Top 3 scores	67%	100%	67%	100%	83%
2	33%	0%	0%	0%	8%
1	0%	0%	33%	0%	8%
0	0%	0%	0%	0%	0%
Bottom 3 scores	33%	0%	33%	0%	17%

Figure 5.41: How people who responded ***Very Likely* to electronic widget management** also answered the Survey Body questions — Look! For Q2 and Q4, 100% of the Very Likely responses were high scores

SUMMARY

- Advanced Filter queries drive the hiding and showing of your data records. By hiding and showing records according to your queries, you affect the responsive information of the Data Dashboard,

- You cannot have an empty row **within** a Criteria range, but **must have** at least one empty row between the Criteria range and the List range.

- If you accidentally leave out a row or column in the List range, your query may do unexpected things.

- With Advanced Filter queries you can **AND** and **OR** between criteria, allowing complex queries.

- Every field has a relationship to every other field. Any query can turn up interesting information about any set of fields.

Chapter 6

Handling Text Fields in Surveys

We've mentioned previously in this book that open-ended text fields — where survey respondents can enter whatever they please — make it more difficult to analyze a survey. This is because querying open-ended text is wonderfully difficult. In addition to that, how would you calculate the *average value* of a text field? Text has no numeric value unless you give it one. Don't misunderstand: open-ended text fields can provide excellent feedback and insights that you didn't anticipate and otherwise might not get, and that's good, because you undertake a survey to *find things out*. The problem with open-ended text fields in simple surveys is that a respondent can enter *almost anything*. Thus, you must be able to deal with *almost anything* in your analysis. That's a tall order. High-end survey organizations may subject such fields to sophisticated computerized text analysis. You may not have that luxury. Yet, *there is a way...*

We don't have an artificially intelligent solution to offer you that can automatically analyze the text entries that your survey may present. But we do have the next best thing: *you*. You're *a naturally intelligent solution*, not an artificial one, and this chapter can help you — at least to a small extent — wrestle in a practical way with the text entries you may receive from surveys that... um... *other people* may have conducted without first seeking your wise counsel. It happens. *C'est la vie*. That's life. You now may be anticipating this old saying that we just made up:

Some successfully avoid open-ended text fields.

Others have open-ended text fields thrust upon them.

If you have had open-ended text fields "thrust upon" you, what follow are some practical ideas about how to handle them. If you have not (yet) had an open-ended text field thrust upon you... congratulations.

Note: Before you embark on a big project of categorizing comments as described, please read through the balance of this chapter to see if you want to go ahead.

How Much Text Can an Excel Cell Hold?

In Excel, a cell can hold **32,767** characters... *but...*

The cell itself can display only the first **1024** of those characters; the formula bar can display all of them.

If you want to determine how many characters are in a cell, use the formula

$$=LEN(<cell>)$$

If your survey hasn't limited the number of input characters in the open-ended text field, you may want to export cell contents from Excel or copy-paste it to view the contents of that field in another program, such as Notepad. 1024 characters equal about 180 English words (more or less). This box holds 111 words.

FIND & SELECT AND TEXT-BASED QUERIES

Microsoft Excel offers two built-in methods to deal with text that do not involve complicated formulas or VBA programming: **(a)** Find & Select, and **(b)** querying with text criteria. If your survey includes a text field, but not many respondents have used it (say, fewer than 5% of them), either of these methods may be adequate.

FIND & SELECT

Find & Select does what its name implies — finds text (in a manner similar to a word processor) and selects cells based on various criteria. Excel lets you find all instances of matching text at once and displays them in a compact and selectable list for your review.

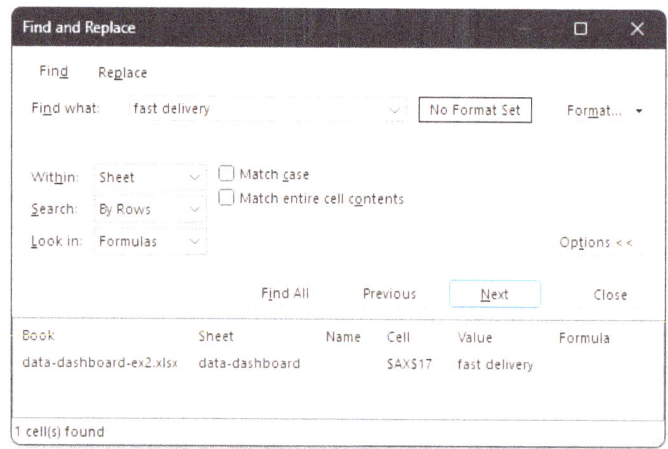

Figure 6.1:   Find All, showing all the cells containing the search text. Click a list item to go to that location.

1. Choose *Home | Editing | Find & Select* to display the Find & Select pulldown.

   All the commands on the Find & Select pulldown menu are thoroughly documented in Excel Help. They allow you to find cells and cell contents in different ways. We're concentrating on **text**.

2. From the pulldown menu, choose **Find**, and then type the word or phrase you're looking for into the Find What field. You can use wildcards, as shown in Table 6.1.

4. Click any of the list items to go to that location on the worksheet.

Table 6.1:   Wildcards for use in Find/Replace

TO FIND	USE
Any single character.	? (question mark)
Any string of characters.	* (asterisk)
The special characters ?, *, or ~	~ (tilde) followed by ?, *, or ~

3. Click **Find All**. Excel displays a list of text cells that include the text in the Find What field (Figure 6.1).

TEXT-BASED QUERIES

Advanced Filter queries against text fields work differently than does Find & Select but exactly as do queries against numerical fields... with *one small gotcha*:

Unless the word or phrase you're searching for comprises the complete content of the field, you *must use wildcards*. Obviously, querying the complete content of a field might otherwise cause a problem if someone has written a lengthy response.

For example, if you want to query the Comment field for the phrase "fast delivery," and you enter the query shown in Figure 6.2...

Figure 6.2:   Enter this, and your query will fail

...your query will return no selection results unless "fast" is the **full and complete content of the field**.

To find a record where the word "fast" is embedded somewhere within the text field, you must use a query with wildcards, as in Figure 6.3.

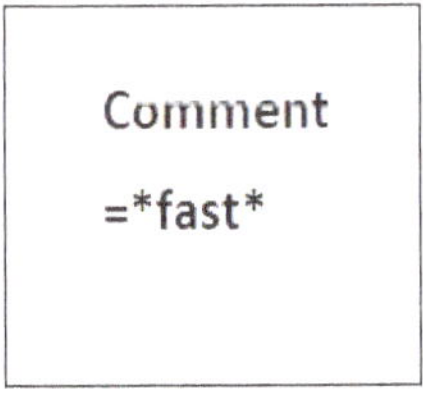

Figure 6.3:   Query, with wildcards — this query returns cells where "fast" appears *anywhere*, as in "fast delivery" but also in "breakfast"

You can combine the wildcards in Table 6.1 on page 98 with the operators in Table 6.2.

Note: With text, the Microsoft method of criteria entry makes more sense. For an explanation, see "How to Specify What You're Looking For" on page 70.

Table 6.2:   Query operators for text searching

OPERATOR	EXAMPLE
= (equal)	**=fast** or **="=fast"** looks for records where the text consists *only* of the single word "fast." Try **=*fast*** (with wildcards) for a field where "fast" appears somewhere in the text, such as "fast delivery."
> (greater than)	**=">fast"** or **>fast** looks for records where text begins with and consists of a single word that is *alphabetically later* than "fast." (The single-word problem applies here, too. You need wildcards.) You can also try **=>fast*** or **>*fast*** and the **?** wildcard.
< (less than)	**="<fast"** or **<fast** looks for records where text begins with and consists of a single word *alphabetically earlier* than "fast." Combine with the wildcards **?** and ***** to help locate a phrase.
>= (greater than or equal to)	**=">=fast"** or **>=fast** looks for records where the single word "fast" or a word later in the alphabet begins the field; combine with wildcards for embedded text.
<= (less than or equal to)	**="<=fast"** or **<=fast** looks for records where the single word "fast" or a word earlier in the alphabet begins the field; combine with wildcards for embedded text.
<> (not equal to)	**="<>fast"** or **<>fast** looks for records where the single word "fast" does not begin a record. Use **="<>*fast*"** to find records where "fast" in combination with anything else does not occur.

Queries against text fields are something of an art form, and you need a reasonable idea of what it is you're searching for. But, as with a simple text search, if you have only a few records that include a text field that holds any content, you may be able to use the two methods of Find & Select and text-based queries.

You can also use text-based queries alongside the next method we'll show you, to refine your results. They're not mutually exclusive. However, that next method requires some work.

SOLUTION: HOW TO BUILD A PROFILE FOR YOUR TEXT FIELDS

You can count non-empty text fields. You can read the content of text fields using the Mark One eyeball or listen to them using a screen reader. You can search them for keywords. But unless you build some method of *profiling and categorizing* your text fields in objective terms, you can't figure the Mean value of topics mentioned in text fields or the ratio of favorable comments to unfavorable comments. Unprofiled text fields must remain *fuzzy* from any kind of quantitative analysis.

A text field can say *anything*. Currently, only a living intelligence can categorize and classify such a field — especially on the kind of budget that's likely to prevail at an organization doing its own "simple survey."

Once classified in some way, you can begin to identify positive, neutral, and negative comments and determine the relative numbers of each. You can identify comments that demand (or suggest) action, comments that must be referred to marketing, sales, or product development — or to legal (*gulp*) — and comments that provide insight into the population that you're surveying... which is why your organization has asked the open-ended question in the first place.

Profiling is a manual process and it takes time. *It is a highly responsible process.* What if the classifier misses something really important? This is one of the reasons we don't encourage open-ended text fields for simple surveys.

A PROFILE INDEXING SYSTEM

You can develop a profile indexing system that includes information such as:

- **Subject of comment.** This is perhaps the most critical aspect of the profiling or indexing process. We discuss how to create such an index list in "Subject" on page 101.

- **Importance of comment.** Say, on a scale from 1–5. Your judgment call.

- **Quality of comment** ("It makes its point" versus "it rambles along with no definite topic"). Another scale from 1–5. This is

something of an academic grade. You can consider it optional, but wouldn't it be interesting to know that all high-quality (or low-quality) comments came from one location or demographic?

- **Positive/neutral/negative tone.** A scale of maybe 1–3, maybe 1–9. (**Why 9?** Nine gradations offer a middle value for "neutral.") Which value signifies the positive and which the negative — 1 or 3? You decide.

- **Tag for the department(s)** that are most affected so that you can refer any pertinent comments to them. You'll need to create an enumerated list; but it should not be too long and you know your own organization best. Let's say: no more than 10 departments or people.

Do you have to do it this way? Absolutely not — but we recommend that you profile or index the responses in some way. You may want to create fields for *Topic01*, *Topic02*, and *Topic03* instead of only one *Subject* per record. Just remember that *it will be **you** who will be filling in the data for all those fields across all 800 responses.* This is not something that your survey respondents do for you. This is another reason why open-ended text fields are difficult to handle.

The big issue with any indexing method is one of maintaining consistency. It is best undertaken by one person rather than by a team for that reason. It is time-consuming and laborious — but you *can* get excellent results.

If you're reading this chapter for tips on how to handle text fields, you probably already have at least one open-ended text field lurking somewhere in your survey data (it can be anywhere; its location among the fields does not matter — and maybe there's more than one). **You will add new profile fields which *no survey respondent ever sees and into which no respondent ever enters a value.*** You can add them next to the text field, or at the far right of the worksheet (and temporarily hide the columns in between if you wish).

In Figure 6.4, we've imagined an open-ended text field called *Comments* that follows the field *How Likely* and its set of potential reasons — but really, it could go anywhere. To the right of *Comments*, we've added the fields *Subject, Importance, Quality, Pos/Neu/Neg,* and *Tag for.* (We'll cover each of these shortly.)

After adding these fields (or fields like them according to your needs and preferences), you can assign numeric profile values in them for each open-ended text field. These values allow you to query for particular kinds of comments or for comments that make specific points positive or negative — without having to read through all the comments again and again.

Of course, you can use text search and text query in addition to this indexing method, too.

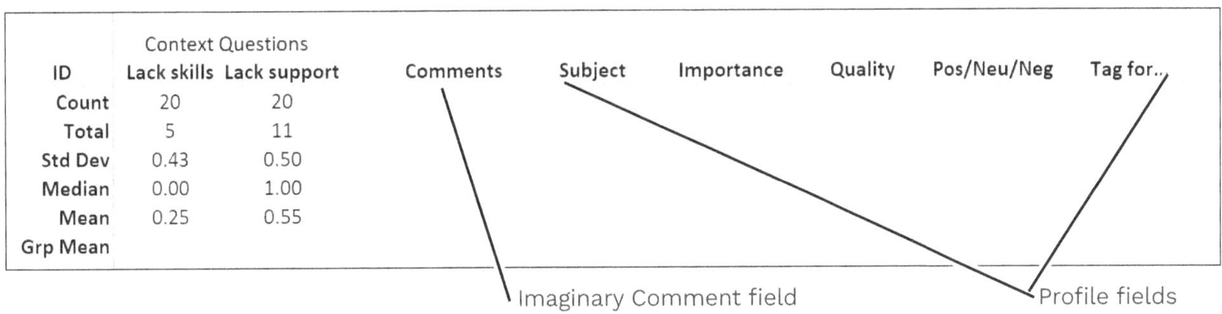

Figure 6.4: Here we have added an imaginary field *Comments* (holding the open-ended text responses from the survey) plus *five other fields* that no respondent ever sees — *they are for your internal use only, but they become part of your survey data*

Note: Remember that Excel can display only the first 1024 characters within a cell (about 180 English words based on an average of 4.7 characters per word and allowing for spaces). If you're not sure you're seeing the complete comment, add another column called **Length** to your records to the right of **Comments** and use the formula *=LEN(<cell>)* where *<cell>* is a reference to the Comments cell for each record, to confirm each comment's full size. You can always review all text in the Formula bar.

SUBJECT

You know the open-ended questions in your own survey even if you didn't write them. For example, they're probably something like this:

- Why did you choose Western Widget as your widget supplier?

- Tell us what you like or don't like about...

- Is there anything else you'd like us to know?

As you might expect, open-ended questions can be endless in their variety. We can't provide you with an encyclopedic list of such questions any more than we can predict how people might answer them.

But YOU might be able to do this.

Before you start looking at what people actually said, begin to make a list of what kinds of things you believe your respondents *might* say. This gives you an organized way to categorize the answers once you begin reading them. Yes, people can (and sometimes do) enter a treatise on African elephants in response to your question. But really, if you're doing a survey about widgets, respondents are likely to stick to that end of the spectrum. *You will add to this list of categories as you go.* For example, in their answers, people might use such phrases as:

- Fast delivery.

- Reasonable prices.

- Excellent support.

- Smooth chocolaty taste.

(Well, maybe not that chocolaty taste answer — but you should be able to anticipate at least *some* of these responses.)

Start your list with topics that you think you might find in the comments, such as delivery, price, support, features — whatever your ideal survey respondent might say to tell you how your customer/club/trade association views your organization and its many fine offerings.

1. Write down the topics you expect to see and put them into a list. Generally, they'll begin to fall into an order and (we hope) groups of similar topics.

2. The comments can be positive or negative in nature; of poor quality or good quality. We're just developing ways to classify *topics* here.

Once you have a beginning set of topics, you can begin to work with the text fields in earnest.

What if there's more than one topic that's applicable to an answer? It's a judgment call — and it's *your* judgment that matters. As we mentioned, you can have Topic01, Topic02...Topic*n*, but someone at your organization (**YOU**) is going to have to fill in all those blank Topics.

We suggest: Each potential subject gets its own number. You assign that number. We suggest numbering subjects within *ranges*, rather than just starting with number 1 and marching off in all directions as you encounter new topics. (See Table 6.3.) That way, you both categorize subjects in general ("delivery") and are able to specify a topic within the category of delivery ("fast" or "on-time"). You'll be able to create queries to find comments by using these numerical subject designators later.

For example, a comment that mentions *delivery, fast* might be 1; a comment that mentions *delivery, on-time* might be 2. A comment

mentioning *delivery, flubbed* might be 3. But all delivery-related comments fall into the Delivery range of 1-20.

Table 6.3: Borrow a page from computer programmers, and allocate more category space than you think you'll need — and you may find that even this might not be enough. Ranges can be as wide as you need, and need not be uniform in size. You can have one category that holds 40 topics and another that holds 10. **Note that categories cannot overlap. You cannot include the same number in two categories.**

SUBJECT	RANGE
Delivery	1–20
Price	21–40
Support	41–60
Features	61–80

As you read through the open-ended text field comments, your list will grow with topics you never suspected could exist. Your classification system must adjust and grow with it. Figure 6.5 shows a representation of the category ranges from Table 6.3 as you might see them in an Excel worksheet.

	Subj Code	Start	End	Count
39				
40	A Delivery	1	20	
41	B Price	21	40	
42	C Support	41	60	
43	D Features	61	80	
44				

Figure 6.5: The categories from Table 6.3 implemented as adjustable ranges in the Data Dashboard; these categories would appear in the Responsive Counts area of the Data Dashboard because they will be counted responsively. **Category ranges cannot overlap.**

Create a responsive count for a range of values

If you list all your Subjects by number you might find yourself with a long column of (say) a hundred *potential* values that you might assign to text in the Comments field — It's very much *unlike* having only three Country values or five Industry types.

It is not practical to use the *SUMPRODUCT*SUBTOTAL* formula as described in Appendix C, "Explaining the Data Dashboard's Most Important Formula" on page 137 (which we use everywhere else for responsive counts on the Data Dashboard).

Why? It's not *practical*; we don't say that the method can't work. It can. However, the problem is that the big formula matches and counts only *one value at a time*. With a Start/End range of Subjects we need to find whether a value matches any one of a the values that *falls within the range*.

We know of no elegant, single Excel formula that can:

- Count a cell if that cell's value is within a specific range of values, and

- Ignore rows hidden by a query so that the count is responsive.

Helper columns to the rescue. While there is no *single* formula that can do what we need, **we can break the problem into two parts** by using Helper columns, as shown in Figure 6.6 on page 104.

- *For each row*, count those Subject values that fall into one of our four example ranges, and put those counts in a helper column for each category. **Because we have Start and End values that we know do not overlap (because we created them that way), a value can fall into only one of the helper column ranges.**

- *SUM* up the counts for each helper column Subject range in a hidden-row-responsive way.

Here are the steps to make these responsive counts work (see Figure 6.6 on page 104):

1. We entered a set of dummy numbers into column BC to represent a set of Subject values that describe the contents of the completely imaginary text field *Comment*.

2. Using the four example Subject categories from Table 6.3 and Figure 6.5 (or any that

are more meaningful to you), create a set of Subject Code names (A Delivery, B Price...), along with a Start and an End value pair for each. You'll be able to adjust these Start/End values as needed later if your Subject ranges change. Leave the column under the Count label blank for now. Those values get calculated with their own formula later.

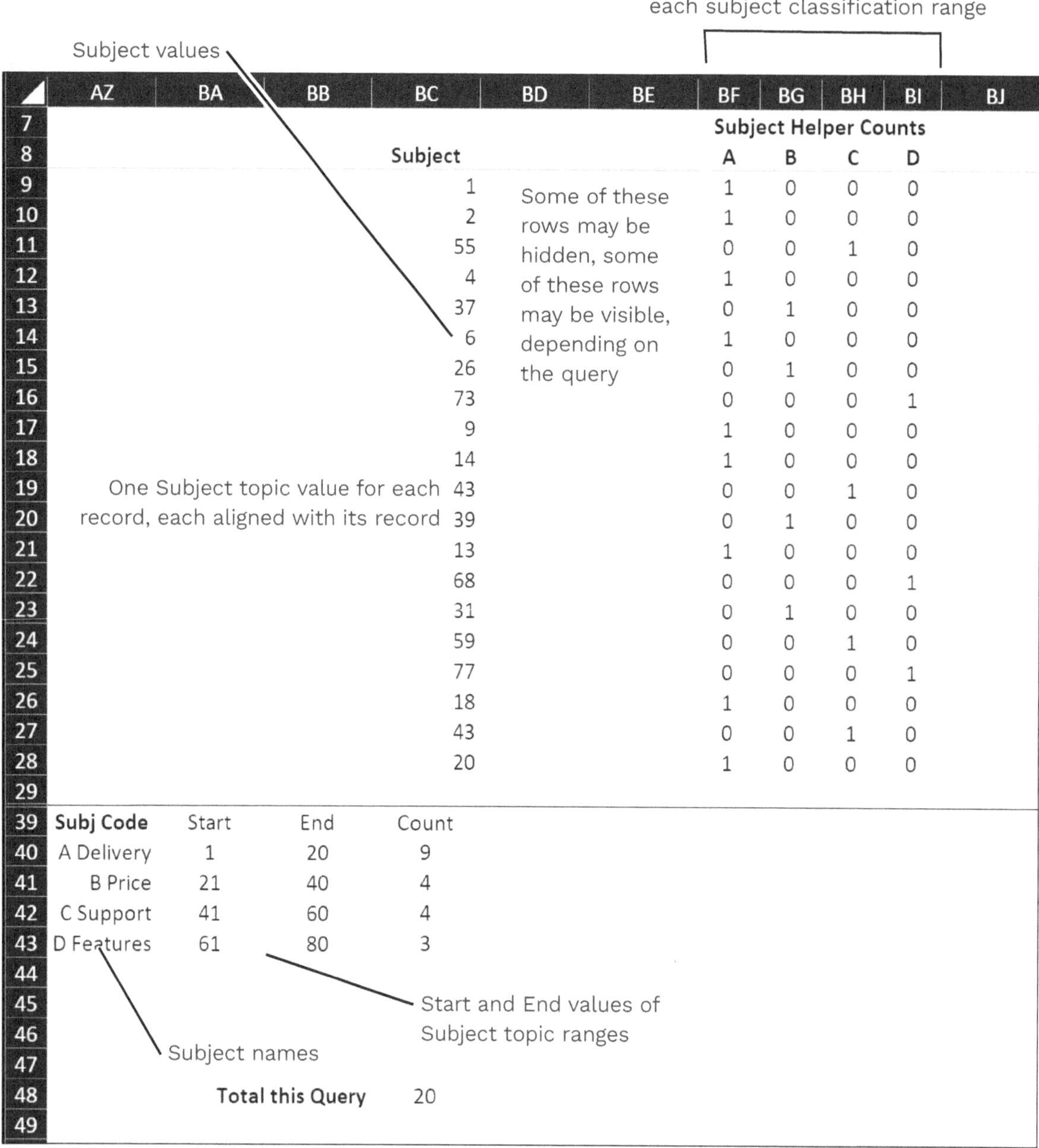

	AZ	BA	BB	BC	BD	BE	BF	BG	BH	BI	BJ
7											
8				Subject			A	B	C	D	
9				1			1	0	0	0	
10				2			1	0	0	0	
11				55			0	0	1	0	
12				4			1	0	0	0	
13				37			0	1	0	0	
14				6			1	0	0	0	
15				26			0	1	0	0	
16				73			0	0	0	1	
17				9			1	0	0	0	
18				14			1	0	0	0	
19				43			0	0	1	0	
20				39			0	1	0	0	
21				13			1	0	0	0	
22				68			0	0	0	1	
23				31			0	1	0	0	
24				59			0	0	1	0	
25				77			0	0	0	1	
26				18			1	0	0	0	
27				43			0	0	1	0	
28				20			1	0	0	0	
29											
39	**Subj Code**	Start	End	Count							
40	A Delivery	1	20	9							
41	B Price	21	40	4							
42	C Support	41	60	4							
43	D Features	61	80	3							
44											
45											
46											
47											
48		**Total this Query**		20							
49											

Figure 6.6: Counting Subject topics in ranges requires a 2-step process

3. As shown in Figure 6.6, create Helper columns for as many Subject ranges as you need. (We show four; one for each Subject range. You might have more or fewer. Don't fill in any values.)

We placed the Helper columns well to the right and beyond the operational Data Dashboard fields. The Helper columns don't need to be adjacent to the Subject values — we show them close for explanation. **However, it is critical that all the rows line up correctly for each record. Each row is one record, and all the values for that record must be on the same row, including values for those records in any Helper rows.** You can't put Helper data just anywhere. These columns all become part of the List range when you do Advanced Filter queries.

4. **Put the following formula into example cell BF9:**

$$=COUNTIFS(\$BC9,">="\&\$BA\$40, \$BC9,"<="\&\$BB\$40)$$

Take a few moments to look at Figure 6.6 on page 104 and **locate the specific cells** used in that formula.

What does this formula do? The *COUNTIFS* function *counts a cell depending on multiple IFs* — in this case, it determines whether **the cell value in BC9 is greater than or equal to** the value in **BA40** (the Start value for Delivery) AND also whether **the cell value in BC9 is less than or equal to** the value in **BB40** (the End value for Delivery). Both *IFs* must be TRUE for the function to count cell BC9. If BC9 is within the range Start-to-End (on row 40), the formula puts a 1 in the cell BF9; otherwise, it puts a 0 in cell BF9.

The >= and <= must be quoted and concatenated using & with the contents of **BA40** or **BB40,** as shown in the formula. (It doesn't work if you forget.)

5. Select the formula in cell BF9 and **fill-right** into BG9, BH9, BI9. These are the columns for the other three Subject ranges, which have their own Start and End pairs, each pair on its own line (lines 41–43).

   We need to adjust the Helper B, C, & D formulas because the Helper columns changed from left-to-right when we filled-right, but the Start and End values they refer to change from top-to-bottom.

6. **Edit the formula in BG9** so that it refers to the Start/End values in **BA41** and **BB41**:

=COUNTIFS($BC9,">="&$BA$41,
$BC9,"<="&$BB$41)

7. **Edit the formula in BH9** so that it refers to the Start/End values on row 42:

=COUNTIFS($BC9,">="&$BA$42,
$BC9,"<="&$BB$42)

8. **Edit the formula in BI9** so that it refers to the Start/End values on row 43:

=COUNTIFS($BC9,">="&$BA$43,
$BC9,"<="&$BB$43)

9. Select the four cells BF9, BG9, BH9, and BI9 and **fill-down** to row 28 (the limit of the Data Dashboard data). This part of your spreadsheet now should look like the top part of Figure 6.6 on page 104. **There can be only a single 1 on any line (because the ranges are mutually exclusive and have no overlap). If you have more than a single 1 on any line, something is wrong (overlapping ranges or you forgot to change a range reference).**

Why fill-right first and then fill-down? As you've seen, you need to adjust the reference to the cells that Start and End the ranges. If you don't correct those references after the first **fill-right,** the references will increment and not refer to the correct position for their Start/End pairs. After making the initial correction, you can **fill-down** and the formula will increment correctly. You *could* fill-down and then fill-right... but then **you'd have to correct all 80 cells** rather than just the first three. It would be even more work if you had 800 records. We are trying to minimize hand-editing.

The Helper columns are now complete.

Adding responsive counts

Just as with other columns of data, you'll want counts for the Subject ranges to respond to whether rows are hidden or shown.

However, because the big formula we use elsewhere does not work here (because of the Start/End pairs), and because we've added Helper columns, *these Subject counts become much simpler.*

We can use the *AGGREGATE* function.

Note: Need a refresher on the *AGGREGATE* function? Find it in the section "AGGREGATE" on page 60.

---

1. As shown in Figure 6.6 on page 104, **into cell BC40 enter the formula:**

=AGGREGATE(9,5,BF$9:BF$28)

What does this formula do? AGGREGATE can perform any of several tasks and it can ignore values in hidden rows. The AGGREGATE function is:

AGGREGATE*(function,option,range)*

In this formula:

- *function* **is 9,** which means perform a *SUM* on the range.

- *option* **is 5,** which means ignore any hidden rows when doing that *SUM*.

- *range* **is the range for the A Delivery Helper column values,** BF$9:BF$28.

The *AGGREGATE* formula *SUM*s up the values of any visible cells in the **A Delivery** Helper column and puts that value into **BC40**.

Note: You cannot use the plain SUM function because it cannot ignore hidden rows.

How it works. The Helper column for A Delivery contains a 1 only for those subject values within the Start/End range for **A Delivery** — all other cells in the A Delivery Helper column contain 0 because they are not within the Start/End range. These rows may be visible or hidden (as determined by a query later). Adding up those visible values — and only the visible values — provides a count of the visible rows where the Subject value falls between the designated Start and End for a given query.

2. **Fill-down** from BC40 into the Count cells in BC41, BC42, and BC43.

3. **Edit the ranges** — remember that the Helper columns increment left-to-right, but the values in BC40–BC43 increment down. Refer to Figure 6.6 on page 104, and enter:

cell BC40 =AGGREGATE(9,5,BF$9:BF$28)
cell BC41 =AGGREGATE(9,5,BG$9:BG$28)
cell BC42 =AGGREGATE(9,5,BH$9:BH$28)
cell BC43 =AGGREGATE(9,5,BI$9:BI$28)

Does this use of *AGGREGATE* need to be wrapped with the umbrella protection against a 0 count of records the way that Responsive Statistics do? No. The function used by *AGGREGATE* here is 9, which is SUM. If there are no records, the SUM is 0 even without any protection.

What to do next. You now have a *responsive count* for your Subject indexing system — the comments that fall within the Subject ranges are counted and they respond to queries.

Add Responsive Percentages and Responsive Statistics. See Figure 6.7 on page 107.

- Create **Total this Query** and **Confirm Total**. They should come up with the same total. We explain the difference between the two calculations in "Responsive Counts" on page 44.

- Create **Responsive Percentages** for each of the subject ranges as explained in "Deriving Responsive Percentages from Counts" on page 54. These need the umbrella.

- Create **Responsive Statistics** for each of the subject ranges, as explained in "Responsive Statistics" on page 59. Statistics such as Median and Mean can give you an overall sense of how the content of comments changes with location and demographics. These need the umbrella.

  There is a fundamental difference between statistics such as Median and Mean for survey scores (such as 0–5) and Median and Mean for classifications such as Subject codes. Classifications are widely dispersed and are not "scores." They're *descriptive values*. Still, because they're numeric, they can have means, averages, mins, and maxes, standard deviations, and all the rest.

- **Query the data to see what happens.** You can query the Subject field using the values you assigned to the Subject field. See how the counts, percentages, and statistics change.

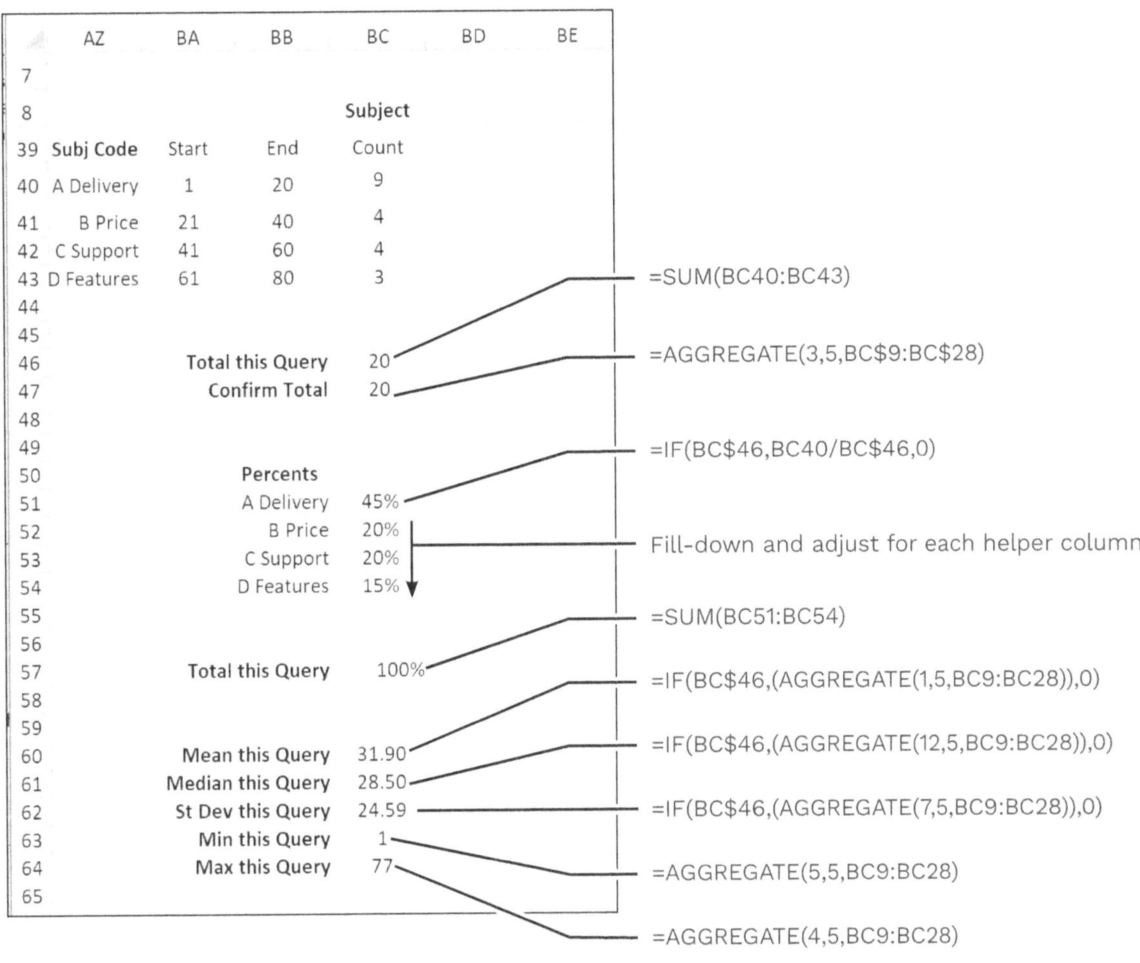

Figure 6.7: Responsive Percentages and Responsive Statistics for the Subject codes.

HOW CAN I USE THE RANGED SUBJECT FIELD WITH A TEXT QUERY?

Even if you query your ranged Subject field for a single value (say, 1 for *Delivery, Fast*), you still might return 50 records from a survey of any decent size. That can be a lot of haystack to search for a specific needle. But remember: The Subject values only *symbolically represent* the contents of the Comments field. **You have access to both the Subject index and the actual content of the Comments field.**

Do an AND query. You can narrow your data in the Data Dashboard if you:

- Enter a single-value criterion for the Subject you're looking for (Delivery, Fast), **AND...**

- On the same Criteria range row, enter a text query for a phrase you remember from that great comment you read.

The Subject index and the text query can quickly locate the record with the comment you are looking for. Read-up on AND and OR queries in "Queries Using AND / OR" on page 72. Read-up on text queries with "Text-Based Queries" on page 99.

WHAT ABOUT THE OTHER FIELDS OF THE PROFILE?

ID	Context Questions		Comments	Subject	Importance	Quality	Pos/Neu/Neg	Tag for...
	Lack skills	Lack support						
Count	20	20						
Total	5	11						
Std Dev	0.43	0.50						
Median	0.00	1.00						
Mean	0.25	0.55						
Grp Mean								

Figure 6.8: Other fields of the profile

The values of the other fields of the profile don't have to be analyzed and grouped in the same two-step way as does Subject. Their variety is more like "your role in the organization" — one of five, six, or seven values, rather than consisting of anything under the sun that requires multiple classification levels.

As other fields of the profile, we suggested:

- **Importance:** scale of 1–5.

- **Quality:** (optional) scale of 1–5.

- **Positive/Neutral/Negative:** You may want to consider a scale of 1–3 or 1–9, with one end of the scale signifying Positive and the other Negative. Neutral would be in the middle. The scale of 1–9 gives you some wiggle-room for degrees or positivity or negativity and because 9 is odd, there is a "middle number."

- **Tag for:** You may want to refer specific comments to various departments or individuals for their consideration or action. Create a numbered list of departments or individuals and put the referral number here (use a 0 for not-referred; we prefer that to leaving the field blank). We can't predict your list, but it should not be too long. Aim for 10 or fewer Code values.

Note: You may remember our mention of the survey "stakeholders" 'way back on page 20. When you tag text fields for referral, you're tagging for them.

Use the big, complex formula for counts

Because these scales are relatively small and consist of individually countable values — unlike the wide ranges of Subject values — no Helper columns are necessary. You can use the single formula for responsive counts as described in Appendix C, "Explaining the Data Dashboard's Most Important Formula" on page 137, and shown (just as an example) in Figure 6.9.

Responsive Percentages and Responsive Statistics for the text-oriented "other fields" are the same numerical-based calculations as elsewhere in the Data Dashboard.

$$=SUMPRODUCT(--(G\$9{:}G\$28=\$F40)*$$
$$SUBTOTAL(103,OFFSET(INDEX(G\$9{:}G\$28,1),$$
$$ROW(G\$9{:}G\$28)-MIN(ROW(G\$9{:}G\$28)),0)))$$

Figure 6.9: An example of the "big, complex formula" used elsewhere in the Data Dashboard to create a responsive count of the set of values in a column of data

In the example formula, the range *G$9:G$28* is the column of data currently being searched to find the value provided in *$F40*.

IT ALL WORKS TOGETHER

The process of reading through and categorizing text fields can be time-consuming, but once done, you should not have to do it again for the results of this survey. You should be able to do an Advanced Filter query and find records with text fields of specific topics with a level of importance and quality that you have set.

Appendix A

How-To: Various Tasks

This appendix collects the major how-to task instructions of the book. Appendix B on page 119 describes the many different ways to use the Advanced Filter query with your survey data.

WANT TO USE OUR DATA? HERE IT IS...

This is the example data we're going to use in this book. You can type it directly into a spreadsheet if you wish. Yup, this is everything. We're trying to keep it simple so that the models will be easy.

	A	B	C	D	E	F	G	H	I	J	K	L	M	N	O	P
1	ID	Know	Country	Likely	Reason1	Reason2	Reason3	Reason4	Q1	Q2	Q3	Q4	Industry	Revenue	Employees	Role
2	1001	1	2	3	0	0	1	1	4	0	0	4	5	?	3	5
3	1002	1	2	2	1	0	0	1	5	2	5	4	4	4	4	3
4	1003	5	3	2	1	1	0	1	4	2	4	3	4	5	3	3
5	1004	2	3	5	1	1	0	0	5	3	4	0	4	1	2	2
6	1005	4	2	5	0	1	0	1	1	2	5	0	4	3	5	4
7	1006	2	2	5	0	1	0	0	5	0	0	5	5	5	2	5
8	1007	2	2	3	0	0	0	0	5	3	3	1	4	5	5	2
9	1008	3	3	1	0	0	0	0	3	4	1	5	5	5	7	3
10	1009	1	2	5	1	0	1	1	5	1	3	3	1	2	6	1
11	1010	1	2	5	1	1	0	1	2	0	4	4	3	1	3	5
12	1011	2	2	4	0	0	0	1	1	1	3	3	4	3	5	2
13	1012	2	3	4	0	1	0	0	4	3	5	5	5	3	4	5
14	1013	1	1	2	0	1	0	0	1	5	2	0	3	3	7	5
15	1014	4	1	3	1	1	0	1	2	0	4	5	1	4	4	4
16	1015	2	1	4	1	1	0	0	5	5	0	0	1	5	6	5
17	1016	1	3	4	1	1	1	0	0	5	5	1	4	3	3	6
18	1017	1	1	2	1	0	0	1	3	1	2	4	3	5	2	5
19	1018	1	1	1	1	0	0	0	5	4	4	3	2	1	1	5
20	1019	1	1	4	0	0	1	1	4	1	1	2	3	1	4	6
21	1020	1	1	1	0	1	1	1	2	3	4	4	2	1	5	2

original-data   data-dashboard

Figure A.1: This is the data we'll be using in the survey models. We want to keep things as simple as possible.

IMPORTING YOUR OWN SURVEY DATA FROM A CSV FILE

With the CSV file copied from its source to your computer (and that source safely tucked away on its velvet cushion in your safe), open the CSV file with Notepad (Windows) or TextEdit (Macintosh) — or your favorite text editor — to give it a quick look for regularity. Figure A.2 shows the contents of a CSV text file that contains our survey data — you can see how everything lines up. Again, your real CSV will be *a lot* bigger. Note that the first line of this CSV file includes column headers. A CSV file that you receive may not have column headers yet, and if it does it will certainly include headers different from these. You can change the headers *after* import into Excel if you want to. Also, this CSV file shows ID numbers for each line (that is, for each record). Your CSV file may not have an ID number assigned yet; you can assign an ID after import.

Keep the original CSV file pristine in case you need to go back to it. Don't edit it directly.

```
ID,Know,Country,Likely,Reason1,Reason2,Reason3,Reason4,Q1,Q2,Q3,Q4,Industry,Revenue,Employees,Role
1001,1,2,3,0,0,1,1,4,0,0,4,5,2,3,5
1002,1,2,2,1,0,0,1,5,2,5,4,4,4,4,3
1003,5,3,2,1,1,0,1,4,2,4,3,4,5,3,3
1004,2,3,5,1,1,0,0,5,3,4,0,4,1,2,2
1005,4,2,5,0,1,0,1,1,2,5,0,4,3,5,4
1006,2,2,5,0,1,0,0,5,0,0,5,5,5,2,5
1007,2,2,3,0,0,0,0,5,3,3,1,4,5,5,2
1008,3,3,1,0,0,0,0,3,4,1,5,5,5,7,3
1009,1,2,5,1,0,1,1,5,1,3,3,1,2,6,1
1010,1,2,5,1,1,0,1,2,0,4,4,3,1,3,5
1011,2,2,4,0,0,0,1,1,1,3,3,4,3,5,2
1012,2,3,4,0,1,0,0,4,3,5,5,5,3,4,5
1013,1,1,2,0,1,0,0,1,5,2,0,3,3,7,5
1014,4,1,3,1,1,0,1,2,0,4,5,1,4,4,4
1015,2,1,4,1,1,0,0,5,5,0,0,1,5,6,5
1016,1,3,4,1,1,1,0,0,5,5,1,4,3,3,6
1017,1,1,2,1,0,0,1,3,1,2,4,3,5,2,5
1018,1,1,1,1,0,0,0,5,4,4,3,2,1,1,5
1019,1,1,4,0,0,1,1,4,1,1,2,3,1,4,6
1020,1,1,1,0,1,1,1,2,3,4,4,2,1,5,2
```

Figure A.2: A comma-separated-values (CSV) file viewed in Microsoft Notepad — compare this data to the data in Figure A.1

Close the CSV file — it does not need to remain open — and then open Microsoft Excel to begin the import process.

Note: Microsoft Excel can directly *open* a CSV file using *File | Open* — but this places all the data into a single cell, not the situation that we want. Instead, we must *import* the CSV file.

Note: Older versions of Excel require you to use *Insert | From Text/CSV*.

1. On a new, blank Excel worksheet, click the cell A1.

   Why A1? Using a blank worksheet and choosing cell A1 is so that your import starts in cell A1. While you can import to any starting cell (and if you're an experienced Excel user, where you import does not make much difference), this book assumes that you're importing your CSV file to cell A1.

2. Click the Data menu.

3. On the Data menu, click the button From Text/CSV (Figure A.3 on page 111). (A command sequence like this is often abbreviated with bars such as *Data | Get & Transform Data | From Text/CSV.*)

   Microsoft Excel displays a standard Open dialog box where you can navigate to and select the CSV file that holds your survey data.

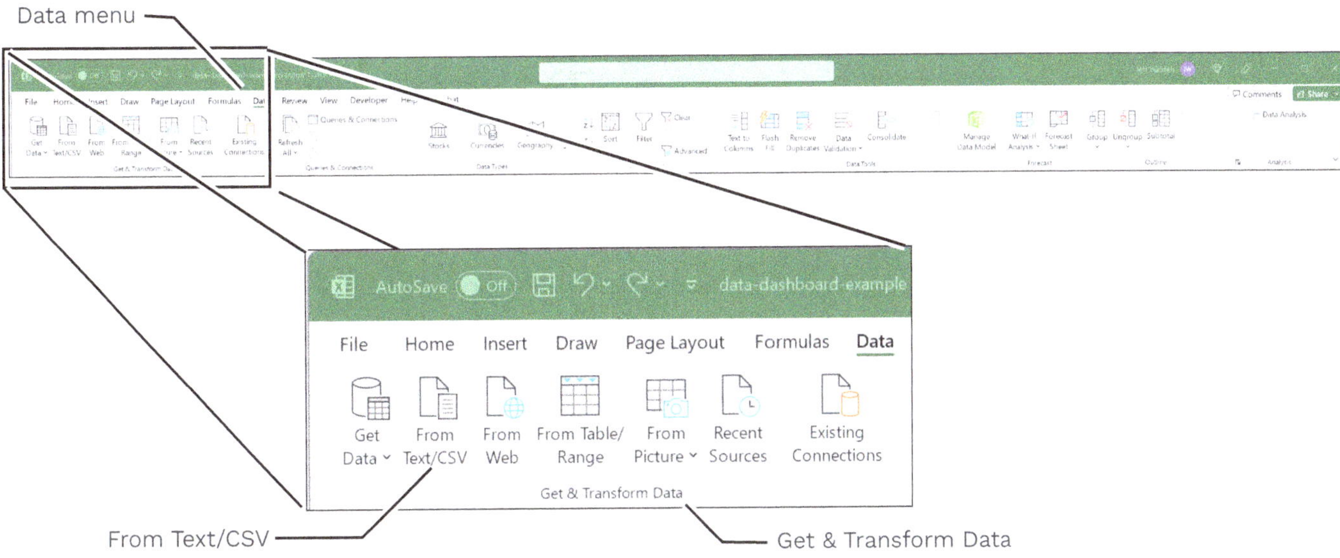

Figure A.3: *Data | Get & Transform Data | From Text/CSV*

4. Select the CSV file from the Open dialog, and then click Open.

Excel displays the Load dialog box (Figure A.4).

Note: The Transform button on the Load dialog box displays the Power Query Editor that can modify your data in various ways as it's being imported. The analyses in this book do not require transformations by the Power Query Editor, and it's not in-scope for this book.

If you have a lot of data, the import process may take a few moments. Excel imports the CSV file as a pre-formatted table (shown in Figure A.5 on page 112) — which we will change.

Why change it? We'll change it because we don't need the data to be displayed in this format.

Load button

Figure A.4: Load dialog box

5. Click Load.

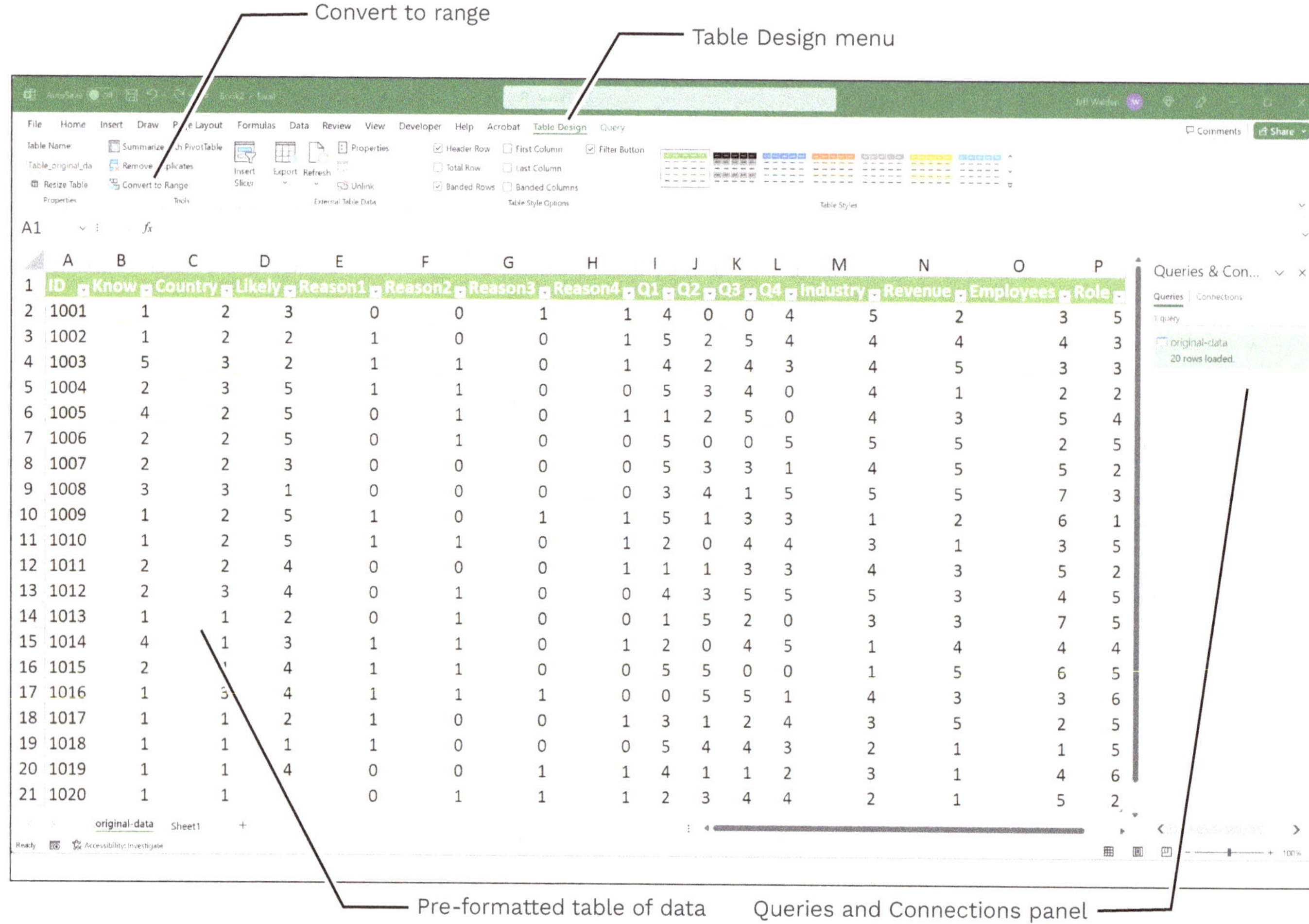

ID	Know	Country	Likely	Reason1	Reason2	Reason3	Reason4	Q1	Q2	Q3	Q4	Industry	Revenue	Employees	Role
1001	1	2	3	0	0	1	1	4	0	0	4	5	2	3	5
1002	1	2	2	1	0	0	1	5	2	5	4	4	4	4	3
1003	5	3	2	1	1	0	1	4	2	4	3	4	5	3	3
1004	2	3	5	1	1	0	0	5	3	4	0	4	1	2	2
1005	4	2	5	0	1	0	1	1	2	5	0	4	3	5	4
1006	2	2	5	0	1	0	0	5	0	0	5	5	5	2	5
1007	2	2	3	0	0	0	0	5	3	3	1	4	5	5	2
1008	3	3	1	0	0	0	0	3	4	1	5	5	5	7	3
1009	1	2	5	1	0	1	1	5	1	3	3	1	2	6	1
1010	1	2	5	1	1	0	1	2	0	4	4	3	1	3	5
1011	2	2	4	0	0	0	1	1	1	3	3	4	3	5	2
1012	2	3	4	0	1	0	0	4	3	5	5	5	3	4	5
1013	1	1	2	0	1	0	0	1	5	2	0	3	3	7	5
1014	4	1	3	1	1	0	1	2	0	4	5	1	4	4	4
1015	2		4	1	1	0	0	5	5	0	0	1	5	6	5
1016	1	3	4	1	1	1	0	0	5	5	1	4	3	3	6
1017	1	1	2	1	0	0	1	3	1	2	4	3	5	2	5
1018	1	1	1	1	0	0	0	5	4	4	3	2	1	1	5
1019	1	1	4	0	0	1	1	4	1	1	2	3	1	4	6
1020	1	1		0	1	1	1	2	3	4	4	2	1	5	2

Figure A.5: Survey data as imported and displayed by Excel

6. Name and Save this tab and spreadsheet.

   We named the tab "Original-Data," and then made sure to save the spreadsheet file. **Why?** Once we get this data into Excel and properly formatted, it becomes an easily accessible **baseline copy** of the data that we will use elsewhere. Redundancy is our friend.

CHANGE THE PRE-FORMATTED TABLE

1. With the pre-formatted table displayed, close the Queries and Connections panel (shown in Figure A.5).

2. Be sure that Table Design is selected on the top menu bar.

3. Select the whole of the pre-formatted table, from top-left to bottom-right (in our case, cells A1 through P21).

4. Click the button *Convert to Range*.

   Why? Convert to Range changes the selected table into a normal range of data cells in Excel. The Table Design and Layout menus go away. Even so, the data you've imported retains the color formatting it arrived with. See Figure A.6.

Note: There is a value to Excel's **table format** and having that data remain connected to its source (here, the original CSV file). That value becomes apparent when the original data changes — new transactions, activity by sales staff, and so forth: a variety of data that is added, deleted, and changed over time can appear automatically in a table. Many Excel examples dwell on this type of data. *Survey data is not transactional* as in such examples. You have completed the survey. The data is very unlikely to change.

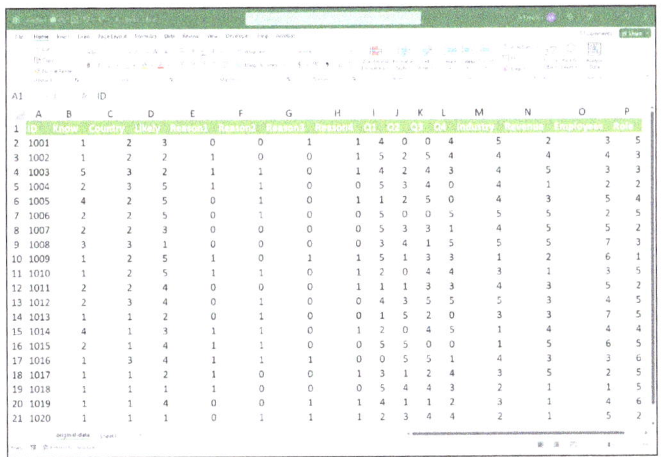

ID	Know	Country	Likely	Reason1	Reason2	Reason3	Reason4	Q1	Q2	Q3	Q4	Industry	Revenue	Employees	Role
1001	1	2	3	0	0	1	1	4	0	0	4	5	2	3	5
1002	1	2	2	1	0	0	1	5	2	5	4	4	4	4	3
1003	5	3	2	1	1	0	1	4	2	4	3	4	5	3	3
1004	2	3	5	1	1	0	0	5	3	4	0	4	1	2	2
1005	4	2	5	0	1	0	1	1	2	5	0	4	3	5	4
1006	2	2	5	0	1	0	0	5	0	0	5	5	5	2	5
1007	2	2	3	0	0	0	0	5	3	3	1	4	5	5	2
1008	3	3	1	0	0	0	0	3	4	1	5	5	5	7	3
1009	1	2	5	1	0	1	1	5	1	3	3	1	2	6	1
1010	1	2	5	1	1	0	1	2	0	4	4	3	1	3	5
1011	2	2	4	0	0	0	1	1	1	3	3	4	3	5	2
1012	2	3	4	0	1	0	0	4	3	5	5	5	3	4	5
1013	1	1	2	0	1	0	0	1	5	2	0	3	3	7	5
1014	4	1	3	1	1	0	1	2	0	4	5	1	4	4	4
1015	2	1	4	1	1	0	0	5	5	0	0	1	5	6	5
1016	1	3	4	1	1	1	0	0	5	5	1	4	3	3	6
1017	1	1	2	1	0	0	1	3	1	2	4	3	5	2	5
1018	1	1	1	1	0	0	0	5	4	4	3	2	1	1	5
1019	1	1	4	0	0	1	1	4	1	1	2	3	1	4	6
1020	1	1	1	0	1	1	1	2	3	4	4	2	1	5	2

Figure A.6: The imported CSV file converted into a "normal" range of Excel cells

5. With the range of imported CSV cells still selected (or re-selected) from top-left to bottom-right, click the Home menu.

6. In the Styles section of the Home menu, click Normal. This changes the cells to an unformatted appearance.

If your spreadsheet is narrow and the ribbon compact, you may have to click Cell Styles to see the style settings, as in Figure A.7.

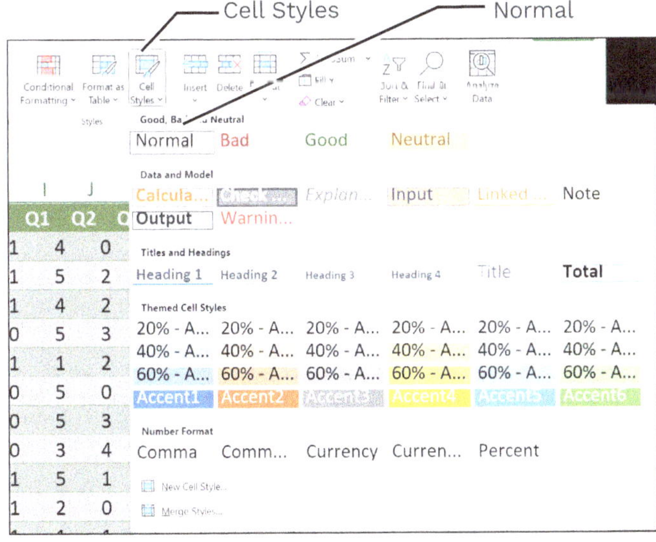

Figure A.7: Cell Styles and Normal

When all this importing and un-doing of format is finished, you should have your CSV data on a spreadsheet tab looking like Figure A.8.

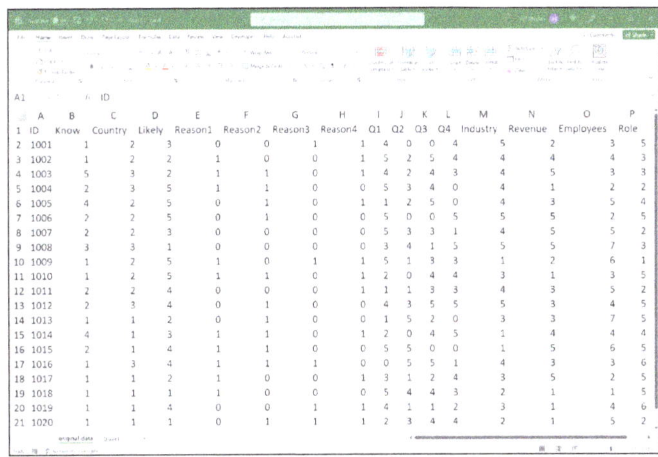

ID	Know	Country	Likely	Reason1	Reason2	Reason3	Reason4	Q1	Q2	Q3	Q4	Industry	Revenue	Employees	Role
1001	1	2	3	0	0	1	1	4	0	0	4	5	2	3	5
1002	1	2	2	1	0	0	1	5	2	5	4	4	4	4	3
1003	5	3	2	1	1	0	1	4	2	4	3	4	5	3	3
1004	2	3	5	1	1	0	0	5	3	4	0	4	1	2	2
1005	4	2	5	0	1	0	1	1	2	5	0	4	3	5	4
1006	2	2	5	0	1	0	0	5	0	0	5	5	5	2	5
1007	2	2	3	0	0	0	0	5	3	3	1	4	5	5	2
1008	3	3	1	0	0	0	0	3	4	1	5	5	5	7	3
1009	1	2	5	1	0	1	1	5	1	3	3	1	2	6	1
1010	1	2	5	1	1	0	1	2	0	4	4	3	1	3	5
1011	2	2	4	0	0	0	1	1	1	3	3	4	3	5	2
1012	2	3	4	0	1	0	0	4	3	5	5	5	3	4	5
1013	1	1	2	0	1	0	0	1	5	2	0	3	3	7	5
1014	4	1	3	1	1	0	1	2	0	4	5	1	4	4	4
1015	2	1	4	1	1	0	0	5	5	0	0	1	5	6	5
1016	1	3	4	1	1	1	0	0	5	5	1	4	3	3	6
1017	1	1	2	1	0	0	1	3	1	2	4	3	5	2	5
1018	1	1	1	1	0	0	0	5	4	4	3	2	1	1	5
1019	1	1	4	0	0	1	1	4	1	1	2	3	1	4	6
1020	1	1	1	0	1	1	1	2	3	4	4	2	1	5	2

Figure A.8: Survey data from the CSV file, imported into Excel, and un-formatted

IMPORTING YOUR DATA FROM AN EXCEL FILE

If your data has been delivered to you as an Excel file (and as long as it's formatted to look as in Figure A.8), getting the data into your working survey spreadsheet is much easier. You can do either:

- Save the original Excel file to a new and different file name on your computer. That effectively makes a duplicate copy of it. Then save the original Excel data file to that thumb drive we mentioned earlier and stash it away on its velvet cushion.

- Select the data set, including the column names, from far top-left to far bottom-right and copy it. Then display a new blank Excel spreadsheet (not just a new tab on the existing spreadsheet), click cell A1 on that new spreadsheet, and paste. Remember to save the original Excel file to the thumb drive and put it away for safekeeping.

You should now have a working Excel spreadsheet that looks like Figure A.8 on a named tab (for example, "Original-Data").

ADD YOUR OWN ID NUMBERS

Perhaps your CSV data did not come with ID numbers for each row/record, or you have set aside any invalid responses, removing them from the data, and want to number only the remaining valid responses sequentially. You can add that here.

1. Copy the contents of the Original-Data tab to a fresh worksheet. **Why?** This leaves Original-Data alone as a backup.

2. On the new worksheet, insert a column for the ID: *Home | Insert | Insert Sheet Column* (Figure A.9). This column can go anywhere, but it's logical to make it the leftmost column.

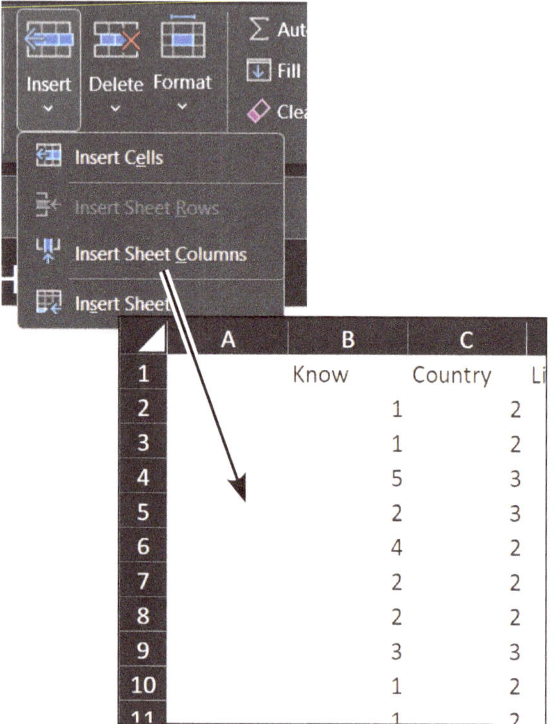

Figure A.9: Insert a column

3. Enter a column name (we named it ID) and a starting number. (Figure A.10.)

4. Select the starting number and highlight the rest of your column of data, down to the bottom of the data. (Figure A.10.)

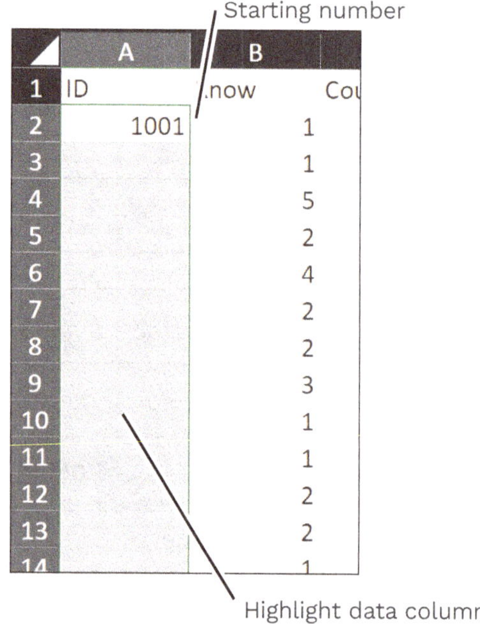

Figure A.10: Starting number and data column

5. With the data column highlighted, choose *Home | Editing | Fill | Series* from the Editing section of the Home menu. (Figure A.11.)

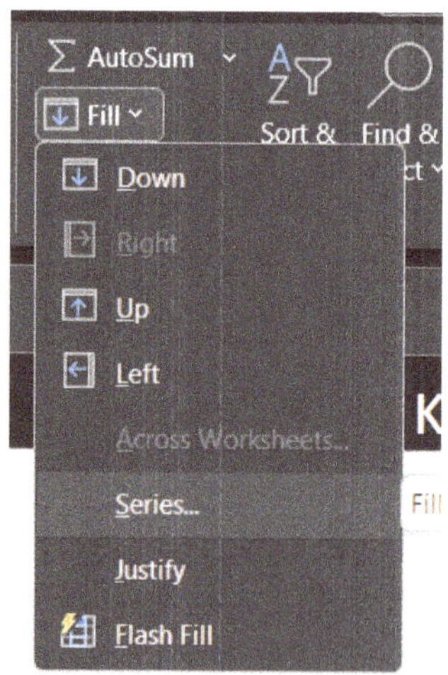

Figure A.11: *Fill | Series*

Excel displays the Series dialog, Figure A.12 on page 115.

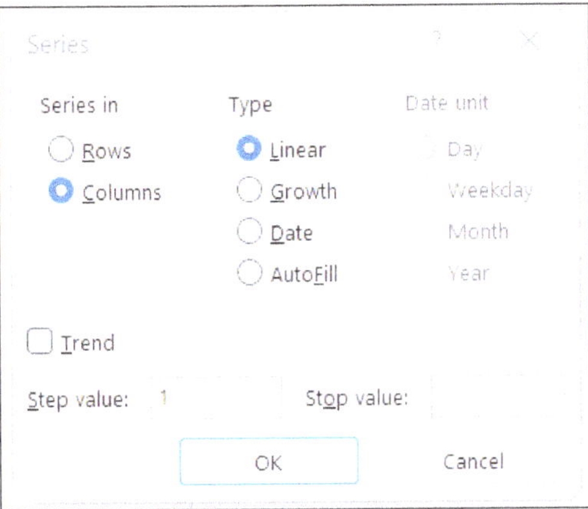

Figure A.12: Series dialog

6. For sequential numbers, make sure that the settings are as shown in Figure A.12, and then click OK.

   Excel adds ID numbers to your data, as shown in Figure A.13.

	A	B	C
1	ID	Know	Country
2	1001	1	2
3	1002	1	2
4	1003	5	3
5	1004	2	3
6	1005	4	2
7	1006	2	2
8	1007	2	2
9	1008	3	3
10	1009	1	2
11	1010	1	2
12	1011	2	2

Figure A.13: ID numbers added to data

Note: It is important that all data columns are the same length — that is, you have no partial records. If you have added too many ID numbers, delete the extras so that you don't create false incomplete records. If you have added too few IDs, add new numbers this same way, starting with the last correct number in the sequence.

BRING YOUR OWN DATA INTO AN EXISTING DATA DASHBOARD

We don't want to make too big a deal of this process, but we did think it deserves its own mention. Think of this section as a checklist.

Bringing data from your own survey into an existing Data Dashboard that you've built along with this book is easy **but it is a time when it's possible to introduce errors into your data**.

- **Make room** for all your new data columns and column names by inserting columns where needed. You may have several Screening questions and many more Context and Survey Body questions. No doubt your Demographics are different, too. Your new Data Dashboard will be wider and much more detailed than our small example. You will have different Code values for each field, depending on your survey's fields.

  Remember that the field names for the Criteria range **must exactly match** the field names for the List range.

- **Make sure** that each field has an appropriate number of answer values (Codes). For example, the Industry field on the sample Data Dashboard has five potential values for Industry type. We worked on a survey recently that had 17 different values. If you have 17 values for Industry... you'll have to set 'em up. This goes double for any open-ended text field data that you want to bring in. (See Chapter 6, "Handling Text Fields in Surveys" on page 97 for more information about open-ended text fields.)

  When the number of Responsive Counts changes, the Responsive Percentages and Responsive Statistics must change with them. The process of adding new fields and changing or enlarging the number of field values means adding to the calculations they require. You already have the formulas; you only need to hook them up to the data.

- **Does your survey include text fields?** Be sure to read Chapter 6, "Handling Text Fields in Surveys" on page 97. In addition to room for text, you'll need room for your text profiling fields and Helper columns, which you can put "out of the way" on the far right of the Data Dashboard.

- **Know the record count** of your incoming data. The Data Dashboard as described in this book uses only 20 rows of data. If you have 800 incoming records... you're going to have to insert *at least* 780 rows. (You can always remove unneeded rows later, but Excel won't automatically make room for the excess if you don't plan for it.)

- **Know where your data is coming from.** Are you getting a CSV file or an Excel file? It almost doesn't matter. With a Data Dashboard all set up, you can just copy-and-paste the new data into the appropriate data columns. You do this column-by-column, highlighting the full length in the Data Dashboard required by the receiving column to hold the new data. Even when bringing in over 50 columns of data, we've found this to be a process that took only a few minutes.

  BE ALERT!
  MAKE SURE RECORDS AND COLUMNS LINE UP CORRECTLY. If you're starting the paste on row 9 and you know it's going to go from row 9 to row 810, data in **EVERY COLUMN** must start on row 9 and end on row 810. No exceptions. *This is the place where being careless WILL corrupt your data.* It's easy to fix by checking against your untouched source material and re-pasting, but don't make that work necessary for yourself. Please.

- **Make sure all your calculations work.** You've added new fields, you've added new potential answers for those fields. You're going to be doing some formula replicating and adjusting. However, if you've built the Data Dashboard, you have all the formulas you need already in place, as well as the knowledge to make new formulas if you need them.

- **Make it all pretty again.** Adding new data can disarrange things. Spend some time tidying up the Data Dashboard, and you'll be ready for new presentations.

Become a Query Ninja

When we built the Data Dashboard, we logically put the query area up top so that the field names for the Criteria range were directly above the field names for the List range. This places both query and data on the same spreadsheet page. It makes queries easy to define and to see the result of your queries reflected in the data and the calculations immediately below them. (Figure B.1) It also keeps the query out of the hide-and-show area (the List range) that makes the Data Dashboard responsive.

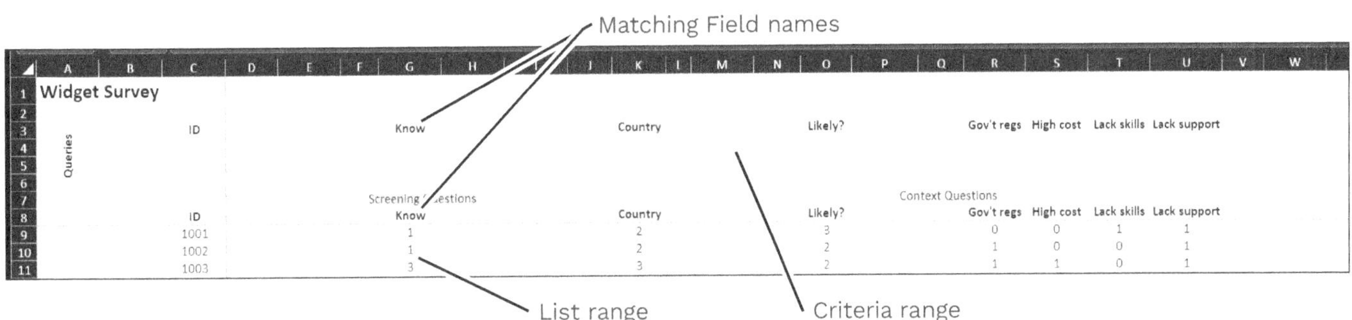

Figure B.1: List range and Criteria range in the Data Dashboard

There are other ways to create queries — other places to put your criteria, and other ways to work with the data.

RULES OF THE RANGE

The range rules continue to hold, *no matter where you put the query.*

- The **Criteria range** must include only the field names and the rows(s) that contain criteria — no blanks. The **List range** must include all data, top-left to bottom-right, or you risk leaving out rows or columns.

- Criteria field names and corresponding List field names must match — **EXACTLY.**

- No empty rows are allowed within the Criteria range. Every row you include in the Criteria range must contain either field names or criteria.

- **There must be a blank (empty) row beneath the Criteria range.** This is true wherever you end up putting your Criteria range. When the Criteria range is above the data — as it is on the Data Dashboard — the empty row separates the Criteria range from the List range.

Can I put these techniques to work in the Data Dashboard? Sure. All these query techniques are compatible with the Dashboard exactly as we have built it.

Um... However. If you're not already familiar with Advanced Filter queries, some of the techniques we show here may take a little practice before you feel confident putting them to work customizing the Dashboard after so carefully building it — especially those that create an effect on a spreadsheet tab other than the tab on which the Criteria range resides or that use Excel macros. **We'll copy the data from the Data Dashboard** by itself into its own worksheet without the distraction of the other calculations. **This is for practice, but what you learn here can be applied to the Data Dashboard as you wish.**

Copy the survey data from the Dashboard, including field names. Then paste that data onto a blank workbook tab. We'll name that tab *Query-Ninja-1*. **Then, remove the blank columns** from the practice data so that it looks like Figure B.2. Queries don't care about the blank columns on the Dashboard; removing them just keeps this practice data tab "tighter."

Later, we'll create two new spreadsheet tabs called *Query-Ninja-2* and *Query-Ninja-3*.

	A	B	C	D	E	F	G	H	I	J	K	L	M	N	O	P
1	ID	Know	Country	Likely?	Gov't regs	High cost	Lack skills	Lack support	Q1	Q2	Q3	Q4	Industry	Revenue	Employees	Role
2	1001	1	2	3	0	0	1	1	4	0	0	4	5	2	3	5
3	1002	1	2	2	1	0	0	1	5	2	5	4	4	4	4	3
4	1003	5	3	2	1	1	0	1	4	2	4	3	4	5	3	3
5	1004	2	3	5	1	1	0	0	5	3	4	0	4	1	2	2
6	1005	4	2	5	0	1	0	1	1	2	5	0	4	3	5	4
7	1006	2	2	5	0	1	0	0	5	0	0	5	5	5	2	5
8	1007	2	2	3	0	0	0	0	5	3	3	1	4	5	5	2
9	1008	3	3	1	0	0	0	0	3	4	1	5	5	5	7	3
10	1009	1	2	5	1	0	1	1	5	1	3	3	1	2	6	1
11	1010	1	2	5	1	1	0	1	2	0	4	4	3	1	3	5
12	1011	2	2	4	0	0	0	1	1	1	3	3	4	3	5	2
13	1012	2	3	4	0	1	0	0	4	3	5	5	5	3	4	5
14	1013	1	1	2	0	1	0	0	1	5	2	0	3	3	7	5
15	1014	4	1	3	1	1	0	1	2	0	4	5	1	4	4	4
16	1015	2	1	4	1	1	0	0	5	5	0	0	1	5	6	5
17	1016	1	3	4	1	1	1	0	0	5	5	1	4	3	3	6
18	1017	1	1	2	1	0	0	1	3	1	2	4	3	5	2	5
19	1018	1	1	1	1	0	0	0	5	4	4	3	2	1	1	5
20	1019	1	1	4	0	0	1	1	4	1	1	2	3	1	4	6
21	1020	1	1	1	0	1	1	1	2	3	4	4	2	1	5	2
22																

Tabs: query-ninja-1 | qn-2 | qn-3 | +

Figure B.2: Data from the Data Dashboard — this is only the List range; we've closed up the columns, left off all the calculations, and did not include the existing Criteria range (we'll be using alternate locations)

WHERE WE'RE GOING

This chapter explains several different ways of setting up Advanced Filter queries.

Version One (page 121) duplicates the hide-and-show type of query used on the Data Dashboard — but from a different location on the same worksheet.

Version Two (page 122) tells you how to create a library of queries for repetitive use that you can cut and paste.

Version Three (page 123) copies data from the List range to another location *without hiding and showing*.

Version Four (page 124) shows you how to copy data from specific fields only.

Version Five (page 124) copies data from the List range to another tab.

Version Six (page 126) puts the query on a different tab from the List range. You can do both hide-and-show and copy queries this way.

Version Seven (page 128) not only executes queries from a different tab, but copies data from the List range to a *third* tab.

Version Eight (page 129) shows you how to create a macro (a short program) that can hide-and-show or copy, and which can accept variable criteria on-the-fly.

VERSION ONE: AN ORDER OF CRITERIA ON THE SIDE

Figure B.3 shows the first place we'll be putting the Criteria range — to the side and slightly below the List area.

Why put the Criteria range below the List range? Why not have it nice and neat and immediately next to our data? Because executing a query can hide and show the various rows of the List range, and our query *hides and shows rows across the full width of the spreadsheet* — you could end up hiding your own query. (Oops) This is also why the query area in the Data Dashboard is located *above* the List range. *The List range on the Data Dashboard is and must be very active.*

If you were implementing Version One in the Data Dashboard, the new Criteria Range could be no higher on the spreadsheet than the Basic Statistics (that is, below the List range). The rows immediately above the Basic Statistics are List range data, and may be hidden from time to time. Thus, we put the new Criteria range down and to the right. **These examples show that you can put the Criteria range almost anywhere that works for you, even on another tab — or even on another worksheet file. We'll get to that.**

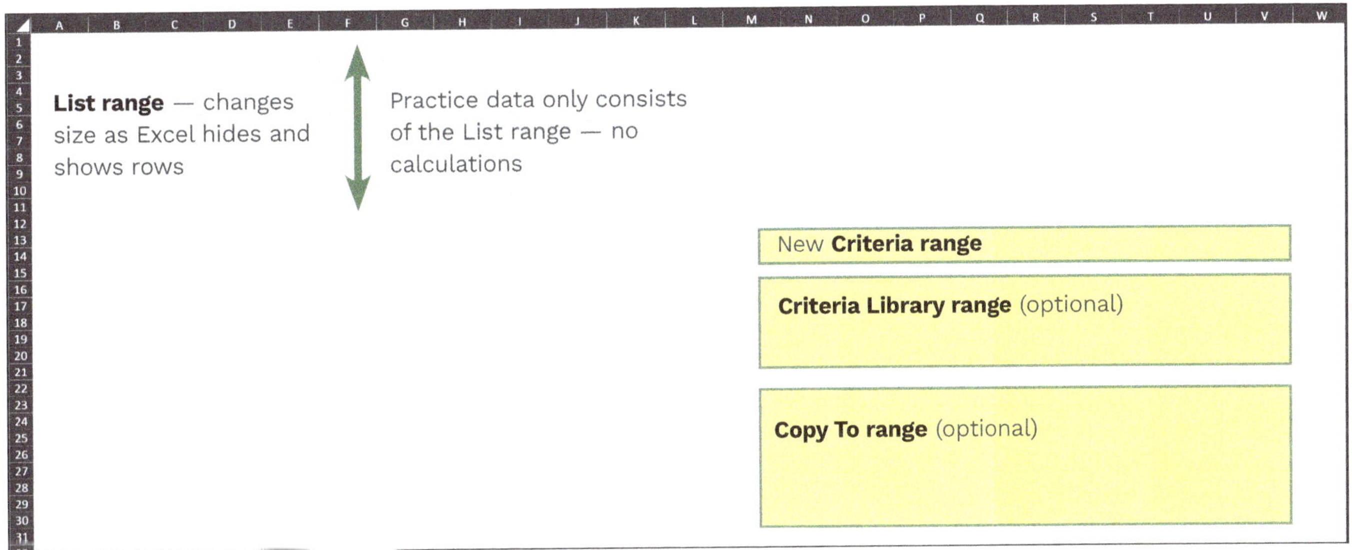

Figure B.3: The practice area — compare it to Figure B.2

1. Copy and paste the headers (and only the headers) from the List range to the new Criteria range at the lower right (see Figure B.3). The headers must match **EXACTLY**.

   If you copy all of the headers, you can use any combination of them in queries. However, **you *can* copy only those headers that you believe you will use frequently** — perhaps Country and the Demographic fields. However, for this example we suggest copying and pasting all headers.

2. Try a query (they work the same as when the Criteria range is located above the List range). For a refresher, see "At Long Last We Do a Query" on page 73.

For example, type 3 under Country, as in Figure B.4.

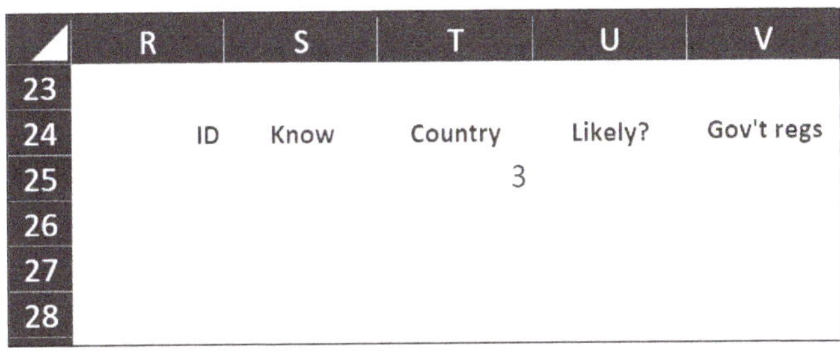

	R	S	T	U	V
23					
24	ID	Know	Country	Likely?	Gov't regs
25			3		
26					
27					
28					

Figure B.4: Version One: Criteria on the Side — see Figure B.3

Note: Make sure that there is a blank row under the Criteria range. *Rules of the Range.*

---

3. Choose *Data | Sort & Filter | Advanced* to display the Advanced Filter dialog box (Figure B.5).

4. Make sure that **Filter the list in place** is selected. This hides and shows rows.

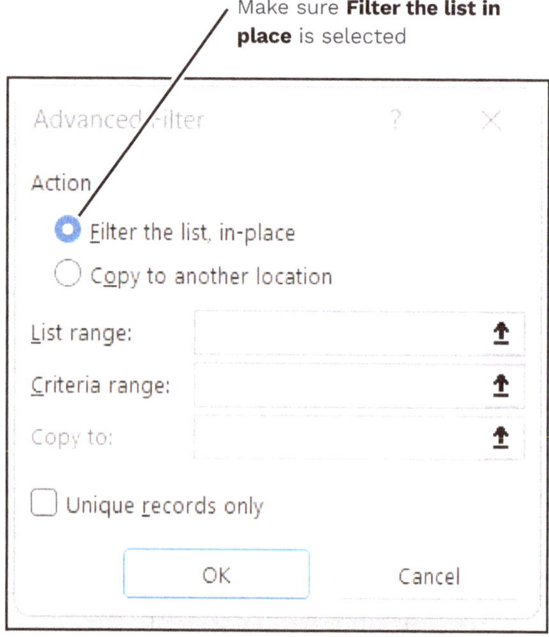

Figure B.5:   Advanced Filter dialog box

5. Define the List range and the new Criteria range by clicking within the List and Criteria fields of the Advanced Filter dialog box, then highlighting the respective ranges. You've done this before with the Data Dashboard.

6. Click OK.

    Excel executes the query and the List range displays only the records where the Country field is 3, as in Figure B.6.

	A	B	C	D	E
1	ID	Know	Country	Likely?	Gov't regs
4	1003	5	3	2	1
5	1004	2	3	5	1
9	1008	3	3	1	0
13	1012	2	3	4	0
17	1016	1	3	4	1
22					

Figure B.6:   All records from Country = 3

7. Click Clear to restore all records to the List range. *Clear does not remove criteria from the Criteria range.*

Note: Did you experience a *query oops*? See "Troubleshoot the Query" on page 84. In our experience, most query problems boil down to having (or not having) a blank row where it must be, or not clicking outside the List and Criteria ranges before clicking Advanced.

VERSION TWO: CREATE A QUERY LIBRARY

If you find that you need to create the same set of queries over and over, or need to create repeatable complex queries using **AND**s and **OR**s, you can create a query library.

A query library is nothing more than a prepared set of criteria that you can quickly copy and paste into the waiting Criteria range. See Figure B.3 on page 121 for location. There are other ways to accomplish often-repeated queries, such as creating a macro query. We do that in "Version Eight: Macro Query (Now You're Cooking with Code)" on page 129. A macro query can still make use of a prepared library.

The widget survey data is simple (in the extreme!), but depending on the complexity of your own survey, you might want to create different Demographic queries or a set of specific Survey Body responses that repeatably reveal the demographics of the organizations that made those responses.

VERSION THREE: QUERIES THAT COPY-TO SOMEWHERE ELSE

You may want to copy a subset of data to another location or tab on your spreadsheet **or even to a completely separate spreadsheet file** for use in tables, graphs, reports, or for some other task. You do this with a Copy-To query.

Figure B.3 on page 121 shows a Copy-To area below both the Criteria range and any query library you may have set up. **Why there?** Because copying data from the List range and placing it somewhere else can take up a variable amount of space *and it over-writes* whatever may be there already. Copy-To does not care what's present in the area it's copying-to.

Note: **The Copy-To process overwrites any cells in its target area.** If you've copied data that you want to keep, you should move it elsewhere before doing the next Copy-To query to that same area (or choose a different Copy-To location). If you Copy-To data that *does not* completely overwrite previous data, some number of rows or columns of old data may be left in place. This can be confusing at the very least. Thus, **make it a practice** to highlight and delete (or move) any data left in the Copy-To range before doing your next Copy-To query to that location.

---

1. Clear any existing query and make sure that the Criteria you've placed in the Criteria range is what you want.

2. Choose *Data | Sort & Filter | Advanced* to display the Advanced Filter dialog box.

3. Select **Copy to another location** and fill in the List range and Criteria range fields as usual (Figure B.7).

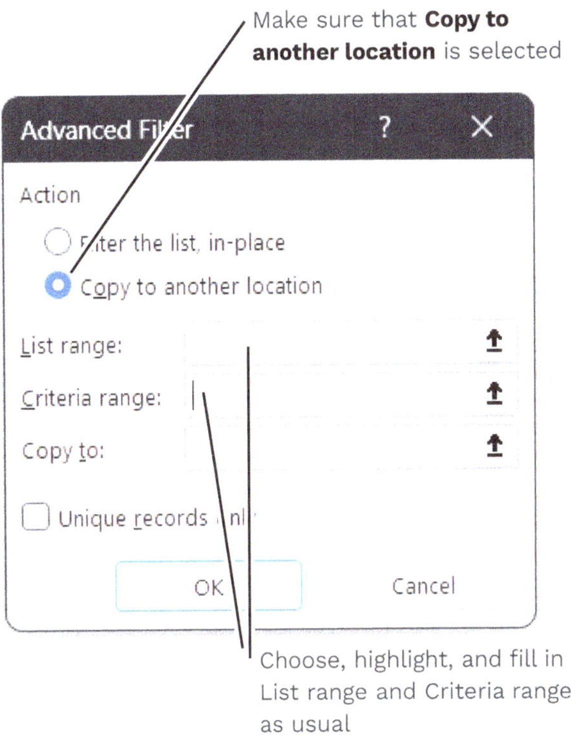

Figure B.7: Advanced Filter dialog box

4. In the Advanced Filter dialog box, click within the Copy-To field and then click **the cell you designate as the top-left location** of the copied data.

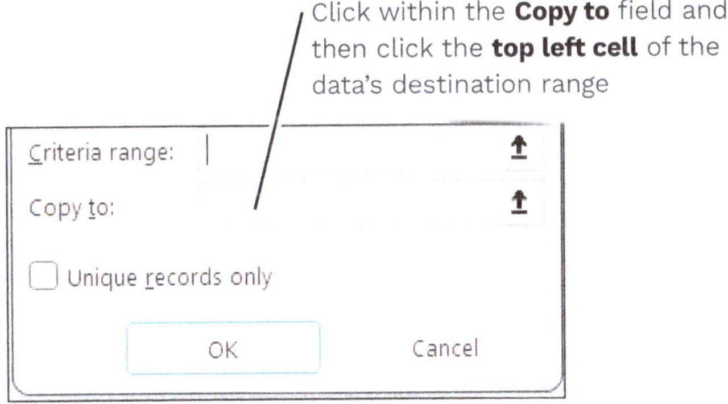

Figure B.8: Copy-To field

Excel copies the rows of data that meet your criteria and places them at the location you designated in the Copy To field.

This time, no data rows are shown or hidden — only copied. See Figure B.9.

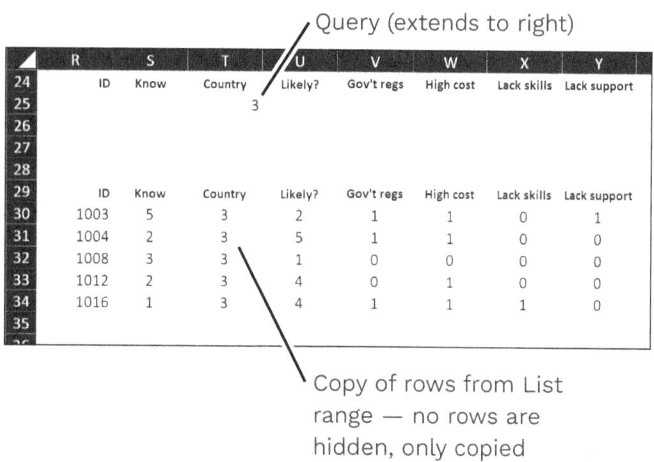

	R	S	T	U	V	W	X	Y
24	ID	Know	Country	Likely?	Gov't regs	High cost	Lack skills	Lack support
25			3					
26								
27								
28								
29	ID	Know	Country	Likely?	Gov't regs	High cost	Lack skills	Lack support
30	1003	5	3	2	1	1	0	1
31	1004	2	3	5	1	1	0	0
32	1008	3	3	1	0	0	0	0
33	1012	2	3	4	0	1	0	0
34	1016	1	3	4	1	1	1	0
35								

Figure B.9: Data is copied to the new location — no rows of data are hidden or shown

VERSION FOUR: COPY ONLY PARTIAL RECORDS

Version Three copies complete rows of records, even if you specify only one field (such as Country) as its criterion.

What if you want to **copy only two fields** — say, Country and Likely — (or three, or four fields…) but no other information from the records? Maybe you want to graph just these particular data; maybe you want only that specific data for a report.

To copy only a limited number of fields, copy and paste only those specific field names so that they are *ready and waiting at the location* where you want the data copied to. See Figure B.10.

Rather than clicking an empty cell to designate it as the Advanced Filter Copy-To location, **highlight the two field names you have waiting to receive the data.** As an example, for the outcome in Figure B.10, put the two-cell range T32:U32 into the Copy-To field.

Only data from the two specific fields you designate — and only from records that meet the criteria, *even if the criteria are not among the two selected fields* — are copied to the new location.

Note: The **EXACT** field names must be present in the Copy-To location.

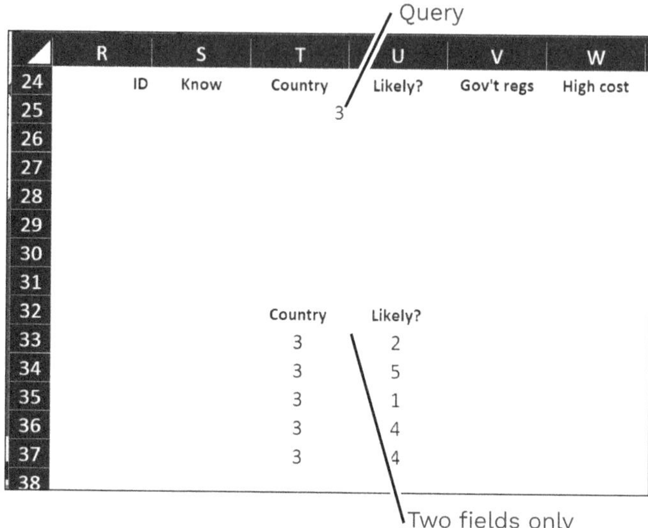

	R	S	T	U	V	W
24	ID	Know	Country	Likely?	Gov't regs	High cost
25			3			
26						
27						
28						
29						
30						
31						
32			Country	Likely?		
33			3	2		
34			3	5		
35			3	1		
36			3	4		
37			3	4		
38						

Figure B.10: Copying data from two fields only — the Copy-To area specifies only the two fields T32:U32

VERSION FIVE: COPY TO ANOTHER SHEET

Let us say that you have created a worksheet tab named **Query-Ninja-2**. On that tab, you want to place data from the List range (on Query-Ninja-1) so that you can make tables, graphs, or reports (or just admire it; we're cool with that).

But, *you do not want* simply to copy and paste data from Query-Ninja-1. No. You want the data to appear on Query-Ninja-2 as if by magic.

Can do.

And yes, you can copy partial records for this, too, using the same field-name selection technique shown in Version Four.

But first: A Word About *The Trick*

This is *The Trick* about queries. This is important. Listen up.
You **must start** *any Advanced Filter query from the spreadsheet tab that is your* **eventual data destination**. (This will be a repeating theme as we continue from here.) We've been doing this, only it's been "invisible" because we've been working only on one tab. Still… keep this in mind: **always start any Advanced Filter query from the destination location.**

Copy to another sheet

1. Verify that your List range and Criteria range already are set up as you want them on the spreadsheet tab **Query-Ninja-1** (or whatever you have chosen to name it), as in Figure B.11.

2. Create a new, empty tab. We'll imaginatively name this **Query-Ninja-2,** as in Figure B.12.

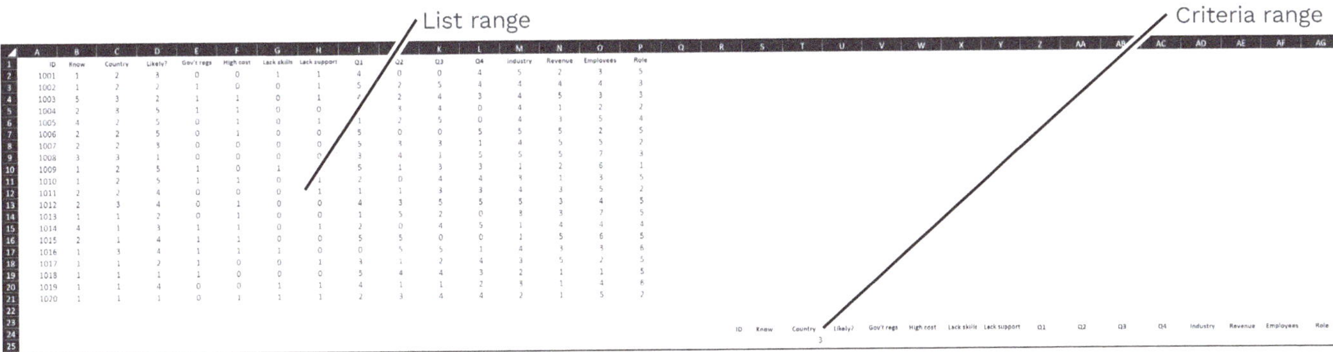

Figure B.11: List range and Criteria range on the spreadsheet tab **Query-Ninja-1**

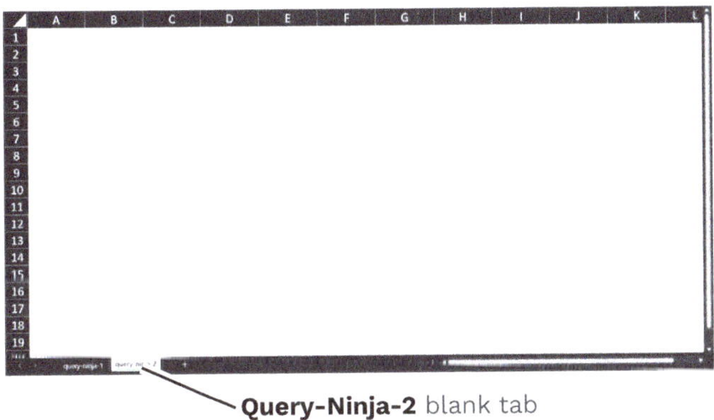

Figure B.12: New, blank Query-Ninja-2 tab

3. Click a cell on the **Query-Ninja-2** tab. Almost any cell will do, but we'll pick cell A1. **This is the spreadsheet cell that designates your destination.** Even though this tab is completely empty, this is where you want the data to end up, and because of that you must start here. Remember: it's **The Trick**.

4. **With the destination Query-Ninja-2 tab displayed and the destination cell selected**, click *Data | Sort & Filter | Advanced*. Excel displays the Advanced Filter dialog box

(Figure B.13). Make sure to select **Copy to another location**.

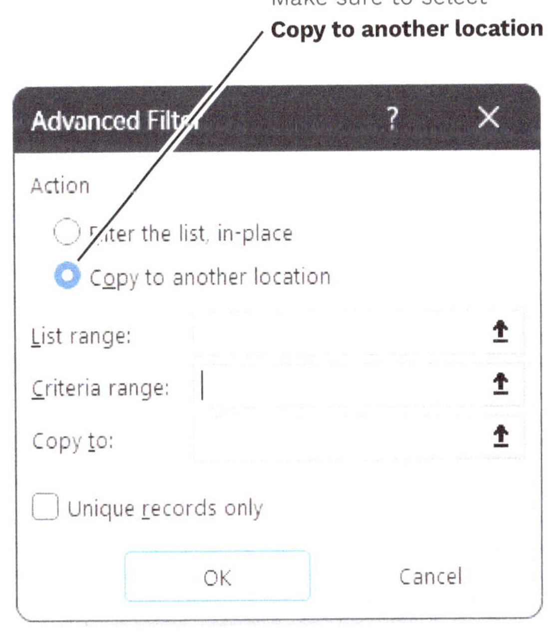

Figure B.13: Advanced Filter dialog box

5. In the Advanced Filter dialog, click within the List range field.

6. Navigate to the **Query-Ninja-1** tab, and select the List range there, as usual. Excel continues to display the Advanced Filter dialog on screen.

7. In the Advanced Filter dialog, click within the Criteria range field. Navigate to **Query-Ninja-1** (if you're not already there), and select the full Criteria range as you have previously.

8. If necessary, navigate to the **Query-Ninja-2** tab.

9. In the Advanced Filter dialog, click within the **Copy-to** field, and then, on the **Query-Ninja-2 tab, click cell A1**.

10. In the Advanced Filter dialog, click OK.

When you click OK in step 10, what should happen? Excel executes the query from Query-Ninja-1, and copies matching data from the Query-Ninja-1 List range to the Query-Ninja-2 tab starting in cell A1 (Figure B.14).

The data on Query-Ninja-2 are *copied only*. All data rows are still present on Query-Ninja-1. (Go check!) No rows are hidden or deleted in the Query-Ninja-1 List range after this query.

	A	B	C	D	E	F	G	H	I	J	K
1	ID	Know	Country	Likely?	Gov't regs	High cost	Lack skills	Lack support	Q1	Q2	Q3
2	1003	5	3	2	1	1	0	1	4	2	4
3	1004	2	3	5	1	1	0	0	5	3	4
4	1008	3	3	1	0	0	0	0	3	4	1
5	1012	2	3	4	0	1	0	0	4	3	5
6	1016	1	3	4	1	1	1	0	0	5	5
7											
8											

Figure B.14: Query-Ninja-2 tab showing the copied data from the List range on Query-Ninja-1

VERSION SIX: QUERY SHEET 1 FROM ANOTHER SHEET

Some of us are better data housekeepers than others. Perhaps you don't want to clutter your Data Dashboard with queries or query libraries.

Instead, you want to query the List range located on the tab **Query-Ninja-1** using a query located on the tab **Query-Ninja-2**.

You can do this. You can **(a)** hide and show rows (for example, on the Data Dashboard — although we'll be using the practice data) or you can **(b)** copy data from the List range — all by using an Advanced Filter query located on a tab different from the one holding the data.

Here's how, shown in Version 6.1 and Version 6.2.

Version Six dot One — make rows hide and show from a query located on a different tab

1. Clear any leftover Advanced Filter queries by clicking *Data | Sort & Filter | Clear*. This restores any hidden data in the List range.

2. Copy the field headers (column names — just the names) from the List range on **Query-Ninja-1**, then navigate to the **Query-Ninja-2** tab and paste the column names starting at cell A1. Remember — the column names must match **EXACTLY**. That's why we copy and paste.

3. Set up your query beneath the column names. In our case, we're going to look for records where Country = 3, as shown in Figure B.15.

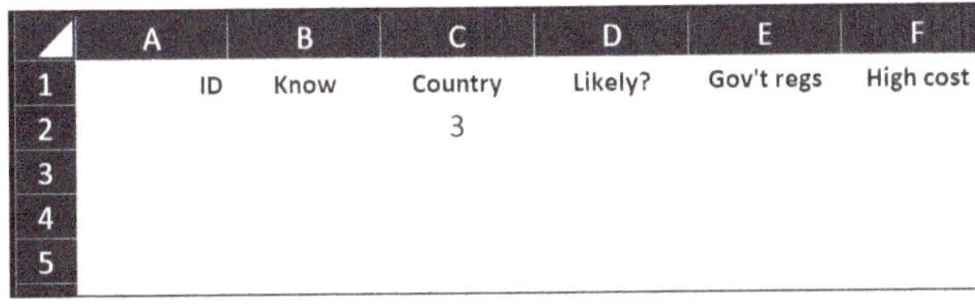

Figure B.15: Query for Country = 3 as it appears on the **Query-Ninja-2** tab

Leave the query on **Query-Ninja-2** and navigate to **Query-Ninja-1**, where we left the List range.

Remember *The Trick*. You **must** always start a query from its destination. Because we are going to be hiding and showing records in the List range on **Query-Ninja-1**, we must initiate the query from the tab where the hiding and showing will take place — **Query-Ninja-1**.

4. With the List range of **Query-Ninja-1** displayed, choose *Data | Sort & Filter | Advanced* to display the Advanced Filter dialog box.

5. Make sure that **Filter the list in place** is selected. (Figure B.16)

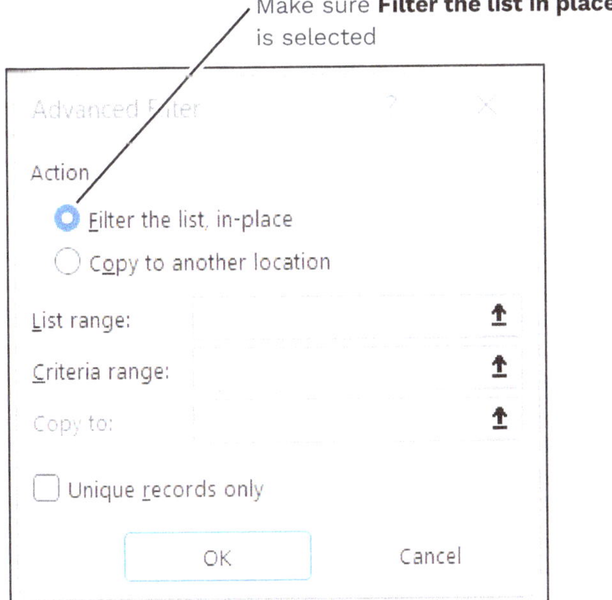

Figure B.16: Filter the list in place

6. In the Advanced Filter dialog box, click within the List range field, and then

highlight the List range on Query-Ninja-1, top-left to bottom-right.

7. In the Advanced Filter dialog, click within the Criteria range field, and then navigate to your criteria: **on the tab Query-Ninja-2**. Highlight all column names and all rows that contain criteria.

8. Click OK.

Back on the tab **Query-Ninja-1**, Excel displays only those rows that contain a 3 in the Country field.

Version Six dot Two — copy List range rows to sheet 2, but no hiding or showing back on Query-Ninja-1

1. Clear any Advanced Filter queries by choosing *Data | Sort & Filter | Clear*. This restores any data that may be hidden in the List range.

2. You should have a test query already set up on Query-Ninja-2. If not, do steps 2 and 3 from the section "Version Six dot One — make rows hide and show from a query located on a different tab" on page 126.

   Remember *The Trick*. You **must** always start the query from its destination. You are about to copy list items to Query-Ninja-2. Therefore **you must start on Query-Ninja-2**.

3. Navigate to **Query-Ninja-2**, the tab where we have the query. (Figure B.17.)

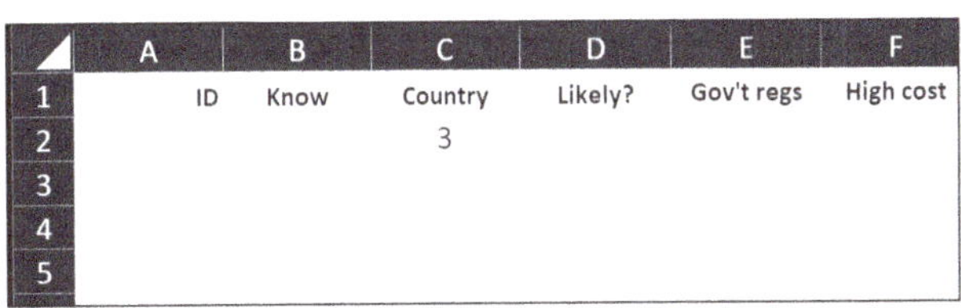

Figure B.17: Query-Ninja-2, where we have the query

4. Choose *Data | Sort & Filter | Advanced* to display the Advanced Filter dialog. Make sure that **Copy to another location** is selected (Figure B.18 on page 128).

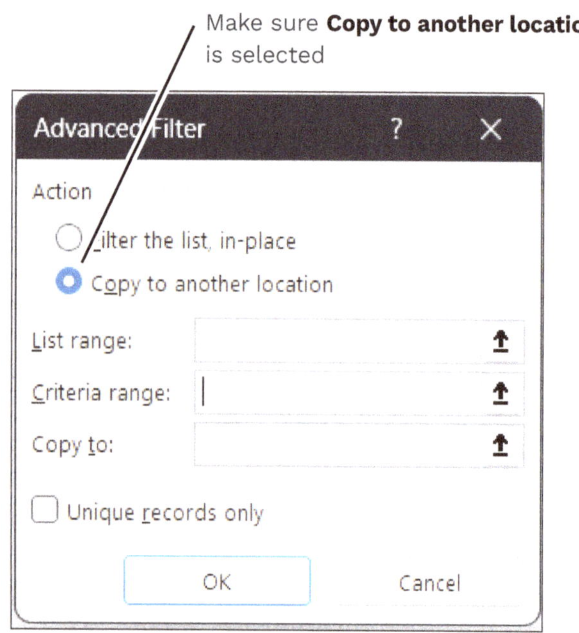

Figure B.18:   Advanced Filter dialog

5. On the Advanced Filter dialog, click within the List range field, then navigate to **Query-Ninja-1** (where the List range is waiting).

6. Select the List range cells from top left to bottom right. Excel returns you to **Query-Ninja-2**, where your Criteria is waiting.

7. On the Advanced Filter dialog, click within the Criteria range field and select the Criteria range.

8. On the Advanced Filter dialog, click within the **Copy-to** field, and then click the cell (on Query-Ninja-2) that you want to be the top-left of the copied data.

9. Click OK.

   Excel copies the requested data from the List range on **Query-Ninja-1** and puts it on **Query-Ninja-2**.

VERSION SEVEN: QUERY SHEET 1 FROM SHEET 2 BUT COPY SHEET 1'S DATA TO SHEET 3

Version Seven is very much like Version Six dot Two, where the List range is on **Query-Ninja-1** and the Criteria range is on **Query-Ninja-2**.

This time, we'll **create another new tab** and call it **Query-Ninja-3** and we'll copy the data to that third tab.

1. Clear any Advanced Filter queries by choosing *Data | Sort & Filter | Clear*. This restores any data that may be hidden in the List range.

2. Your query should still be set up. If not Copy the field headers (column names — just the names) from the practice List range on Query-Ninja-1, then navigate to the Query-Ninja-2 tab and paste them starting at cell A1. Remember — the column names must match **EXACTLY**.

3. Set up your query beneath the column names. In our case, we're going to look for records where Country = 3, as shown in Figure B.19.

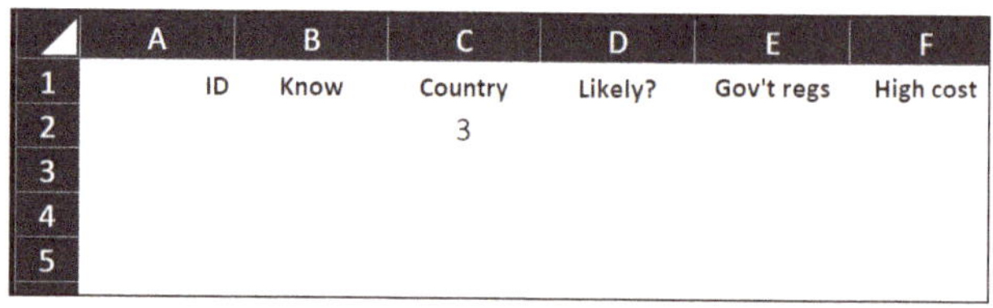

	A	B	C	D	E	F
1	ID	Know	Country	Likely?	Gov't regs	High cost
2			3			
3						
4						
5						

Figure B.19:   Query-Ninja-2, where we create the query

Remember *The Trick*. You **must** always start the query from its destination. You are about to copy list items to **Query-Ninja-3**. It doesn't matter where the data is; it doesn't matter where the query is. **We must start on the destination: Query-Ninja-3.**

4. Navigate to **Query-Ninja-3**; this tab is completely empty.

5. Choose *Data | Sort & Filter | Advanced* to display the Advanced Filter dialog. Make sure that **Copy to another location** is selected (Figure B.20).

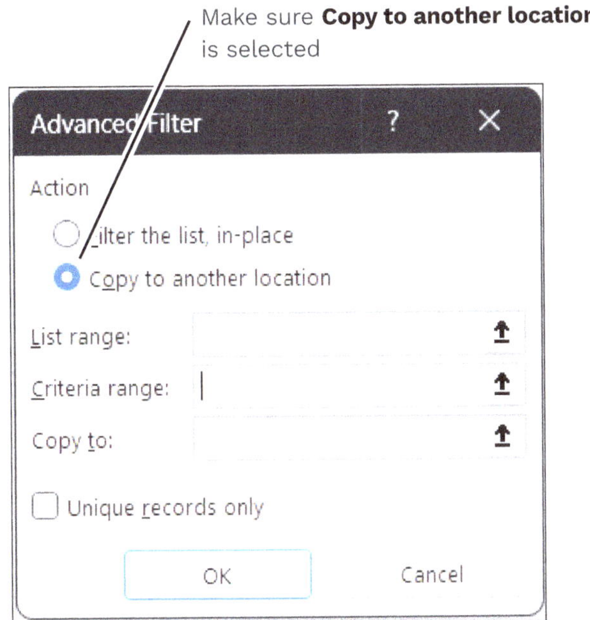

Figure B.20:   Advanced Filter dialog

6. On the Advanced Filter dialog, click within the List range field, then navigate to **Query-Ninja-1** (where the List range is waiting).

7. Select the List range cells from top left to bottom right. Excel returns you to **Query-Ninja-3**, the empty destination tab. The Advanced Filter dialog should be open.

8. On the Advanced Filter dialog, click within the Criteria range field, then navigate to and select the Criteria range from **Query-Ninja-2**.

9. On the Advanced Filter dialog, click within the **Copy to** field, and then navigate to **Query-Ninja-3** and click the cell that you want to be **the top-left of any copied data**.

10. Click OK.

    Excel copies the requested data:
    …from the List range on Query-Ninja-1
    …according to the Criteria on Query-Ninja-2
    …and puts it on the tab Query-Ninja-3.

VERSION EIGHT: MACRO QUERY (NOW YOU'RE COOKING WITH CODE)

Excel's built-in Visual Basic for Applications (VBA) programming language can automatically create a small computer program called a *macro* that can execute on demand using various combinations of criteria that you enter as you wish.

This book cannot fully document all aspects of programming with Visual Basic for Applications — there are many good books and websites focused on that one topic. What we want to demonstrate is how to create and use a macro with Advanced Filter queries in a survey worksheet environment. Unfortunately, we must leave additional experimentation as an exercise for the student.

You trigger the macro with a key combination you choose (such as Control-Shift-L or Control-P). The macro looks at the criteria you have entered and then executes the Advanced Filter query *according to its programming*.

When you create a workbook that includes one or more macros (and assuming that you want to save and not throw away those macros), you must save the workbook file with a .xslm filename extender (for example, query-ninja.xslm) — that is, as a macro-enabled Excel workbook file.

Note: When creating a macro that uses Excel's Advanced Filter, it is vitally **important to remember *The Trick*.** Wherever you end up putting your List range, Criteria range, Copy to range, or even if you Filter in place, **always trigger the macro from the tab where you want the results — the destination**.

And there's yet another gotcha. When you create a macro, you trade away some flexibility in return for some convenience. To create the macro, you must define a **fixed-size Criteria range** and a **fixed-size List range.** (A fixed-size List range is common with survey data; after all, you don't want to ignore any of it). You'll also define a **specific Copy-To destination** where the macro will *always* put any copied data — *always* — which means that you can't put data just anywhere when you run the macro. Your macro will always put copied data in the same place, whether anything is already there or not. *It overwrites*. Macros thus require… um… *a little forethought*.

- **If you want a macro that only delivers data from a couple of fields,** rather than delivering the entire record, you can do that. We saw that technique with "Version Four: Copy Only Partial Records" on page 124. BUT, that macro will copy only those two fields and never any others.

- **If you want to a macro to filter by any or all of several Criteria with both AND and OR** (OR requires more than one row of Criteria), you can — but your Criteria range then must always include more than one row, each of which contains criteria — *because you cannot have an empty row inside the Criteria range, and the Criteria range is fixed and defined inside the macro.*

The Solution. Create a set of macros to do your bidding and perform different types of filtering operations using a given List range and various combinations of Criteria ranges…

Only you can decide whether a set of pre-programmed macros (with variable criteria) is more practical for you than a query library or defining an Advanced Filter operation on the fly when and as you need it.

When you create a macro, you must save your Excel workbook file as a macro-enabled workbook file — .xlsm. It's that or delete the macro. Be aware of this requirement.

Tip: You can "fool" a macro that demands a multi-line OR query into acting as a single-line AND query by putting the same query value(s) for the same field(s) on more than one line. Essentially, this says, "search for 1 OR 1." All such fields must match on all lines of the query.

Version Eight dot One: a macro to filter the List range in place using a query on the same tab

This macro hides-and-shows rows in the List range — just like we do manually with the Data Dashboard.

1. On tab **Query-Ninja-1** (where the full List range is located), make sure that you have copied the field names from the List range and placed them below and to the right of the List range, as in Figure B.3 on page 121. The field names must match **EXACTLY**.

Note: As you have learned with query Versions One through Seven, you can put your Criteria range on another tab and this method will still work. We're showing the simplest way to hide and show, with List and Criteria ranges on the same tab (similar in layout to the Data Dashboard). The tabs you use are less important than *The Trick*: **always begin the Advanced Filter process at its destination.** Because we are hiding and showing rows, the tab that holds the List range is the destination.

---

2. Add a criterion (or two) to the single row beneath the Criteria range field names. The Advanced Filter will execute using these criteria when you create it, but they are really just placeholders.

3. With the tab that contains the List range and Criteria range displayed, choose *View | Macro | Record Macro* (Figure B.21).

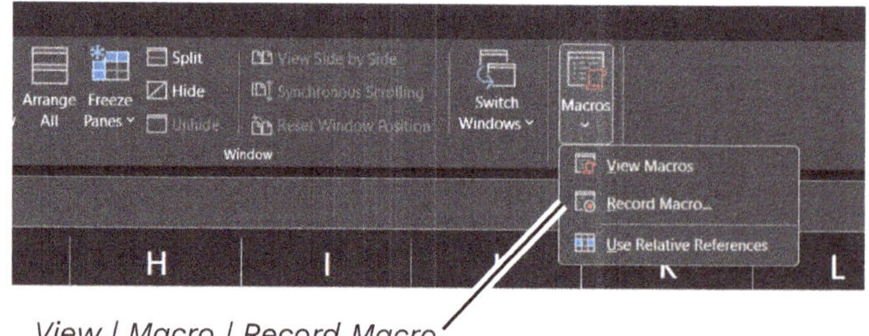

View | Macro | Record Macro

Figure B.21:   Start the macro recording process

This action displays the Record Macro dialog (Figure B.22 on page 131).

The Record Macro dialog box is where you name the macro and provide it with a shortcut key combination (there are other ways to trigger the macro, but keyboard shortcuts are the most usual).

Note: **Recording the macro is not time-sensitive. Relax.** There is no clock ticking. The macro will record any mouse clicks and menu choices, however, so **don't click randomly around the worksheet** — you'll only have to edit out those clicks later in the *macro review and editing process*.

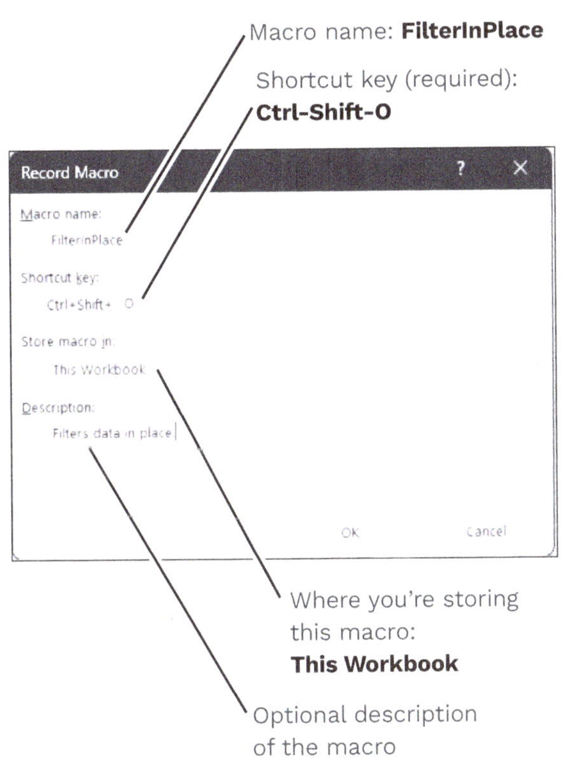

Figure B.22: Record Macro dialog box

4. Name the macro with a descriptive name. You can name the macro anything up to 254 characters. However, Microsoft does not allow spaces or non-alphabetic characters such as slashes, dashes, dollar signs, or underlines. The programmer's convention is to capitalize the name at each word internally like this: **FilterInPlace.**

(This practice is colloquially known as "CamelCase," because there is usually a hump or two in the middle.)

5. Type a shortcut key combination. Excel requires that the combination start with Control (Option on Mac). In Figure B.22, we've added Shift-O, so the combination that triggers the macro is **Ctrl-Shift-O**. (Option-Shift-O on Mac.)

6. Store the macro in **This Workbook**. This keeps the macro with your data.

7. Optionally, enter a description of the macro, so that you (or others who use the spreadsheet later) can determine what the macro does without having to read the code or guess. Because of ***The Trick*** it is good practice to record where to trigger the macro (that is, from which tab, in a multi-tab workbook, for example).

8. Click OK. Now Excel begins recording the macro in earnest.

9. Choose *Data | Sort & Filter | Advanced*. Excel displays the Advanced Filter dialog, with which we have become so familiar.

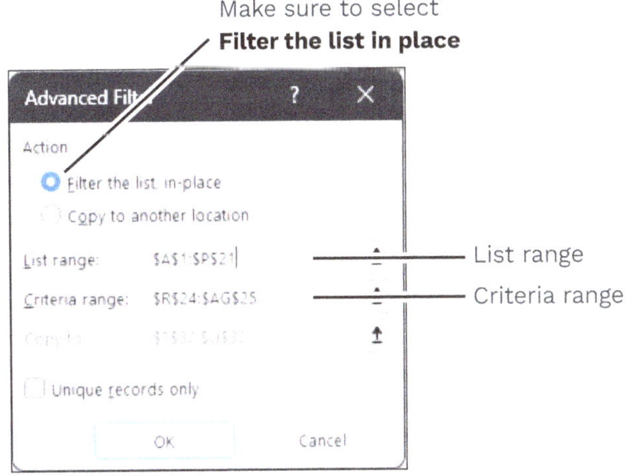

Figure B.23: Advanced Filter dialog box

10. Make sure that you have selected **Filter list in place** (this makes the List range hide and show); and then click within the List range field and highlight the List range; then click within the Criteria range field and highlight the Criteria range.

11. Click OK. Excel executes the Advanced Filter.

12. Choose *View | Macros | Stop Recording*. The macro recording stops.

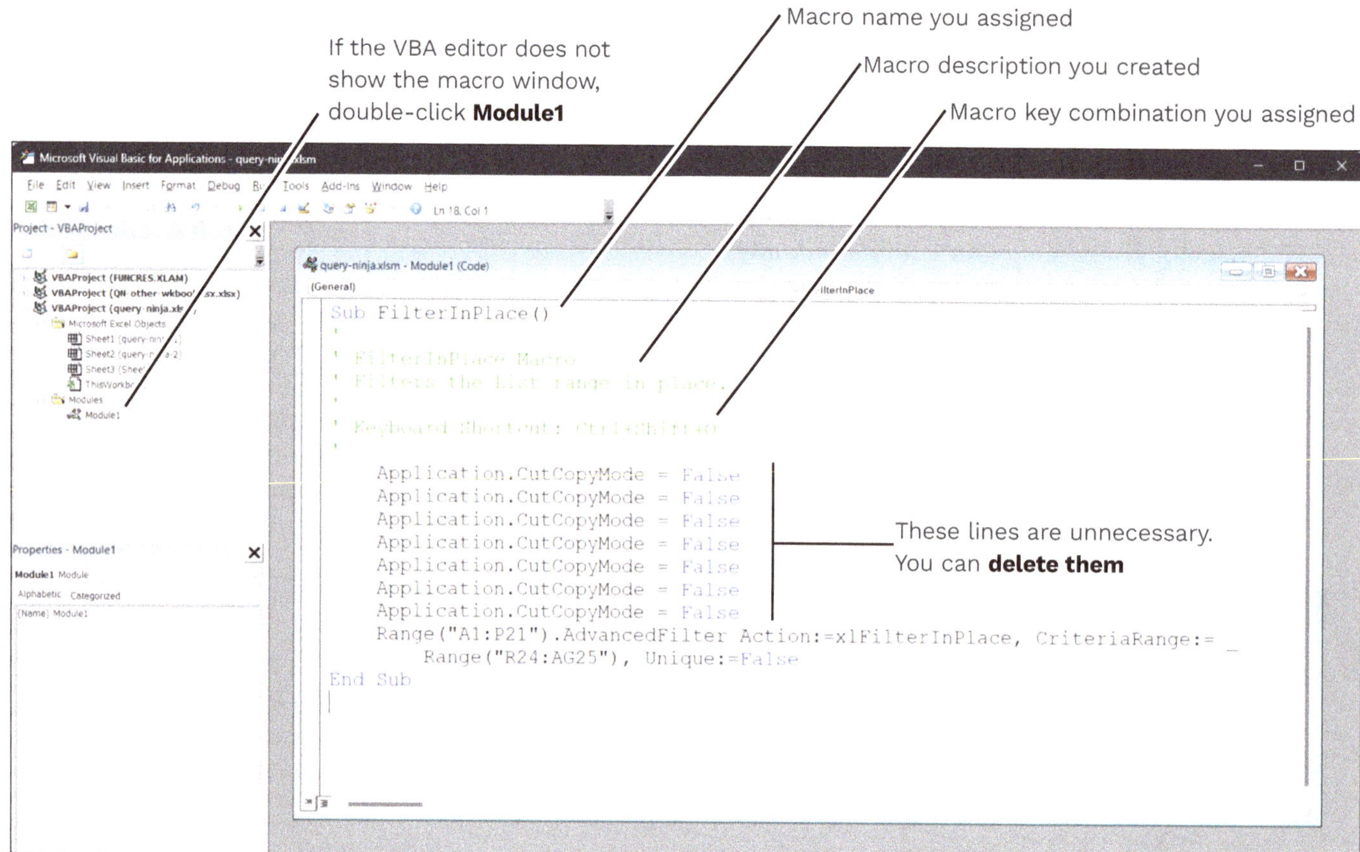

Figure B.24: Excel's Visual Basic Editor (VBE) showing the **Ctrl-Shift-O** macro

Review and edit the macro

Inevitably, the macro will contain unnecessary programming code just because you recorded it rather than programmed it directly.

Press Alt-F11 (Windows) or Opt-F11 (Mac). Excel displays its Visual Basic Editor (VBE), as in Figure B.24.

If VBE does not show the macro code, click *VBAProject (query-ninja.xslm)* or the name you have given to your workbook, and then **double-click Module1,** as shown in Figure B.24.

1. Delete the lines that read:

Application.CutCopyMode = False

You may have a greater or lesser number of these lines decorating your macro code. In Figure B.24, there are seven. They're generated by mouse movements and clicks during the recording of the macro (we took screen shots; that generated these lines).

Keep the following lines of code. They perform the macro actions:

Range("A1:P21").AdvancedFilter Action:=xlFilterInPlace, CriteriaRange:=Range("R24:AG25"), Unique:=False
End Sub

You should recognize *Range("A1:P21")* as the top-left and bottom-right of the List range, and Range("R24:AG25") as the Criteria range.

If you have clicked somewhere, adjusted a column width, or performed some other action before clicking *View | Macros | Stop Recording*, there may be additional lines between the macro code proper and the words **End Sub**.

If so, you can delete those lines. **DO NOT DELETE THE *CODE* OR *END SUB*.**

2. **Click the VBE Save icon** or choose Save from the VBE File menu (not Excel's File menu) to save the macro, as in Figure B.25.

   After saving the VBE macro, you can close the Macro window.

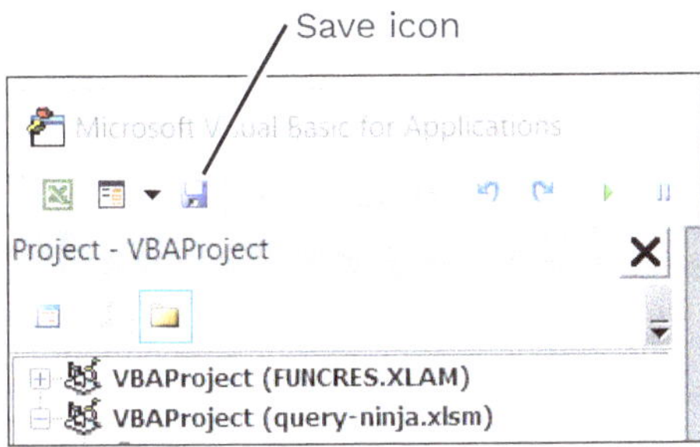

Figure B.25:   Save the macro

3. **Save the workbook file.** If this is the first time you've saved the spreadsheet with a macro on board, Excel displays a Save As dialog box to allow you to save the file as a macro-enabled spreadsheet (with a .xlsm filename extension — for example, query-ninja.xlsm), as in Figure B.26.

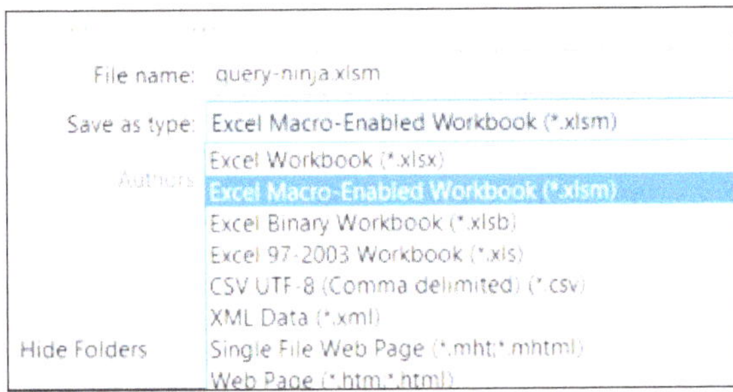

Figure B.26:   Saving a macro-enabled worksheet

Run the macro

Because of **The Trick**, you also **must run the macro from its destination** — not just anywhere. Fortunately, our hide-and-show criteria and the data on which it works are both on the same tab.

1. Clear any existing query. Choose *Data | Sort & Filter | Clear*. This restores any rows hidden by the process of creating the macro.

2. Make sure that you're displaying the tab **Query-Ninja-1** — this is the tab where we have placed both the data and the query.

3. Enter query values beneath the Criteria field names. In Figure B.27 on page 134, we entered 1 below Country and 5 beneath Q1. This is an **AND query** (both criteria are on the same row).

   For a refresher on And and OR queries, see "Queries Using AND / OR" on page 72.

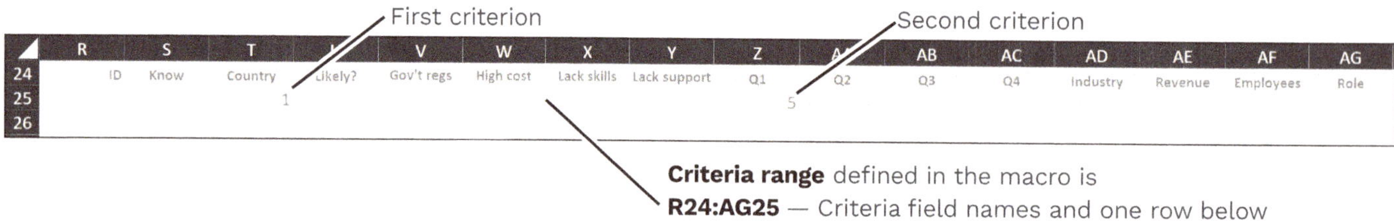

Criteria range defined in the macro is
R24:AG25 — Criteria field names and one row below

Figure B.27: Entering criteria preparatory to executing the macro

4. Press **Ctrl-Shift-O** (*Opt-Shift-O* for Mac).

   Excel executes the query. It hides and shows rows according to your criteria. *That's that.*

   Clear the query and try different criteria. Each time you execute the query with Ctrl-Shift-O, Excel reads the current criteria that you have entered into the Criteria range, and performs the Advanced Filter query based on those criteria.

Note: Ctrl-Shift-O always reproduces the same AND query — just with different (or fewer or more) criteria on the same row. If you want to limit returns to fewer fields or if you want to do an OR query, you must save a new macro and assign it a different shortcut key combination. Ctrl-Shift-O can *only* do this single specific Advanced Filter query — albeit using various criteria.

View available macros and their options

After you have created a library of several macros, you will realize that you need some way to remember what macros appear in a worksheet and what they do. Someone else who uses your worksheet may need to discover what macros you have programmed and what your macros do.

Excel provides a way for you to view a list of existing macros.

1. Choose *View | Macros | View Macros* (Figure B.28.)

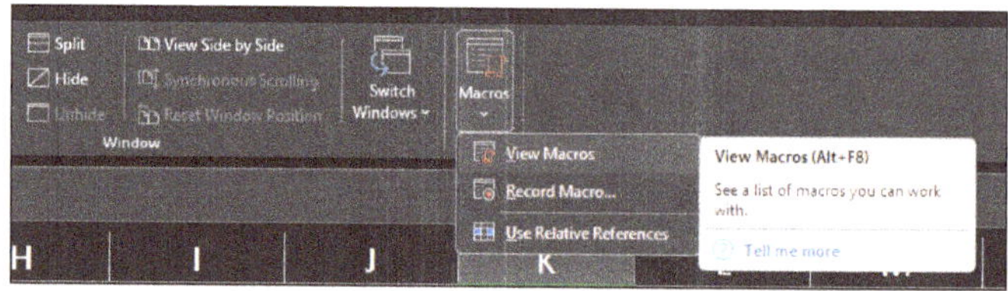

Figure B.28: View macros

Excel displays the Macros dialog box, Figure B.29. The Macros dialog box displays a list of the macros available to you. We have created only one macro: **FilterInPlace**.

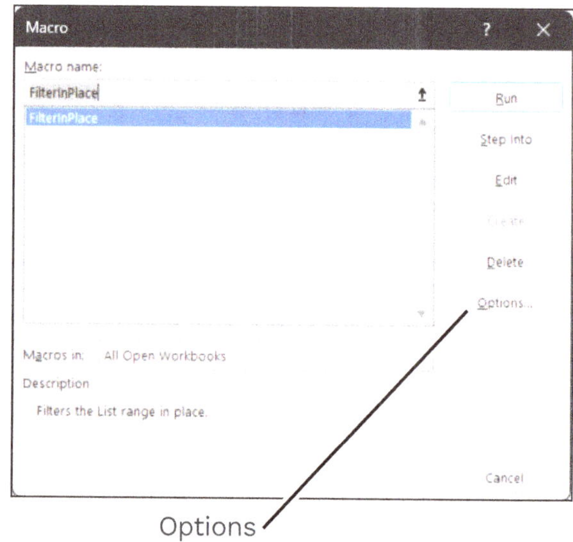

Figure B.29: Macros dialog lists macros and lets you run, edit, and assign new keyboard shortcuts

2. With the Macros dialog box displayed, you can:
   - **Run a macro.** This is the alternative to using the keyboard shortcut to trigger a macro. Select the macro, and then click Run. Be sure to remember **The Trick**, and display the Macros dialog to run a macro only when you are *at the destination of the macro.*
   - **Step Into** (a programming/debugging activity not covered in this book).

- ○ **Edit.** We did this in the previous section, "Review and edit the macro" on page 132.
- ○ **Create** a macro from scratch (beyond the scope of this book).
- ○ **Delete.** If you want to remove a macro permanently (and perhaps start over).
- ○ **Options** (change the shortcut key combination and description).

3. Click Options (Figure B.29). Excel displays the Macro Options dialog box, Figure B.30.

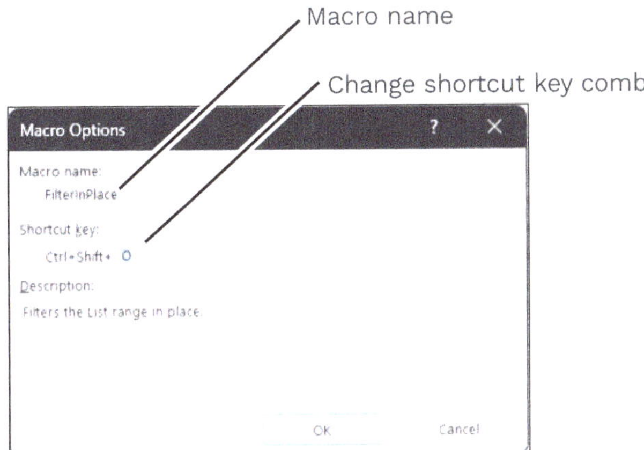

Figure B.30: Macro Options dialog box

In the Macro Options dialog box you can **(a)** change the shortcut key combination and **(b)** modify the description of what the macro does.

4. Make any changes you want, and then click OK (or Cancel) to close the Macro Options dialog.

5. Click Cancel again at the Macros dialog box. You have viewed the Macros in your worksheet and their options.

Note: Modifying the shortcut key combination changes the keystrokes that trigger the macro. *It does not change the keyboard shortcut comment inside the macro code, as shown in* the green text in Figure B.31 on page 135. You must change this manually, if you wish.

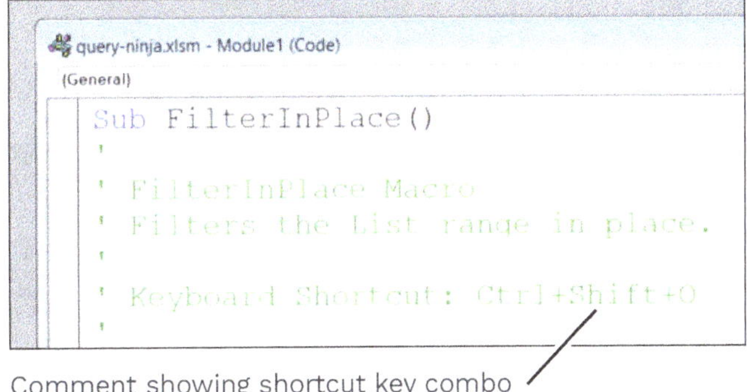

Comment showing shortcut key combo

Figure B.31: Comment line within the macro showing the keyboard shortcut combination.

You can modify this comment by editing the VBA code. (See "Review and edit the macro" on page 132.) Highlight the O, and type J (for example), then press return. The text turns green. *You must press return*.

The apostrophe (') at the beginning of the line signifies a comment. Lines beginning with the apostrophe do not execute. They are there only as "comments." Do not remove the apostrophes.

Version Eight dot Two: macro to copy

In this final macro version, we create a query that places data on the tab **Query-Ninja-2**. The List range and the Criteria range remain on **Query-Ninja-1** (but of course, you can put the Criteria range elsewhere as we showed in "Version Seven: Query Sheet 1 from Sheet 2 but Copy Sheet 1's Data to Sheet 3" on page 128. You can also copy only the data for specific fields, as shown in "Version Four: Copy Only Partial Records" on page 124.

Really, Advanced Filter queries and macros are mix-and-match in a lot of ways.

1. Clear any existing Advanced Filter queries (*Data | Sort & Filter | Clear*).

2. On **Query-Ninja-1** (where the data resides) add a criterion (or two) to the single row beneath the Criteria range field names. These criteria are just placeholders.

3. With the tab **Query-Ninja-2** displayed (this is the destination, where the copied data will end up, in accordance with **The Trick**), choose *View | Macro | Record Macro* (Figure

B.32). This action displays the Record Macro dialog (Figure B.33 on page 136).

Figure B.32: Start the macro recording process

Note: Recording the macro is not time-sensitive. There is no clock ticking.

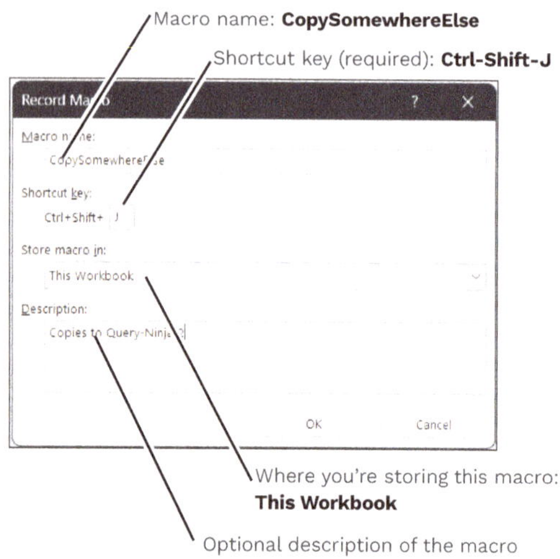

Figure B.33: Record Macro dialog box

4. Enter a name for the macro. We chose **CopySomewhereElse**.

5. Enter a shortcut key combination for the macro. We chose **Ctrl-Shift-J**.

6. Store the macro in **This Workbook**.

7. Optionally, add a description of the macro ("Copies to Query-Ninja-2").

8. Click OK. The macro begins recording.

9. Choose *Data | Sort & Filter | Advanced*. Excel displays the Advanced Filter dialog box, Figure B.34.

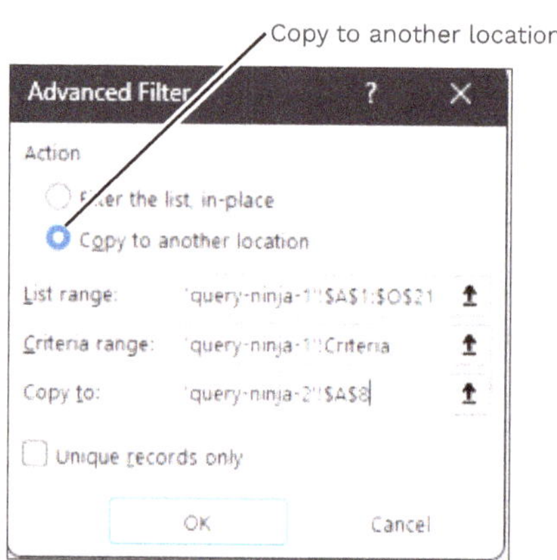

Figure B.34: Copying to another location using a macro

10. Make sure you have selected **Copy to another location**.

11. Click within the List range field (you may need to erase what's there), navigate to **Query-Ninja-1**, and highlight the List range.

12. Click within the Criteria range field (you may need to erase what's there), navigate to **Query-Ninja-1**, and highlight the Criteria range. Remember — the Criteria range location and size become permanent parts of the macro.

13. Click within the Copy to field, navigate to the tab **Query-Ninja-2**, and pick an empty cell for the upper-right corner of the data you will be copying to this tab. We chose **$A$8**.

14. Click OK. Excel executes the query and copies the data that matches your criteria to **Query-Ninja-2**, starting in cell A8.

15. Choose *View | Macro | Stop Recording*. Excel stops recording the macro.

16. Review and edit the macro programming code, as shown in "Review and edit the macro" on page 132.

17. Run the macro. Replace the original criteria with different values. Remember to start at the destination, then trigger the macro (Control-Shift-J for **Windows** or Option-Shift-J for **Mac**).

You are now an official Query Ninja.

Explaining the Data Dashboard's Most Important Formula

If you're like us, you want to know how the formulas in the Data Dashboard work — with particular attention to the largest and most complex formula on the worksheet. The explanation is complex because some of it takes place hidden within Excel's internal computing machinery. **You must use Excel 2010 or later to build the Data Dashboard.**

The most important formula in the Data Dashboard appears in Figure C.1. This formula counts those fields that match the answer code values (1, 2, 3, 4...) but counts them only when a particular record is visible. We call this, "the big, complex formula" because... well... it's big and really complex — *and not at all intuitive.*

This Appendix starts with the basics, then a simplified explanation, and then goes into *a lot* of detail.

| G40 | | *fx* | =SUMPRODUCT(--(G$9:G$28=$F40)* SUBTOTAL(103,OFFSET(INDEX(G$9: G$28,1),ROW(G$9:G$28)-MIN(ROW(G$9:G$28)),0))) |

	D	E	F	G	H	I	
8				Know			
39		Knowledge	Code	Count		Country	C
40	Very knowledgeable		1	10			US
41	Knowledgeable		2	6			Canada
42	Somewhat		3	2			UK
43	No knowledge		4	2			
44							
45							
46		Total this Query		20		Total this Q	
47		Confirm Total		20		Confirm 1	
48							

Figure C.1: The big, complex formula is far from intuitive, difficult to parse (pick apart), and part of its operation is hidden inside Excel's computing machinery — but it works correctly and reliably. You can test it.

WHY THIS APPROACH? HOW IS IT "RESPONSIVE"?

In Chapter 4 on page 33, we stated that whatever formula we chose had to:

- **Count the number of times** that each separate answer value appeared in the survey data (that is, for *each* question, how many times did people answer 1, 2, 3, or 4) and...

- **Respond to whether the row containing that answer was visible or hidden**. We do not want the formula to count an answer value if it is hidden (by a query or manually), and it must count a value if it is visible. We call this kind of counting *responsive* because the counts change depending on which rows the Data Dashboard hides or shows after an Advanced Filter query.

Note: **Versions of Excel as early as 2007 can execute the big formula correctly.** ***HOWEVER...*** The *AGGREGATE* function used elsewhere in the model was introduced in Excel 2010. **The Data Dashboard cannot work as described in this book without using *AGGREGATE*.** Check your version of Excel at *File / Account*. There may be alternative ways to re-create the responsive calculations performed by *AGGREGATE*, but this book does not cover them.

Figure C.2 shows the big formula as it appears in the Excel formula bar.

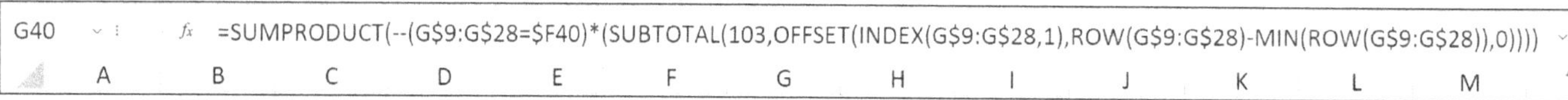

Figure C.2:   The big, complex formula as it appears in the Excel formula bar

Here is the formula written out:

$$=SUMPRODUCT(--(G\$9{:}G\$28{=}\$F40)*$$
$$SUBTOTAL(103,OFFSET(INDEX(G\$9{:}G\$28,1),$$
$$ROW(G\$9{:}G\$28)-MIN(ROW(G\$9{:}G\$28)),0)))$$

Figure C.3:   A formula that can count visible cells that match a target value; this one comes from cell **G40** in Figure C.1 on page 137; it's looking for its target value in cell **$F40**

In the Data Dashboard example, the data range for all fields starts on row 9 and ends on row 28 (20 records) — thus the sample range shown in Figure C.3 is G$9:G$28 for the data in column G.

A QUICK "TOP-LEVEL" EXPLANATION OF THE FORMULA

Component functions of the formula are:

SUMPRODUCT
SUBTOTAL
OFFSET
INDEX
ROW
MIN

By definition, the *SUMPRODUCT* function **sums up the products of (at least) two identically sized arrays.** In the case of our formula, one array is created by G\$9:G\$28=\$F40 and the other array is created by all the functions following *SUBTOTAL*. We think of this as Part 1 and Part 2; but it's one formula, all wrapped by *SUMPRODUCT* — which sums up the product of the two arrays.

```
=SUMPRODUCT(
    --(
        G$9:G$28=$F40)*          ———————— Part 1 —
                                  SUMPRODUCT
                                  array

    SUBTOTAL(103,
        OFFSET(
            INDEX(
                G$9:G$28,1),
                ROW(            ———————— Part 2 —
                    G$9:G$28)-   SUBTOTAL array
                MIN(
                    ROW(
                        G$9:G$28)),
            0)))
```

Figure C.4: Two parts of the formula, *SUMPRODUCT* and *SUBTOTAL*

- **SUMPRODUCT:** ("Part 1" through the * in Figure C.3 and Figure C.4) determines which cells in the data range **match** the target value (in **\$F40**). It creates an *internal array* (you can't see it) for the entire range (G\$9:G\$28 in the example) where 1 signifies that the cell value is equal to the target value and 0 signifies that the cell is not equal to the target value. **This array is invisible to the user.** *This part of the formula does not "know" if a row is hidden; it knows only if a cell in a row of the range matches the target value.*

- **SUBTOTAL:** ("Part 2," and the balance of the formula in Figure C.3 and Figure C.4) creates another invisible internal array that enumerates the cells in the entire range. The *SUBTOTAL* function identifies which elements of the array are located on hidden rows and assigns those elements a 0. Rows that are visible get a 1. *This part of the formula does not "know" if a cell matches the target; only if it is hidden.*

At this point, there are two equal arrays of 1s and 0s in memory, each array corresponding to the entire range — G\$9:G\$28. One array represents the target-matching row with a 1 and a non-target-matching row with a 0, and the other array represents a visible row with a 1 and a non-visible row with a 0.

- **SUMPRODUCT array X SUBTOTAL array** multiplies the array of 1s and 0s that match the target from Part 1 by the array of 1s and 0s that signifies if a row is hidden from Part 2 and sums up the result. **These arrays are internal and invisible to the Excel user.** Table C.1 shows the truth table that the formula uses to evaluate each cell and the multiplication of their values:
MATCH X VISIBLE = COUNT.

Table C.1: *SUMPRODUCT* sums the product of the two arrays, resulting in a count only of cells that are both visible and that match

MATCH?	VISIBLE?	PRODUCT TO SUM
1	1	1
1	0	0
0	1	0
0	0	0

THE LONG-WINDED EXPLANATION

Relax. Get a cup of tea. Settle back. We apologize for the length of all this material.

An Excel worksheet displays a formula on one or more lines in the formula bar (Figure C.5), but Figure C.6 shows the big formula as a programmer might think of it, with each succeeding function or argument on a separate line. As with any mathematical expression, open and closing parentheses must balance. An arrangement like this makes this balance easier to see.

Figure C.5: The big formula on the Excel formula bar

Let's pick this apart.

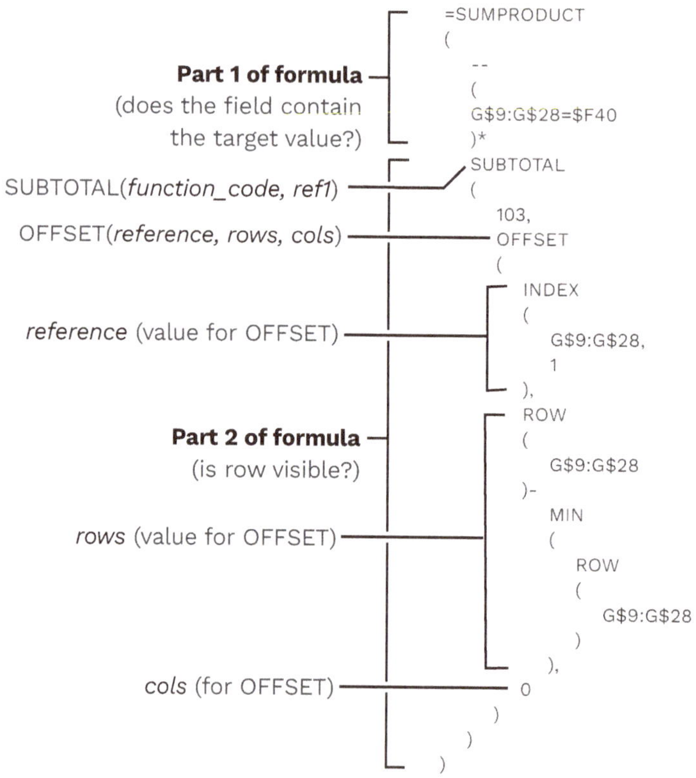

Figure C.6: The big, complex formula as a programmer might see it, with the component parts on separate lines and listing the arguments of the functions used in *SUBTOTAL*

PART 1: DOES THE FIELD CONTAIN THE TARGET VALUE?

Part 1 of the big formula determines whether a field in the range contains the target value. The expression **G9:G$28=$F40** creates an array of 1s and 0s in memory that represents each of the cells in the range. A 1 means that the cell contains the target value and 0 means that the cell does not.

SUMPRODUCT

SUMPRODUCT sums the products of at least two **same-sized** ranges. It can sum a single range, too, but that is simply equivalent to *SUM*.

SUMPRODUCT's syntax is:

Syntax:
SUMPRODUCT(*array1* [,*array2*] [,*array3*]…)

SUMPRODUCT sequentially multiplies its first array by the corresponding array(s) in its set of arguments, and then it sums the results. Figure C.7 shows what happens when SUMPRODUCT multiplies two or more ranges with and without a *test*. (A *test* is the =3 or =2 expression in Figure C.7. It is also the =$F40 expression in Figure C.5.)

H18				A	B	C	D	E
1					Range B	Range C	B*C	Range E
2					4	6	24	10
3					3	8	24	20
4					5	2	10	30
5					1	9	9	40
6					2	3	6	50
7					3	2	6	60
8					2	2	4	70
9								
10				SUMPRODUCT((B2:B8)*(C2:C8))	83		83	
11				SUMPRODUCT((B2:B8=3)*(C2:C8=2))	1			
12				SUMPRODUCT((B2:B8=3)*(C2:C8))	10			
13			SUMPRODUCT((B2:B8=3)*(C2:C8=2)*(E2:E8))		60			

Figure C.7: *SUMPRODUCT calculations* with and without a *test* value for the array

As shown in Figure C.7, the *SUMPRODUCT* formula in **B10** (a merged cell) multiplies the values in Range B by the corresponding values in Range C and then sums them. Column D performs an equivalent multiplication and cell **D10** sums those products and provides the same answer.

However, when you provide one or more of the arrays in *SUMPRODUCT* with a *test* as shown in cells **B11, B12,** and **B13**, you create TRUE/FALSE or 1/0 arrays in memory and it is those arrays that are multiplied — not the values of the cells.

For example, in cell **B11**, *SUMPRODUCT* creates an array identifying which cells in column B are equal to 3 and another array that identifies which cells in column C are equal to 2. When those two arrays are multiplied, only one pair (row 7) are both TRUE. 1 X 1 = 1. Thus, the result in **B11** is 1 (not 2 X 3 = 6).

In cell **B12**, the first array identifies the value 3 in column B with an array of 1s and 0s, the second array simply uses the corresponding values in column C because column C has no test. When the arrays are multiplied and then summed together — (1 X 8) + (1 X 2) = 10.

We can step through Excel's evaluation of the formula in **B13**. Select the cell **B13** and choose *Formulas | Formula Auditing | Evaluate Formula*. Excel displays the Evaluate Formula dialog, as in Figure C.8. Click Evaluate at each step.

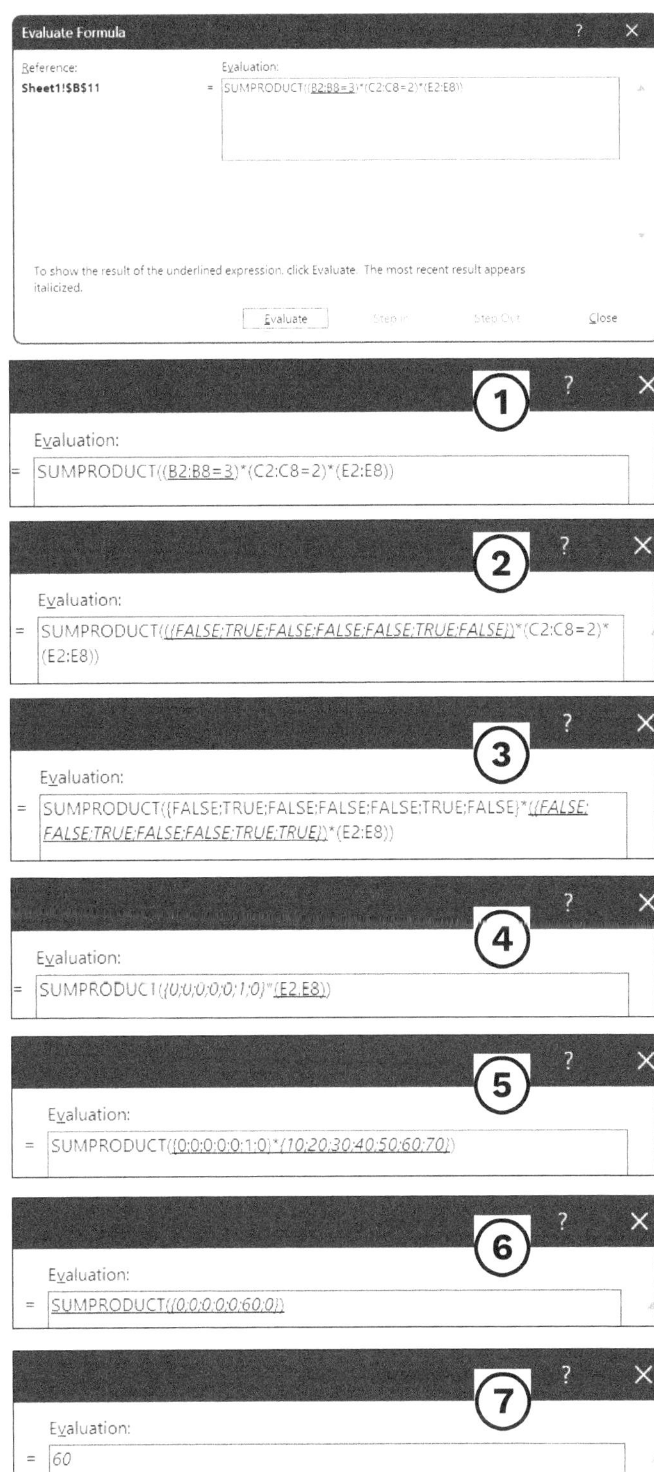

Figure C.8: The step-by-step evaluation of the formula in cell **B11**

In **(1)**, Excel evaluates the first array for cells that contain 3. It creates an array of TRUE and FALSE values, as in **(2)**.

In **(3)**, Excel does the same thing for the second array. It then multiplies the two TRUE/FALSE arrays together as 1s and 0s, and shows that result in **(4)**.

The third array, (E2:E8), does not include a test — only a range of values. In **(5)**, Excel multiplies the TRUE/FALSE product of Ranges B and C with the values of column E and sums the result. Image **(6)** shows that result — 1 X 60 = 60.

When the big formula begins with

$$SUMPRODUCT(--(G\$9:G\$28=\$F40)$$

that portion of the big formula creates an array in memory of 1s and 0s that is equivalent in size to the data range of that column of the survey, and that array identifies (with 1s) those rows of the range that contain the value found in **$F40**. All other elements in the array are 0.

SUMPRODUCT then multiplies that first array by the array created *in the second part of the formula.*

PART 2: IS THE ROW VISIBLE?

The second part of the formula creates an array that shows which rows in the range are visible. The array of the second part of the formula that *SUMPRODUCT* multiplies is created by:

SUBTOTAL(103,
OFFSET(
INDEX(G\$9:G\$28,1),
ROW(G\$9:G\$28)-
MIN(ROW(G\$9:G\$28)),0))

SUBTOTAL acts as a wrapper for an internal array created using the *OFFSET* portion of the formula. *SUBTOTAL* accepts the array that *OFFSET* feeds it — and then *SUBTOTAL* counts (sets to 1) any element of the array if it is visible and sets it to 0 if it is hidden, thus "not counting" it.

Let's review the syntax of the five components.

SUBTOTAL

SUBTOTAL returns the result of one of the functions in Table C.2 applied to one or more references (or ranges) according to the value of *function_num* that you supply.

Syntax:
SUBTOTAL(*function_num, ref1* [,*ref2*]...)

Table C.2 lists the functions available to *SUBTOTAL*. Function numbers 1–11 apply *SUBTOTAL*'s function to all values in the *reference* (that is, in *ref1, ref2, etc.*); function numbers 101–111 ignore hidden rows when applying *SUBTOTAL*'s function. *SUBTOTAL* itself is thus sensitive to whether a row is visible or not.

ref1 identifies the data on which *SUBTOTAL* acts — one cell, several cells, range, or array.

The hidden-versus-visible aspect of *SUBTOTAL* **works only when data appear in a column** (as in our survey), not when the data appear along a row. *SUBTOTAL* always requires a numeric argument for its *function number*.

In the big formula, the function number **103** tells *SUBTOTAL* to perform a *COUNTA*. *COUNTA* *enumerates* non-blank cells (including cells containing text, errors, and empty text cells: ""). Don't confuse "count" with "add up" (function numbers 9 and 109 would do that). SUBTOTAL creates an array where 1 signifies a visble row and 0 signifies a hidden cell.

Table C.2: *SUBTOTAL* functions

LOOKS AT ALL ROWS	IGNORES HIDDEN ROWS	DOES THIS
1	101	AVERAGE
2	102	COUNT
3	103	COUNTA
4	104	MAX
5	105	MIN
6	106	PRODUCT

LOOKS AT ALL ROWS	IGNORES HIDDEN ROWS	DOES THIS
7	107	STDEV[1]
8	108	STDEV.P
9	109	SUM
10	110	VAR[1]
11	111	VAR.P

OFFSET

OFFSET supplies the *ref1* argument to *SUBTOTAL*. *OFFSET* is a critical function for the formula. It supplies the list of cells that *SUBTOTAL* must count.

Syntax:
OFFSET(*reference, rows, cols* [,*height*] [,*width*])

reference is the base location of the offset, the "start-cell." In the big formula, *reference* refers to a single cell. The value for *reference* is:

$$INDEX(G\$9:G\$28, 1)$$

which identifies the *first cell in the example range G\$9:G\$28*.

rows specifies the **row** of the upper-left cell with reference to the start-cell. The value for rows can be positive (up), 0, or negative (down) from the reference start-cell (identified by *INDEX*). In the big formula, the value for *rows* is:

$$ROW(G\$9:G\$28)-MIN(ROW(G\$9:G\$28)$$

The value for the *rows* argument in *OFFSET*, *ROW(G\$9:G\$28)-MIN(ROW(G\$9:G\$28)*, is **critical for understanding how the formula works**. We'll get to that explanation in "How It All Works" on page 144.

cols specifies the **column** of the upper-left cell with reference to the start-cell. The value for *cols* can be positive (right), 0, or negative (left) of the reference cell. In the big formula, the value for

cols is **0**, which means there is *no horizontal offset* from the reference column, G\$9:G\$28.

height, width (both optional) refer to the number of rows (height) or columns (width) that you want the *OFFSET* function to return. These are optional, and the big formula ignores them.

INDEX

INDEX returns the value of an element in the table, range, or array selected by its row and column arguments. In the big formula, *INDEX* is provided with the data range (G\$9:G\$28) and the value 1. This identifies the first row in the range. Because there is no column number value, it identifies the first cell in that range.

Syntax:
INDEX(*array, row_num* [,*col_num*])

array is a table, array, or range.

row_num is the row in the array whose value to return

ROW

Returns the row number of *reference*.

Syntax:
ROW([*reference*])

reference is the cell or range of cells for which you want the row number. Because G\$9:G\$28 is a vertical array, *ROW* returns the row numbers of *reference* as a vertical array.

MIN

MIN returns the smallest, or *minimum*, number among its arguments.

Syntax:
MIN(*number1* [,*number2*]...)

---

[1]   It is unclear from Excel Help whether functions 7 and 107 refer to STDEV.S or the older STDEV and whether functions 10 and 110 refer to VAR.S or the older VAR.

number1 can be a number, name, array, or a reference that contains numbers.

HOW IT ALL WORKS

The formula works with internal arrays. This is, frankly, not intuitively obvious from the appearance of the formula. ***ROW* returns an array.** It's easy to think of *ROW* as returning a single row number (which it can do), but *ROW*'s *reference* argument can return **a range of cell rows**, not just a single value. Microsoft states in the Excel Help: "If *reference* is a range of cells, and if *ROW* is entered as a vertical array, *ROW* returns the row numbers of a *reference* as a vertical array."

That said, all *SUBTOTAL* requires is its *function number* (to control what it does and what it sees) and a *reference* (the entity upon which it needs to perform its function).

In the big formula, the content of *SUBTOTAL*'s *reference* argument is:

OFFSET(
INDEX(G$9:G$28,1),
ROW(G$9:G$28)-
MIN(ROW(G$9:G$28)),0)

Let's say we're dealing with a single, vertical column of cells in our survey data (the column G$9:G$28, for instance). We'll call that column "*range*."

OFFSET needs the following arguments: *OFFSET(reference, rows, cols* [,*height*] [,*width*]) We can forget *height* and *width*. We are left with *reference*, *rows*, and *cols*.

In the *specific case* of the formula:

reference = *INDEX(range, 1)* = a single starting-cell located at the top of *range*. This is a single value, a single cell. We'll call this *start-cell*.

rows = *ROW*(range)-*MIN*(*ROW*(range)). This construction *returns an internal array* of row numbers of all the cells within *range* **MINUS** the minimum row number of *range* — which is the lowest-number row in *range*. This produces an internal array of values that begin with the value 0.

cols = 0 = no horizontal offset for the cells. This value must be present, but other than assuring that it is there and that it is 0, we can ignore it.

Important: *The* rows *argument creates an array.*

Look more closely at *OFFSET*'s *rows* argument. The first instance of *ROW* creates an internal array of row values from its *range*. See Figure C.10 on page 145. Then, **from each of those array values in turn,** the *rows* argument subtracts the row value of the first cell (identified by the *MIN* of the *ROW* of *range*), so that the resulting array values start at 0. See Figure C.10, Figure C.11, and Figure C.12 on page 145.

For example, the *ROW* array values from the range G$9:G$28 are:

{9, 10, 11... 28}

If you subtract *MIN(ROW(range))* that is, the minimum row value of that range — which is 9 — from each element of the array, you get the array:

{0, 1, 2...19}

for our 20 rows of example data.

At this point, internally, *OFFSET* looks like this:

OFFSET(start-cell, {invisible array of 0-based row offsets}, 0)

Thus, *OFFSET* hands off to *SUBTOTAL* as *SUBTOTAL*'s *ref1* argument an internal array of the row numbers of *range*, re-stated as {(*start-cell*)+0, (*start-cell*)+1, (start-cell)+2, (*start-cell*)+3...(*start-cell*)+19}. This **entire array** is returned to *SUBTOTAL* as its *ref1* argument. *You just can't see it.*

***SUBTOTAL*'s function number is set to 103.** This number tells *SUBTOTAL* to perform a *COUNTA* on *ref1* — the array of cell row values supplied by *OFFSET* — **but also to be sensitive** to whether the cell is hidden or visible. Each element of the array (a row) that is visible is counted (enumerated) as a 1, each element of the array that is hidden is counted as a 0. In this way, *SUBTOTAL* creates an array that signifies whether a row is hidden or visible.

STEP-BY-STEP IN EXCEL

The following series of screen shots (Figure C.9 through Figure C.15) illustrate various parts of *SUBTOTAL*'s calculation of the "is it visible?" array count.

OFFSET — in this case — produces a VALUE error unless it's wrapped in another calculation. (We wrap it in *SUBTOTAL*.) As a result, we can't show that part of the calculation by itself. However, you can verify that it works by entering this series of formulas for yourself.

F13	∨ :	f_x
	A	B
1	values	
2	2	
3	4	
4	3	
5	1	
6	5	
7	1	
8		
9		

Figure C.9: A set of random example values in a column representing survey data

B10	∨ :	f_x =ROW(A2:A7)	
	A	B	C
1	values		
2	2		
3	4		
4	3		
5	1		
6	5		
7	1		
8		ROW	
9			
10		2	
11		3	
12		4	
13		5	
14		6	
15		7	
16			

Figure C.10: The *ROW* function, showing the array it creates of the row numbers for *range*. Only the cell **B10** is populated with the formula; cells **B11–B15** "spill over."

C10	∨ :	f_x =MIN(ROW(A2:A7))	
	A	B	C	D
1	values			
2	2			
3	4			
4	3			
5	1			
6	5			
7	1			
8		ROW	MIN(ROW)	
9				
10		2	2	
11		3		
12		4		
13		5		
14		6		
15		7		
16				

Figure C.11: *MIN* applied to *ROW*. *MIN(ROW(range))* returns the value of the lowest-numbered row within *range*, in this case, row 2.

Figure C.11 shows the *MIN(ROW(range))* construct identifying the minimum row number in the range A2:A7 (not the *value* in that location; just the *row number*).

D10	∨ :	f_x =ROW(A2:A7)-MIN(ROW(A2:A7))	
	A	B	C	D
1	values			
2	2			
3	4			
4	3			
5	1			
6	5			
7	1			
8		ROW	MIN(ROW)	ROW-MIN(ROW)
9				
10		2	2	0
11		3		1
12		4		2
13		5		3
14		6		4
15		7		5
16				

Figure C.12: *ROW(range)-MIN(ROW(range))* in cell **D10**. As with *ROW* in Figure C.10, this also returns an array that "spills"; D10–D15 shows how this construct provides a 0-based array. The values in column D are the values in the array produced by *ROW* in column B *MINUS* the minimum row value in column C.

E10	⌄ ⁝	fx	=INDEX(A2:A7,1)		
	A	B	C	D	E
1	values				
2	2				
3	4				
4	3				
5	1				
6	5				
7	1				
8		ROW	MIN(ROW)	ROW-MIN(ROW)	INDEX
9					
10		2	2	0	2
11		3		1	
12		4		2	
13		5		3	
14		6		4	
15		7		5	
16					

Figure C.13: *INDEX* identifies the top "start-cell" in *range* — again, not the cell value but the row

INDEX identifies the single top or "start-cell" in *range*. Note that this identification is not precisely the same process as finding the minimum row in *range*, although the two methods result in identifying the same row value.

F10	⌄ ⁝	fx	=SUBTOTAL(103,OFFSET(INDEX(A2:A7,1),ROW(A2:A7)-MIN(ROW(A2:A7)),0))				
	A	B	C	D	E	F	G	H
1	values						
2	2						
3	4						
4	3						
5	1						
6	5						
7	1						
8		ROW	MIN(ROW)	ROW-MIN(ROW)	INDEX	SUBTOTAL	
9							
10		2	2	0	2	1	
11		3		1		1	
12		4		2		1	
13		5		3		1	
14		6		4		1	
15		7		5		1	
16							

Figure C.14: The range F10–F15 shows the count produced by *SUBTOTAL* when fed the array by *OFFSET*. In this figure, all cells in the range A2:A7 are visible.

Having been fed its *ref1* array of row values by *OFFSET*, *SUBTOTAL* performs a *COUNTA* (of non-empty cells) on the array, enumerating all rows in *range* and placing a 1 in column F when the row is visible and a 0 when it is not. The formula appears only in cell **F10**; its values "spill" into the cells from **F11–F15**.

You can test this formula by hiding random rows in the range A2:A7.

F10	˅ ⋮	f_x	=SUBTOTAL(103,OFFSET(INDEX(A2:A7,1),ROW(A2:A7)-MIN(ROW(A2:A7)),0))					
	A	B	C	D	E	F	G	H
1	values							
2	2							
5	1							
6	5							
7	1							
8		ROW	MIN(ROW)	ROW-MIN(ROW)	INDEX	SUBTOTAL		
9								
10		2	2	0	2	1		
11		3		1		0		
12		4		2		0		
13		5		3		1		
14		6		4		1		
15		7		5		1		
16								

Figure C.15: Rows 3 and 4 are hidden. This figure shows that *SUBTOTAL*'s count responds to hidden rows. *SUBTOTAL* still considers all the cells in *range*, but it correctly applies a value of 0 to the rows that are hidden.

In Figure C.15, we have hidden rows 3 and 4. The count produced by *SUBTOTAL* correctly identifies these two rows as hidden, and denotes them with a 0. Note that the *number of values* in column F remains constant — one for each row in A2:A7 whether hidden or not.

WINDING IT ALL UP

Here is the big formula again:

=SUMPRODUCT(--(G$9:G$28=$F40)*
SUBTOTAL(103,OFFSET(INDEX(G$9:G$28,1),
ROW(G$9:G$28)-MIN(ROW(G$9:G$28)),0)))

The formula produces two arrays of equivalent size but hidden in memory:

- The Part 1 array, where 1 represents the row of a cell that contains the target and 0 represents the row of a cell that does not contain the target.

- The Part 2 array, where 1 represents a row that is visible and 0 represents a row that is not visible.

- Both arrays are the same size because they both refer to the same range.

SUMPRODUCT multiplies one array by the other and sums the result.

1 x 1 = 1 = target value x visible
1 x 0 = 0 = target value x not visible
0 x 1 = 0 = not target value x visible
0 x 0 = 0 = not target value x not visible

When you sum up the product array, you obtain *the number of visible cells that contain the target value.*

www.ingramcontent.com/pod-product-compliance
Lightning Source LLC
Chambersburg PA
CBHW080024260726
48658CB00007B/2459